Goddard, Kentucky

Goddard
School Memories

Influence of the Common School Movement
Goddard, Kentucky
Fleming County

A Historical and Genealogical Reference
Ginny Helphinstine Reeves
161 Helphinstine Road
Wallingford, Kentucky, 41093
2020

Train up a child the way he should go, and when
he is old, he will not depart from it.
—Proverbs 22:6

GINNY REEVES

ISBN 978-1-0980-6831-8 (paperback)
ISBN 978-1-0980-6832-5 (digital)

Christian Faith Publishing, Inc.
832 Park Avenue
Meadville, PA 16335
www.christianfaithpublishing.com

Printed in the United States of America

Ginny Helphinstine (Reeves)
Author
Goddard School, Fourth Grade
1954

Contents

Foreword...9

1   Local, State, and National Beginnings................................13
     Fleming County Common Schools Established...................15
     School Laws and Changes 19

2   The Common Schools at Goddard 24
     Contract Between Teacher and Trustees.............................32
     Sanford School Number 50 Student Census, 1898, 1899......33
     Sanford School, Number 52, Subdistrict 10 1898, 1899 36
     Sanford School, Number 52, Subdistrict 10 1903 39
     Goddard School, Number 52, Subdistrict 10 42
     Goddard School Number 52, Subdistrict 10 1909 43
     Sanford Oak Grove Common School Number 53.................46
     Sanford Oak Grove Common School Number 53 1903........50
     Oak Grove School Goddard Number 53 1907 53

3   The New Goddard School 1909 59

4   Subdistrict Trustees and Compliance with Laws...................73

5   Moonlight Schools..79

6   School Census..81

7   Goddard School Lunchroom 86

8   Reflections on Attendance and Discipline 96

9   Curriculum and Textbooks...102

10   Goddard School Teachers...120

11 Student and Teacher Dress 159

12 School Programs and School Trips 162

13 Clubs and Activities 168

14 Eighth Grade Graduations 176

15 The Goddard School PTA (Parent-Teacher Association) 182

16 Goddard School Bus Drivers..............................184

17 Consolidation and the Closing of Goddard School 189

18 Sale of Goddard School....................................198

19 Students Who Attended Goddard School by Decade 200
    Goddard School Census Report 1911 200
    Census Report of School Children Goddard School 1916...206
    Goddard School Census Report 1918 210
    Census Report of School Children Goddard School,
        Subdistrict Number 35 1920s 216
    Students in the 1930's 225
    1940s Students Some names smeared from flood
        damage. The 1947 books are missing. 238
    1950s Students..250

20 Marriages of Goddard School Students 262

Index of Students Who Attended Goddard School.....................265

Goddard School Bibliography 289

General Index..293

Foreword

Goddard School Memories is an illustrated history of the influence of the common school movement, developed by Horace Mann of Massachusetts, with a goal to provide free education for all, regardless of wealth, heritage, or class. Moral education was the heart of the curriculum. Kentucky first approved common schools in 1821. Fleming County established the schools in 1841. The principles of the common schools were used in US President Teddy Roosevelt's country life movement in 1908, addressing poor living conditions and social problems in rural America. The Goddard School was built in response to President Roosevelt's country life movement. Goddard School personnel practiced Horace Mann's theme from Proverbs 22:6 ("Train up a child the way he should go, and when he is old, he will not depart from it") until the closing in 1960.

This documented history of the Goddard School reveals that many things are known about the Goddard School. County and school records determine that one of the original sites was located one-fourth of a mile from the later site and could be found on Wilder Loop on the Tom Hurst property. The first structures were log one-room schools (number 50, number 52, number 53, and number 54) and were first called field schools, subscription schools, and then common schools. Field schools and subscription schools lasted only three months. Common schools were free education for all and lasted five months.

The last Goddard School, a consolidation of the one-room schools, was located next to the Goddard Church on land purchased from Joseph Malin Plummer in 1909. This structure, built by N.J.

Ferguson, was first a one-room building and was later remodeled by adding two classrooms and a lunchroom.

Oral histories reveal many memories of former students of Goddard School: teachers, cooks, bus drivers, recesses, discipline, attendance, programs and school trips, school clubs, and eighth grade graduations.

Some of the fondest memories among those who attended were that students of all ages and abilities worked together as a family. Older students helped younger students, and more able youngsters tutored those struggling along. Programs and socials involved the total Goddard community and the Goddard Methodist Church. Teachers were highly regarded by family members.

Many reasons exist for writing this book. It was constructed, in large part, from materials and knowledge generated from researching county records, school records, oral histories, newspaper clippings, and personal knowledge. I attended all eight grades at Goddard School in its last years. In addition, my grandmother attended the first Goddard School. My father, my husband, my sister, great aunts, and cousins also attended the Goddard School. I have been collecting information and interviewing people for many years. Now many are deceased, but I still have their memories. Little has been written about the common school movement and the history of education in Kentucky and Fleming County. Few reports have been written about Goddard School.

First, the book can be used for browsing. It has engaging anecdotes full of adventure, humor, and tragedy.

Second, it is a comprehensive history of rural education and common schools in Kentucky, specifically Fleming County, detailing social, cultural, and educational events. State and local curriculum, teaching methods, textbooks, and common school requirements are given.

Third, it is a valuable resource for museum interpretation, providing comparison of rural education and town provisions, even in Fleming County. The Goddard School teachers were expected to carry out many duties. Teachers instructed as many as one hundred students in moral education, reading, arithmetic, writing, orthography (spelling), geography, history, physiology (health), and life science. Besides teaching, the teacher was responsible for cleaning and sometimes repairing the school. Part of this job included arriving at school early enough to get fires going to warm the school before the students arrived. Goddard School teachers did not have teaching supplies, electricity (for many years), indoor plumbing, running water, central heating, janitorial services, telephones, and other needed items that were provided in Flemingsburg schools.

Fourth, the book provides a database of students with parents' names who attended Goddard School and has the potential to unlock family history questions. The Goddard community was part of the Western movement, and people live in homes all over the world.

Finally, this book provides documentation that Goddard, Kentucky, was once a vibrant community before the community withered and died and families moved on.

Goddard School was located in Goddard, Fleming County, Kentucky, a place with green farmlands and Sand Lick Creek, bound by Pea Ridge. The ridge, with an elevation of 1,201 feet, captured the beauty of the valley below. Beagles and blue tick hounds flashed through the pines and oak trees as they chased foxes, rabbits, and squirrels into the sacks of older men, where women dressed chickens, picked blackberries, canned tomatoes and green beans, and made homemade biscuits too good for this world. It was a place where playing the banjo and piano loud was nearly as important as playing it right, where the first frost meant hog-killin' time and the mouth-watering smell of cracklins would drift over the valley of Goddard school from giant iron pots, and students had fresh sausage sandwiches in their lunch, and where Burley tobacco leaves blew off the wagons and hung like scraps of clouds in the branches of trees.

Almost all the houses were painted white. The barns, corn cribs, buggy houses, and hen houses were generally white washed. Many places were bordered with white picket fences and had good gardens and yards full of flowers.

Goddard School community was about one hundred miles from Lexington, Kentucky, ninety miles from Huntington, West Virginia, seventy-five miles from Cincinnati, Ohio, and nine miles to the nearest town, Flemingsburg.

Very few residents saw a mint julep, but several sipped home brew or moonshine from mason jars from local stills. Men paid for their plain-plank houses and a small farm by farming, where Burley tobacco was king. They coaxed crops to grow in the grey clay that no amount of fertilizer would ever turn into rich bottomland. The women worked themselves to death—gardening, canning, cooking, and taking care of large families. Our parents and the students, when they got old enough, worked like dogs in the farm fields as many did not have tractors in those days. If my father ever had a full day of rest in his life, I cannot remember when. Most of our parents wanted us to get an education so that we could have a better life.

Every Sunday morning, the word came forth at the Goddard Methodist Church, next to the Goddard School, where preachers promised that the soul of man never dies.

The Goddard School closed at the end of the 1959 to 1960 school year and was consolidated with Fox Valley Elementary. While great strides have been made in education, there is much from the past that can still be learned and utilized. The rural Goddard School provided adventures of growing and learning with experiences for the child in the church, community, nature, books, and imagination.

Thank you to all who gave your time to share your memories of Goddard School. This book would not have been possible without you!

Thank you to Dr. Brian Creasman, superintendent of schools, Kristie Jolly, and Angie Stephens at the Fleming County school board office for allowing me to research the old records.

Chapter One

Local, State, and National Beginnings

Fleming County and the state of Kentucky had a slow development of education in the early beginning of the state. No provision was made for education in the Kentucky constitutions adopted in 1792 and 1800 respectively. (1) It was 1807 before a governor referred to the subject in his annual address. In that year on December 30, Governor Christopher Greenup said the statement below:

"It is certainly very desirable to have our youth's education among us as it must be evident by their temporary emigration to seminaries in Eastern parts of the United States." (2)

It was 1816 before a governor spoke seriously about the need of a public school system for all children. Governor Gabriel Slaughter addressed the legislature: "Nothing is more worthy of your attention than the promotion of education…by diffusing through the County seminaries and schools for the education of all classes of the community; making them free to all poor children, and the children of poor persons." (3)

The decade 1820 to 1830 was a time of trouble and unrest for Fleming County as it was for Kentucky and the United States. The Panic of 1819 was followed by years of depression. The Bank of Flemingsburg closed, and no new mills, ferries, or new roads were developed. For free education, it was a major setback. A major legislative act for the purpose of establishing common schools in Kentucky had been approved on December 18, 1821. A literary fund was to be distributed to the counties to fund the common school movement. On April 1, 1822, the Fleming County Court appointed commissioners to divide Fleming County into sixteen school districts. However, the hard times that followed the Panic of 1819 found it necessary for the state to use the literary fund, and no distribution was made. (4)

The common school movement was developed by Horace Mann, and its goal was to provide free education to all, regardless of wealth, heritage, or class. Common schools would level the playing field between rich and poor students. The Civil War produced a degree of consensus among most Americans about the need for common schools. People were made aware that division on a major issue, such as slavery, could destroy the country. (5) Horace Mann often quoted Proverbs 22:6: "Train up a child the way he should go, and when he is old he will not depart from it." For Horace Mann, "Moral education was the heart of the curriculum." (6)

Temperance and slavery were the primary moral issues of the day. Moral education was based on the Ten Commandments. Obedience to these commandments preserves the sanctity of family, property, marriage, and truth.

Fleming County had to wait another twenty years to participate in the common school movement.

During those twenty years, many private schools developed. The academy at Flemingsburg continued to operate. It had sold its land endowment before 1812 at prices ranging from ten cents to one dollar an acre. In 1825, the trustees of the academy were made elective. The academy trustees elected on January 2, 1837, were D.K. Stockton, Thomas Fleming, John Donaldson, Thomas Porter, John A. Cavan, and James Throop. (7)

Creighton was one of the teachers. (8) In 1878, the county court disposed of the seminary building by selling it, thus bringing to an end the county academy system. (9)

In addition to the academy, the celebrated William McGuffey ran a private school in Flemingsburg. In Fleming County, private individuals built an undetermined number of subscription schools and field schools on their land. In the records of December 1827, there is mention of a schoolhouse on Licking River near Alexander and Stockton's Mill, and in November 1826, Scioto Evans transferred one-half acre of land to J.D. Bell, Loma Cormack, and Harry Kemper as trustees for the Columbian School House, which the neighborhood had already built on the land for one cent. (10) Thomas M. Crain was named an early teacher in Foudraysburg, later called Hillsboro.

In the Fleming County Records of 1840 to 1850, references are made to the Sylvan Shade School on Fox Creek, the Bum Schoolhouse above Matthew's Mill on the road to the crossing of Fox Creek, the Lewis Crain Schoolhouse at Hillsboro, the Temperance School at Fairview, and Fant's Schoolhouse on the road from LeForge's old mill to the Clover Road. In setting up the common schools, use was made as far as possible of the field school buildings already erected. (11) The field schools normally lasted no more than three months. Early field school textbooks were church hymnals, the Bible, *The Pilgrim's Progress*, and almanacs. The goal was to read, write, and cipher to the rule of three. (12)

Andrew J. Cox of Flemingsburg had a school where he charged tuition and was very prominent in 1866.

The Fleming County Court appointed the commissioners and set up the system of common schools in 1839. The commissioners divided Fleming County into fifty school districts, having a school population of two thousand seven hundred twenty-two children. (13) This meant taxation for the voters. The law gave voters the option of supporting or refusing the school, and votes were held in districts in late 1840 and early 1841. The taxation issue caused considerable opposition. In September 1842 in one district, Robert Stewart protested to the circuit court against the levying of the tax and had his protest upheld by the court. (14)

Fleming County common schools were established in 1841. The Fleming County Court Order Book G, page 85 gives the Commissioner's Report of February Term 1841, giving the names of heads of families with the numbers of children of school age in each family. (15) The report was accompanied by a map of the county showing the common school districts as they were then established.

This report was signed by Commissioners Joseph Seacrest, Mathas Morrison, and Jesse Summons. To understand this map, one must realize the roads were very different at that time. Route 32 had not been developed.

District 49 Order Book G, page 83 gives part of the Goddard area. (16) The heads of household included the following:

William Babbs
William Lewis
James Muse
Mrs. Idyner
Mrs. Conrad
Jesse Patterson
William Hurst
Amos Sutton
John Doyle
A. Gardner
Thomas Staggs
Id Davis
John Norriee
John Iound
Joseph Plummer
Mrs. Kirk
Ben Hartley
Harvey Miller
Mrs. Jordan
Lewis LeForgee

District 29 included the Goddard-Hillsboro vicinity. The Fleming County Court Order Book G, page 85 lists the following heads of households for District 29: (17)

William Emmons
Gamaliel Freeman
Alexander McRoberts
Wm. Vansandt

St. Clair Emmons
James Faris
Mrs. Dearing
Alexandria McRoberts
Jonathan Walton
Nelson Fant
James Bartley
Jesse Evans
Griffin Evans
Bryant Routt
Samuel Moreland
Bazil Hurst
James Story
Elijah Story
Mrs. Lloyd
John Summitt
Sutton Isaac
Charles Nealis

Rev. H. C. Northcott in his *Early History of Hillsboro* describes many of the heads of households listed in District 29 of the commissioner's report in 1841 and where they lived. The Goddard Road is what we now call Routt Road, but it extended over to Parkersburg. "The road to Poplar Plains from the road to Goddard's Mill and Church at the lower end of Mr. Freeman's farm, the road to Poplar Plains turning northwest while the Goddard road followed up to the head of that branch of Locust and passed through what was known as Copper's Gap, and thence down a small stream which emptied into the Sand Lick Fork of Fox. It passed the old Tom Rawlings' farm, mentioned heretofore as the home of Wm. S.T. Graham. Above this farm lived Jesse Evans, some half-mile northeast of the Graham home." (18)

Rev. H. C. Northcott describes what one of the schools was like in District 29 in Hillsboro and the vicinity of the first common schools in Fleming County, which included the Goddard area.

"When I was very small, there was what remained of an old schoolhouse on our farm, about 20 yards west of the dirt road lead-ing to Flemingsburg. But there was a good schoolhouse on the farm near its southern border, about 200 yards west of the same road. It was built of logs with "cat-in-clay" chimney at each end, with fireplaces wide enough and deep enough to take in logs 4 to 5 feet long and a foot or more in diameter. It had one window on the north side made by cutting out a log and inserting a long sash of one pane depth. Opposite this, on the inside, was a writing desk extending all the way across. That is where I first used a pen. I was in my 5th or 6th year when I first went to that school." (19)

"Douglas I. Winn was the teacher. He was a good arithmetician, a splendid penman and a good instructor. He ruled his school kindly and was generally esteemed by patrons and pupils. The morals of the pupils were cared for: profanity, falsehood, and obscenity were forbidden, and truthfulness and all other moral qualities were enforced. Morally, it was a model school. Mr. Winn taught there several years. Afterwards, one session was taught by John Walton, son of Aunt Sally. He had lost a foot by getting it caught by a tree he had cut down. It was amputated just above the ankle and he walked with a crutch. He was not a success as a teacher and did not continue long, but became a constable. The only other teacher in that schoolhouse was Samuel Moreland. He was successful, but Mr. Winn succeeded him and the last before it was tom down. Mr. Winn did not attempt to teach grammar, geography, or philosophy." (20)

"Then followed a schoolhouse a mile south of Hillsboro, on the east side of the road on the farm of William Crain. I think the material of the old one was used to build it. Mr. Winn taught there and my younger brother and I attended. One morning Mr. Winn asked me, 'Henry, did you folks see the phenomena last night?' I told him I did not know what a phenomena was. He explained that great showers of stars had fallen, shooting stars, they call them. I told him that was the first I had heard of it and that I did not think anyone of our family saw them, and so it turned out. But many did see them and were terrified, thinking the end of the world and the judgment Day were at hand. Such a scene would not now seem so fearful, as science has shown that this was only an unusually heavy overflow of a regular astronomical occurrence every November. I have always regretted that I did not see one of the great displays of creative power and glory. But after this time, Mr. Winn was employed at Fant's School House and we attended there. But he had become dull of hearing, could not know near all the mischief going on, even in school hours, and he was unable to maintain discipline and gave up the school. Another teacher there was a Mr. Route of Nicholas County, I think. But he was not capable of controlling such a mob of boys, though qualified in other respects." (21)

"Thomas Richeson came next and he was the last teacher I knew at Fant's School House. Later I attended a school in Hillsboro, the schoolhouse having been transformed from a blacksmith shop, about 20 by 40 feet, warmed by a large stove in the center. Thomas M. Crain was the teacher when I attended there and I studied philosophy and improved my grammar." (22)

As new common schools developed there were not enough school masters to staff them. Up until this time, only men were teachers. Each district would provide a school for all children. Women were now trained to teach, but married women were often barred from the classroom, and women with children were not allowed to teach.

School Laws and Changes

In 1870, Kentucky made the position of school superintendent a public office. He or she was elected for a two-year term. Superintendents rode horseback or buggies to visit the schools.

The Fleming County, Kentucky Settlement Book 4, Page 307 (Fleming County Clerk's Office) gives the Annual Settlement with Teachers for the year ending 1874, by W.A. Morrison: Common School Commissioner. The report does not tell the name of the school, only a list of the teachers and the number of the school, which follows:

1. D. I. Eckman
2. Wm. F. Conway
3. W. F. Rogers
4. John Samuels

5. Phares Throop
6. Tom A. Graham
7. Isiah Dillon
8. E. F. Hamm
9. Y. Phelps
10. E. Robinson
11. A. D. Gross
12. ?Vickers
13. Mrs. Yates
14. Wm. H. George
15–16. Wm Hart
17. Jas Sousley
18. Wm. Allen
19. T. M. Cantrell
20–21. S. O. Williams
22. J. Simdrian
23. J. Simdrian
24. W. W. Cartmell
25. Milford Overly
26. Elias McKee
27. A. B. Chadwick
28. Allen Evans
29. James Reeves
30. Gilmore
31. McKee
32. Andrew Fountain
33–34. Mrs. Morly
35. Tor Primer
36. J. W. Stamper
37. Miss M. E. Prather
38. J. P. Cord
39. Wm. A. Wood
40–41. Miss Caywood
42. James Dawson
43. Johnson Russ
44. S. C. Madden

45. Bailey Bryant
46–47. D. J. Stapleton
49. John R. Carpenter
50. E. Jones
51. O. Estill
53. Alice Staggs
55. J. Kirk
56. R. D. Money
58. J. W. Gordon
59. M. Eva Dickey
60. Hutchinson
61. Sam Hull
62. Jas. Jones
63. Miss Bell Davis
64. Miss Lucky Pleak
65. Mrs. Clarke
68. L. J. Cord
69. Theo Alexander

Total payment to these teachers is $6,849.80 for five months. Signed by J. E. Smith, presiding judge, Fleming County

In 1875, the state school superintendent started offering teacher institutes in the local area for teachers to gain additional training.

In 1882, Milford Overley was elected as commissioner in Fleming County. Overley's title was changed to superintendent of schools in 1884. Overley made major improvements in the schools in Fleming County. When he became commissioner, there were only two brick schoolhouses in the county, with seventy-four one-room houses, half of them (37) being log houses. In 1883, the county schools were redistricted. People felt Overley should be called the Father of Education in Fleming County. (23)

In 1897, C.G. Whaley was superintendent of Fleming County schools and gave a two-year report to the state superintendent of public instruction. "Our county does not show up as well as I should like, but you will notice that we have made some advances. Our attendance has increased, but not as much as it should be, on account of laxity in trustees and others in enforcing our compulsory educational laws, yet I am glad to say that this law has brought some children in school that otherwise would have stayed at home. Our schoolhouses are in better condition than ever before, and I am safe in saying that the standard of teachers has never been up to where it is today. Yet, with all this, there is much that needs to be accomplished before our schools are up to the standard we would all like to see them." (24)

Mr. Whaley reported that there were sixty-nine white and seven colored districts in Fleming County in 1895 to 1896. School was taught for five months in sixty-eight of these schools, with one school having more than five months. By this time, many of the log houses had been upgraded to frame, with only six log houses, sixty-one frame houses, and two brick houses remaining. Goddard's (called Sanford then) four schools were still log. Of the sixty-eight schools, forty-six were furnished with globes, maps, charts, etc. Goddard was not among the forty-six. The number of teachers who taught in the common schools were forty men and thirty-eight women. Men were paid forty-three dollars per month while women were paid thirty dollars and two cents per month. G.W. Leahy was the White Institute conductor for professional development. The colored schools did not have a teacher institute. (25) In 1895 to 1896, the percentage of attendance based on the census (those eligible to attend were thirty-six percent male and thirty-eight percent female attendance based on enrollment) was sixty-three percent male and sixty-eight percent female. Students over eighteen who enrolled were sixty male and sixty-eight female. (26)

1. J.J. Dickey. "Fleming County History." _The Fleming Gazette._ February 24, 1931. Dickey Scrapbook. p. 19.
2. Christopher Greenup. _Executive Journal, 1804 to 1808._ MSS. in possession of Kentucky State Historical Society, Frankfort, Kentucky.
3. Frankfort: Gerard and Kendall. _Journal of the Senate of the Commonwealth of Kentucky 1816._ 1816. pp. 18 to 19

4. Robert S. Cotterill. *History of Fleming County, Kentucky: The First One-Hundred Years, 1780 to 1880.* D. 192.

5. Jenchs and Riesman, D. *The Academic Revolution.* Garden City, New York: Doubleday, 1968.

6. Horace Mann. *Twelfth Annual Report.* Dutton & Wentworth, 1849. p. 107.

7. Deed Book U. p. 24

8. Cotterill, op. cit. 243

9. Cotterill, Ibid. p. 335

10. Cotterill, Ibid. p. 192

11. Cotterill, Ibid. p. 263

12. James Rawlings, "History of Mason County, Kentucky Schools." Maysville, Kentucky, unpublished, p.2. (Available at Kentucky Gateway Museum Center, Maysville, Kentucky.)

13. Cotterill, Op. cit. p. 245

14. Cotterill, Ibid. p. 245

15. The Fleming County Court Order Book G, p. 85

16. Order Book, Ibid. p. 83

17. Fleming County Court Order Book G, Ibid. page 85

18. Rev. H.C. Northcott, *Early History of Hillsboro,* http://kykinfolk.org/fleming/hillsborol.htm, p.12.

19. Ibid

20. Northcutt, Ibid. p. 15

21. Northcutt, Ibid. p. 15

22. Ibid.

23. Cotterill, op. cit. p. 340.

24. Report of the Superintendent of Public Instruction of the State of Kentucky for Two Scholastic Years ended June 30, 1897. Louisville: George F. Felter Printing Company, 1897. p. 351.

25. Ibid. p. 353

26. Ibid. p. 352.

Chapter 2

The Common Schools at Goddard

According to the records of the Fleming County schools, when the county schools were redistricted in 1883, the county school district had four Goddard (Sanford) schools, listed as numbers 50, 52, 53, and 54 in Subdistrict 10. Subdistricts were used until April 25, 1936, when the school board changed the districts again. Flemingsburg was an independent school district until it merged with the county school district in May 22, 1936. (1)

It is thought one of the first Goddard schools, number 52, was located in the general vicinity of Tom Hurst's farm. The old schoolhouse deteriorated and was not satisfactory. It was later used as a com crib. This was located on Wilder Loop in the vicinity of Jean and Larry Porter's property. The students served were east of Goddard and in the immediate Goddard area.

The new second school was a log one-room school in the woods of Professor Tom Hurst, later owned by daughter and son-in law, Wells and Verna Hurst Campbell. The school was called Sanford Oak Grove, number 53. This school served just above Goddard and toward Wallingford on what is now Wooley Road. All Goddard (Sanford) one-room ungraded log schools were part of the common school movement. It is not known where the other two schools were located at Sanford (Goddard). Many students went to age twenty. The regular school year only lasted five months in the year. Attendance was not compulsory. Many of the older boys missed several days in the farm harvest season.

Mr. Tom Hurst was a teacher, and as was his daughter, Miss Verna Hurst. Maude Morrison, before she married Oscar Helphinstine, also taught there a very short time. It was not proper for a lady after she married to teach school at that time.

In 1893, when Maude Morrison started to Sanford's Oak Grove School, number 53, as a student, she still had to deal with the slavery issue. The Confederate boys carried sticks around like they had rifles and threatened shy Union girls, such as herself. Her sisters, Anna and Lulu, and she shivered when they passed the bare spot in Mr. Zeke Jones' field that resulted from her schoolmates' daily replaying their family's side in the war. Several parents of children in the school fought in the Tenth Kentucky Calvary and Sixteenth Kentucky Infantry and still lived in Goddard. They were William A. Gooding, William H. Williams, W.K. Ham, J.W. McIntire, D.E. Staggs, J.W. Hammond, J.W. Gardner, S. K. Gulley, and others. (2) Some skirmishes had taken place nearby at Plummers Landing and Poplar Plains, and the divided sentiments continued.

Maude Morrison had some great teachers in her Goddard Oak Grove School. She loved Miss Molly Waltz because she came and spent the night with each of the students to get to know them and their parents.

Another favorite teacher of Maude's, Mr. Jesse Littleton, son of Columbus and Rose Ann Littleton, was married to Margaret McDaniel and lived at Sanford (now Goddard). He was known for having students provide entertainment on a stage in one end of the classroom. Mr. Littleton's brothers, William, Charles, and Bruce, and sister Minnie, formed a quartet. Maude said, "They really could sing! I wonder how popular they would have been if they had lived in the days of radio and television." Mr. Littleton taught Maude the love of music. Minnie was the mother of Owen Story, who later taught at Goddard School and Fleming County High School. Mr. Jesse Littleton died of typhoid fever shortly after he taught at Oak Grove.

Maude's special cousins Milton Morrison, Heytor Morrison, Elisha Morrison, and Wallace Hunter were also teachers as well as

Himmer McGregor, Morton Davis, Frank Evans, May Zimmerman, Clyde Flannery, Mike Littleton, Maggie Campbell, Myrtle Hickerson, Nell Davis, and Rosco James. Maude's sister, Lulu Morrison, finished her last year of teaching at Oak Grove. Sometimes these teachers may have one hundred pupils at a time. Some of the textbooks used were *Webster's Speller, McGuffey Readers, Ray's Arithmetic,* and *Harry's Grammar.*

Maude Morrison's last teacher, and perhaps the one who influenced her most, was Professor Tom Hurst. Maude did not have transportation to attend high school at Flemingsburg, so Professor Hurst taught her advanced skills for several years. He had additional training somewhere in Ohio. Professor Hurst taught Maude advanced arithmetic and algebra and also grammar as heavy subject in diagramming and parsing. He was the first teacher to teach her writing, which inspired her to start writing poetry. He especially liked her poem "Four Sun Beams," which she had written in her notebook. She kept this notebook from her school days, and now her granddaughter has it. She continued to write poetry. (3)

Subscription schools offered the additional option of going to school in the spring and summer for three months. Maude's father always paid her way. Teachers also accepted furs, food, bacon, com, tobacco, and whiskey as pay. They were called subscription schools because they were supported by pro rata subscription of the farmers in the community who wanted some additional schooling for their children. (4)

The teachers at the Oak Grove subscription schools were Mrs. Charles Jones (Allie Lewis Jones) and Miss Erie Evans. Maude Morrison enjoyed the subscription schools because one had additional curriculum and students from other common schools in the area attended. She enjoyed Jack Evans, Miss Erie Evans' youngest brother, who attended the Emmons School; Mary Ellen Greene, grandchild of Jerry Murphy and Julia Atchison, who also attended the Emmons School; Minnie and Lucy Plummer, children of Joseph Mallon Plummer by his last wife, Lou Ross, who attended the Plummer School; and others.

Maude passed her test for completion from the common school with flying colors! At that time, school was not graded. Different levels of the basics were taught. She was enjoying learning so much that she decided she wanted to be a teacher. Maude wrote poems about her first school days.

Civil War School Days

The tales meditative to me as a child
Of the happiest moments and things not so mild
That my parents recounted will ever outlast
My own sheltered childhood; for days that were past
Were branded with stigma and brought to my breast
The stir of emotion of those years of unrest.

That old trampled bare spot in Zeke Jones' field
To my eager questions would true stories yield
That barren half-acre took longer to hear
Than the heart of the Nation, for it could still feel
The tread of school-children in organized play
Taking sides 'gainst each other, The Blue and the Gray.

The one-room log schoolhouse could tell could it speak
Of the serious conflicts that occurred week by week
As the boys played soldier armed only with sticks
And fought with each other, or practiced sly tricks
On some Reel's daughter, or left in a whirl
Of confusion and terror some shy Union girl.

The homespun-clad children who, shaking with cold
Would walk somewhat faster and pretend to be bold
Past the huge leafy houses that were the den
Of the hogs of the woodland, and sometimes, of men
Who sick and unshaven, had lost all their pride

And from comrades in action had wandered to hide.

The fathers spoke words that were stinging as bees
When they met at the school-house to elect their trustees.
The man so selected had only one plan—
To teach in this district, we choose a strong man
The nervous old teacher gained control of the school
By the number of knuckles he warped with his rule.
The lessons were lengthy and not understood
But the pupils gained knowledge from their school in the wood. (5.)

Maude Morrison Helphinstine, "Along the Buffalo Trail," permission
by Frances Helphinstine and Virginia Helphinstine Reeves

A PTA of the Olden Days

When Molly taught,
(May her soul be blest)
The P.T.A. was at its best.
No home was so crowded or ill fed
That Molly couldn't share a bed.

Her pupils were her joy, delight,
And Molly went to spend the night
With each of them; She meant to know
Why they were bright or they were slow.

Pride in their eyes I still can see,
"Miss Molly's going home with me";
And their cold lunch she shared next day.
Oh yes, Miss Molly knew the way
To gain the confidence of all
And be her pupils large or small
The grades they made were always good
Because Miss Molly understood.

She celebrated Arbor Day
And fathers came and cleared away
The brush, and trimmed with care
The trees that God had planted there.

After the dinner that mothers brought
Were children's speeches. Thus she sought
And found a happy-go-lucky way
For a very successful P.T. A.

Report Card of Maude Morrison
Sanford Oak Grove School 1895
The name Sanford was changed to Goddard.
Mollie Waltz, Teacher

About Molly Waltz, teacher
Maude Morrison Helphinstine (6)

To be a teacher, one had to pass a very difficult test. If one scored below seventy-five, she failed and could not teach.

Maude Morrison discussed teaching with her older sister, Lulu, who was teaching at Bluebank, Kentucky, at this time. Because she knew Maude had enjoyed some of the teachers she had had in the subscription schools, such as Mrs. Allie Lewis Jones and Miss Erie Evans, Lulu suggested that Maude start teaching at the subscription school at Oak Grove to see how she liked it. Lula warned Maude of some of the pranks the big boys might pull on her, like turning the outhouses over, putting tacks in her seat, or putting skunk oil in her pocket when she is helping another student.

Maude purchased her reading books and was ready to go to work.

Just three weeks after she started teaching in the subscription school, she became very ill with double pneumonia. She then had complications and was sick for three years and not able to teach. During this time, she did much thinking. She knew it was not proper for a young lady to teach after she was married! She knew she needed to start developing her skills to run a household. Her mother taught her to cook, sew, quilt, can, and garden. Her mother's half-sister, Aunt Bell, who was not the easiest to live with, came to live with Maude's family during this time. Her father, who was having some major issues with his health from injuries sustained in the Civil War, taught her some business skills with the running of their 200-acre farm, which she decided to implement.

Maude's teacher, T. F. Hurst, had a contract to continue teaching for the regular six months. The teacher's contract was between the teacher and the trustees of the district. The following is the contract for T. F. Hurst, teacher at Goddard School number 53 in 1906.

Contract Between Teacher and Trustees

This Article of Agreement entered into on the 12 day of July 1906 witnesseth that T. F. Hurst, holding a 1st Class certificate, has contracted with the Trustees, Lewis Staggs, C.W. Staggs and W. K. Ham, Trustees of District No. 53, in the county of Fleming, state of Kentucky, to teach the Common School of Said District for the term of 6 months beginning on September, the 3rd day of 1906, in accordance with the Common School Laws and the Rules and Regulations prescribed in pursuance thereof by the State Board of Education, for the sum of Public Money.

Said District has a census enrollment of _____pupil children.

The said teacher hereby holds himself subject to the legal supervision and direction of said Trustees, and to the visitation and lawful authority of the County Superintendent, the said Trustees reserving the right to suspend said Teacher at any time whatever, for any of the causes specified in Common School Laws.

It is also agreed that the fires shall be regularly made and the floor regularly swept in said house, during said term, by the said teacher, the said Trustees providing the fuel and brooms thereof.

(Signatures) C. J. Scott, Chairman
Lewis Staggs, Trustee
C. W. Staggs, Trustee
W. K. Ham, Trustee
T. F. Hurst, Teacher

Note: Section 81—The Contract between Teacher and Trustees shall not be entered into before the first of July of the Calendar year in which the school is to begin.
Note: Sections 83, 134, and 136: Contract must be made at a meeting called for the purpose, all members of the Board present, or after personnel notice to absent member, specifying time, place and purpose of the meeting.

Sanford School Number 50
Student Census, 1898, 1899

Father's Name	Child's Name
Rolla Arnold	Frank Arnold
	Eddie Arnold
	Ottie Arnold
William and Mariah Beckett	Iva B. Beckett
	Charlotte Beckett
	Laura Beckett
	John S. Beckett
Matt and Minerva Bramel	Bettie Bramel
	Anna B. Bramel
	Emma Bramel
	Kirby Bramel
America Bristow	Ida Bristow
Ed and Mollie Carpenter	Early Carpenter
	Goldie Carpenter
Lizzie Carpenter	Belt Carpenter
	Eva W. Carpenter
	Clarence Carpenter
	Alice Carpenter
William (Watt) and Hattie Carpenter	Fay Carpenter
	John Skeen
Abe and Sallie Cline	Sida W. Cline
	Mary B. Cline
Mrs. C. C. Craig	Theodore Bass
William and Melvina Dearing	Levada Dearing
	Una Mae Dearing
	Eddie C. Dearing

Frank and Alice DeBusch

Omar DeBusch
Rillie DeBusch
Eddie DeBusch
Frank DeBusch

James and Motie Doyle

Irvin Doyle
Alice Doyle
Elmer L. Doyle

John and Betsy Doyle

Lula Doyle

Miles H. and Elizabeth Doyle

Mary R. Doyle
Rolla H. Doyle
Frank Doyle
Elias C. Doyle

Nelson and Margerette Gooding

Hattie E. Gooding

Wesley Gooding

Susan Gooding
Thomas F. Gooding
Minnie Gooding
Emma Gooding
Solomon W. Gooding
Retha Gooding

John Grimes

Marshall Parks

James W. and Annie Ham

M. Ham
Carie Ham
Essey Ham

Elizabeth Hartman

Ina E. Hinton
Rosa Hinton

James and Annie Hines

Ida Hines
John L. Hines
Ollie Hines
Robert P. Hines

J. D. Hinton

Robert D. Hinton
Mary Hinton

S. R. and Alice Hinton

Bruce Hinton
Callie Hinton
Nellie Hinton
Lonnie Hinton
Ollie Hinton

John and Zillie Hurst

Roy Hurst
Howard Hurst

Dudley Jordan

Louise Jordan

Perry and Ruth Manning

Anna F. Manning
Minnie Manning
Emma Manning
Gleanor Manning
Rosa Manning

John H. and Allie Mathews

Jennie W. Mathews
Mammie Mathews
Daugherty Mathews

Miranda A. McRoberts

Mary McRoberts

P.M. Samuels

Willie Samuels

Alexander and Lizzie Staggs

Denzel Thacker

David E. Staggs, Sr.

David E. Staggs, Jr.

George and Eddie Tincher

Lizzie Tincher
Mahala Tincher

Taylor and Lizzie Waltz

Lula M. Arnold
Charles Waltz
Robert Waltz

Sam and Rutha Williams

Millie H. Williams
Stella Williams
Flora Williams
Ida Williams

Robert H. and Mary Yantis

Thomas Yantis

Sanford School, Number 52, Subdistrict 10 1898, 1899

Parent	Child	Age
Lott Bramble	Ida Bramble	7
William Carpenter	Emma Carpenter	15
	Mirtle Carpenter	18
	Orval Carpenter	12
	Oscar Carpenter	8
James Gorman	Elder Gorman	
	William Gorman	8
Branson Gulley	Eunice Hughes	7
John Gulley	Matilda Gulley	6
	Rachel Gulley	8
Walker K. Ham	Clyde Ham	12
	Hattie Ham	10
	Jack Ham	19
	Minnie Ham	15
	Thomas Ham	8
	Allen Ham	
Dixie James	Ottn James	7
Mary C. James	Bessie James	14
	Ethel James	10
	Osel James	
	Thomas James	18

Oscar S. James	Arthur James	
	Boswell James	
	Fannie James	
	Girtha James	
	Hittum James	11
	Iva James	
	Lela James	
	Millard James	
	Omer James	10
	Ora W. James	
	Pearl James	6
	Armor James	
Edgar Jordan	Gertrude Jordan	7
William G. Jordan	Dow Jordan	14
	Lulin Jordan	16
	Mage Jordan	19
	Omar Jordan	10
	Otis Jordan	7
Larry D. Kirk	Charles H. Kirk	19
Shelton Parker	Early A. Parker	14
	Green Parker	17
	Iva Parker	
	John S. Parker	7
	Steley M. Parker	11
Joseph M. Plummer	Julia Plummer	7
	Lucie Plummer	13
	Minnie Plummer	14
George W. Pugh	Luther E. Pugh	15
Charles W. Staggs	Mirtie Staggs	
	Ollie Staggs	18
	Tulley Staggs	16
	William Staggs	13

James T. Staggs	Archie Staggs	
	Bussel Staggs	14
	Jessie Staggs	10
	Pearl Staggs	8
	Walter Staggs	7
Lewis (Louis) Staggs	Frank Staggs	13
	Hattie Staggs	8
	Hord Staggs	18
	Irene Staggs	7
	Joseph Staggs	10
	Ward Staggs	13
Ralleigh Staggs	Claude Staggs	6
	Cora Staggs	15
	Laura Staggs	15
	Stewart Staggs	10
William Staggs	Marvin Staggs	8
William Thacker	Annie Thacker	18
	Frank Thacker	9
	Jeanette Thacker	15
John Thompson	Alonzo Leaverball	19
	Evert Thompson	8
	Jessey Thompson	15
William Welch	Burt (Albert) Welch	19
	Ben Welch	9
	John Welch	12
	Matilda Welch	15
	Morton Welch	
	Rachel Welch	7
	Sarah Welch	7
	William Welch	13

Mary (Mrs. Charles)	Charles H. Baird	18
Williams	Grover Cleveland Baird	12
	James Edward Baird	15
	Shila Williams	6
	Thomas Williams	9
	Ben Williams	
Hiriam Yazell	Charley Yazell	
John H. Yazell	Leslie Yazell	10
	Lethia Yazell	9
	Lutie Yazell	7
	Luther Yazell	10

Sanford School, Number 52, Subdistrict 10 1903

Parent	**Child**
Lott Bramble	Ida Bramble
	Ora Bramble
	Mary Bramble
William Carpenter	Emma Carpenter
	Mirtle Carpenter
	Orval Carpenter
	Oscar Carpenter
James Freeman	Alice Fischer
Thomas Grayson	Ora Grayson
Blanche Gulley	Minnie Hughes
C. W. Ham	Amy Ham
	Gilbert Ham
	Ethel Ham

Walker K. Ham	Clyde Ham
	Hattie Ham
	Allen Ham
Mary C. James	Bessie James
	Ethel James
	Osel James
	Thomas James
Oscar S. James	Arthur James
	Boswell James
	Fannie James
	Girtha James
	Lela James
	Omer James
	Pearl James
William G. Jordan	Dow Jordan
	Omar Jordan
	Oris Jordan
James Kirk	Mary Kirk
	Leona Kirk
Shelton Parker	Early A. Parker
	Iva Parker
	Stella M. Parker
Joseph M. Plummer	Julia Plummer
	Minnie Plummer
Charles W. Staggs	William Staggs
H. R. Staggs	Marvy Staggs
James T. Staggs	Archie Staggs
	Russell Staggs
	Pearl Staggs
	Walter Staggs

Lewis (Louis) Staggs	Frank Staggs
	Hattie Staggs
	Hord Staggs
	Irene Staggs
	Joseph Staggs
Raleighn Staggs	Claude Staggs
	Harvey Staggs
	Laura Staggs
	Stewart Staggs
William Thacker	Frank Thacker
John Thompson	Luther Thompson
	Evert Thompson
	Jessey Thompson
William Welch	Ben Welch
	John Welch
	Morton Welch
	Mary Welch
	Sarah Welch
	William Welch
Mary (Mrs. Charles) Williams	Stellie Baird
	Grover Cleveland Baird
	Ben Baird
John H. Yazell	Leslie Yazell
	Lethia Yazell
	Lutie Yazell
	Luther Yazell

Goddard School, Number 52, Subdistrict 10

Note: Sanford has been changed to Goddard
1907

Lott Bramel	Ida Brammel	Dec. 21, 1891
	Ira Brammel	June 6, 1894
	Mary Brammel	Sept. 10, 1896
	Lester Brammel	June 12, 1899
	Minnie Brammel	Mar. 14, 1901
William Dearing	Yants Dearing	Feb. 20, 1890
	Mary R. Dearing	Jan. 31, 1897
John Eubanks, guardian	Grillie Sender (?	1893
Annie Gardner	Essa Ham	Aug. 1, 1889
	Carry Ham	Mar. 23, 1898
	Ewin Ham	May 15, 1897
Branson Gulley	Enis Hughes	Jan. 9, 1891
Walker K. Ham	Allen Ham	Oct. 21, 1890
Sam Hammonds	Brice Hammonds	Sept. 6, 1889
O.S. James	Omar James	Jan. 7, 1890
	Pearl James	Oct. 4, 1891
	Boswell	April 21, 1893
	Grithey	Dec. 27, 1895
	Lida B. James	Oct. 24, 1896
	Lucy James	May 29, 1899
W.E. James	Osel James	Sept. 6, 1891
W.J. Jordan	Otie Jordan	Jan. 20, 1891
Jess Kirk	Mary E. Kirk	Sept. 28, 1893
	Leona Kirk	Mar. 30, 1895
	Arthur Kirk	July 20, 1897
	Matilda Susan Kirk	June 19, 1899

Shelton Parker	Stella M. Parker	Oct. 11, 1889
Benjamin Plummer	Carl Plummer	Jan. 15, 1900
James Pugh	Pearl Pugh	July 13, 1891
	Jane Pugh	May 15, 1899
C.W. Staggs	Lutie Staggs	Jan. 24, 1893
James C. Staggs	Pearl Staggs	Mar. 28, 1890
	Wallie Staggs	Nov. 13, 1891
	Archie Staggs	July 26, 1895
Lewis Staggs	Hattie Staggs	July 21, 1889
	Joseph Staggs	Aug. 10, 1892
	Irene Staggs	May 3, 1895
	Mamie Staggs	June 16, 1899
Raleigh Staggs	Claude Staggs	Oct. 19, 1891
	Harry Staggs	Aug. 15, 1895
	Dorcas Staggs	Oct. 21, 1899
William Staggs	Marvin Staggs	Aug. 12, 1890
William Thacker	Frank Thacker	1889
Jno. Thompson	Everett Thompson	May 17, 1891
	T. Luther Thompson	May 9, 1895

Goddard School Number 52, Subdistrict 10 1909

William Bailey	Ella M. Bailey	August 17, 1898	10
	Frank E. Bailey	April 18, 1900	9
	Amy E. Bailey	Sept. 16, 1902	7
William Dearing	Yants Dearing	Feb. 20, 1890	14
	Mary R. Dearing	Jan. 31, 1897	12

Sarah Evans, guardian	E.O. Sandes	April 19, 1897	12
Robert Fieman	M.W. Fieman	Nov. 10, 1902	6
W.K. Ham	Allen Ham	Oct. 21, 1890	18
Thomas Hammond	Melvin Hammond	October 4, 1902	6
Charles Hughes	E. Hughes	Jan. 9, 1891	18
W.H. Humphries	B. Humphries	March 11, 1901	7
O.S. James	Omar James	Jan. 7, 1890	19
	Pearl James	Oct. 4, 1891	17
	Boswell James	April 21, 1893	15
	Gritney James	Dec. 27, 1895	13
	Lida B. James	Oct. 24, 1896	11
	Lucy James	May 29, 1899	10
W.E. James	Osel James	Sept. 6, 1891	17
Ga. Jones	V. Jones	Jan. 4, 1902	7
Alice Jordan	G. Jordan	May 12, 1891	17
	B. Jordan	Nov. 7, 1894	14
	Y. Jordan	Aug. 13, 1897	11
	L. Jordan	Aug. 19, 1901	8
	B. Jordan	June 14, 1903	6
W.J. Jordan	Otie Jordan	Jan. 20, 1891	18
Jess Kirk	Mary E. Kirk	Sept. 28, 1893	15
	Leona Kirk	Mar. 30, 1895	14
	Arthur Kirk	July 20, 1897	11
	Matilda Susan Kirk	June 19, 1899	9
	M. Hayden Kirk	Feb. 3, 1901	8
	James F. Kirk	June 6, 1903	6

William Lawrence	Mae Lawrence	Dec. 4, 1900	8
C. Mattox	E.O. Mattox	May 3, 1902	7
Samuel McClure	H. F. McClure	July 17, 1889	19
	D. F. McClure	Feb. 6, 1897	12
Jas. McIntire, guardian	H. Hammond	Feb. 6, 1891	18
Shelton Parker	Stella M. Parker	Oct. 11, 1889	19
Benjamin Plummer	Carl Plummer	Jan. 15, 1900	9
	Lester Plummer	Nov. 3, 1902	6
George Plummer	Jewel Plummer	June 17, 1903	6
J.D. Pugh	S. J. Pugh	May 18, 1898	10
	E. Z. Pugh	July 4, 1901	7
G. W. Royce	Ray S. Royce	Dec. 16, 1901	7
Thomas Shoemaker	A. L. Shoemaker	Dec. 12, 1892	16
Thomas Shoemaker,	Mattie Craig	August 7, 1890	18
guardian	Calvin Craig	August 7, 1892	16
	Charles M. Craig	March 7, 1886	14
	Mary Craig	September 29, 1902	6
C.W. Staggs	Lutie Staggs	Jan. 24, 1893	16
James C. Staggs	Pearl Staggs	Mar. 28, 1890	19
	Wallie Staggs	Nov. 13, 1891	17
	Archie Staggs	July 26, 1895	13
Lewis Staggs	Hattie Staggs	July 21, 1889	18
	Joseph Staggs	Aug. 10, 1892	16
	Irene Staggs	May 3, 1895	13
	Mamie Staggs	June 16, 1899	10
	Alime Staggs	Dec. 20, 1901	7

Raleigh Staggs	Claude Staggs	Oct. 19, 1891	17
	H. Staggs	Aug. 15, 1895	13
	D. Staggs	Oct. 21, 1899	10
	H. Staggs	Aug. 29, 1901	7
Jno. Thompson	E. Thompson	May 17, 1891	18
	T. L. Thompson	May 9, 1895	14
Charles Yazell	Edna M. Yazell	Oct. 13, 1900	8
	Leonard R. Yazell	May 13, 1903	6
J. H. Yazell	Luther Yazell	Oct. 28, 1892	16
	Lotie Yazell	Sept. 5, 1893	18
	Leslie Yazell	Feb. 4, 1895	14
Nelson Yazell	Lena Yazell	Sept. 24, 1894	14
	Clarence Yazell	Mar. 6, 1897	12
	Ernest Yazell	Nov. 13, 1898	10
	Vern M. Yazell	May 24, 1900	9
	Harold Yazell	June 28, 1902	6

(Some teachers do not give complete information.)

Sanford Oak Grove Common School Number 53

Student Census 1898, 1899
Sanford, Kentucky

Father's Name	Child's Name	Age
G. D. Bramel	Calla Bramel	7
	Dora Bramel	11
	Marie Bramel	6
Sam Bratton	Arthur Bratton	9
Sarah Evans	Chester Evans	10
	William Evans	16

J.W. Faris	Curtis Yazell, guardian	7
	William Yazell, guardian	6
	James G. Faris	7
	William C. Faris	9
James F. Faris	Gertrude Faris	7
	John R. Faris	6
Henry Gaines	Elbridge Gaines	7
	Elmer Gaines	12
	May Gaines	10
	Muriel Gaines	6
William Gooding	Clarence Hickerson	11
Jas Grayson	Arnet Grayson	18
	Doss Grayson	14
	Joseph Grayson	16
	Omar Grayson	12
C.N. Ham	Amy Ham	6
Charles W. Hammond	Early Hammond	14
	Emma Hammond	18
	Harvey Hammond	7
John T. Hammonds	H. Walter Jones	16
James M. (Levina F. Hedges)	Arthur Hedges	16
	Floyd Hedges	17
	Lloyd Hedges	17
	Mary Hedges	13
V. G. Hedges	Ollie Lee Hedges	6
J. W. Hunter	Elmond Hill	
	Hinton Hunter	9
	Lulie Hunter	14
	Morgan Hunter	18
	Nellie Hunter	16
	Orvil Hill, guardian	14
	Ralph Hunter	11

James Hurst	Bessie Hurst	
	Dudley Hurst	6
	Lula W. Hurst	10
	Lyda F. Hurst	6
	Nelson Hurst	19
	Rhoda Hurst	15
	Robert Hurst	11
Tom F. Hurst	Alice Hurst	9
	Verna Hurst	6
D.A. Jackson	Omer Jackson	11
	Robert Jackson	9
W. J. James	Bertha L. James	8
	Roscoe James	7
James S. Knapp	E.H. Knapp	16
	Eva L. Knapp	17
	Irvin H. Knapp	15
	Millie Knapp	
	Rulla Knapp	14
	Stella Knapp	6
J. Frank Littleton	Charles Littleton	7
	Chester Littleton	8
	Lulu Littleton	6
Myrina Luman	Charles Hickerson	6
James McIntyre, guardian	Clark Maxey	12
Elisha S. Morrison	Frankie Morrison	9
	Mary L. Morrison	16
	Martha Lyons Morrison	8
	Nellie Morrison	10
Henry Clay Morrison	Eliza Maude Morrison	13
E. S. Morrison	Lida M. Morrison	12
Mrs. Martha Muse	Pearl Story	19

J.F. Plummer	Ann Plummer	9
	Elbert Plummer	17
	Hiriam Plummer	6
	Marshall Plummer	16
	Omer S. Plummer	11
	Robert Plummer	12
Elizabeth E. Reeves	Clarie Bratton	6
Carl Rickert	Mattie Rickert	15
	William Rickert	19
Hiram Rickert	Charles Gooding, guardian	15
	Donna Rickert	8
	Lela Rickert	7
	Ona Rickert	8
	Stella Lee Rickert	
U.C. Royse	Estella Royse	7
	George Royse	19
T.W. Shepherd	Alice Shepherd	
	Ames Shepherd	
	Bess Shepherd	
	Ethel Shepherd	
	Hittum Shepherd	
C. P. Vise	Ann Vise	8
	Ola Vise	8
	Omer Vise	9
	Rola Vise	10
	Tullie Vise	13
Floyd Waddle	Alice Waddle	11
	Clifford Waddle	6
	LeVada Waddle	9
	Major R. Waddle	12
W. H. Williams	Dora Williams	18
	George Williams	18
	Nora Williams	16

Hiram Yazell	Ally Jane Yazell	12
	Charles P. Yazell	16
	James T. Yazell	18
	John Samuel Yazell	9
	Joseph M. Yazell	14
	Minnie Yazell	7

(Some teacher records give the age of the child instead of the birthday. Depending on the teacher, dates may vary.)

Sanford Oak Grove Common School Number 53 1903

Goddard, Kentucky

Father's Name	Child's Name
John Bolin	Lillie B. Bolin
G.D. Bramel	Calla Bramel
	Marie Bramel
	May D. Bramel
	Milford Bramel
William Dearing	Una Mae Dearing
	Yantis Dearing
	Mary Dearing
Sara Evans	Chester E. Evans
	E. O. Sands
James M. Faris	Anabell Faris
	John Ransome Faris
	Stellie Faris
John Faris	Basil Faris
	Curtis Yazell
	James G. Faris
	John Faris
	William B. Faris
	William Yazell

John W. Faris

Carl Faris
James Gordon Faris

Kittie Faris

John B. Faris
Unis Faris

Henry Gaines

Elbridge Gaines
Alma Gaines
Mary Gaines
Murriel Gaines
Nellie Gaines

William Gooding

Clarence Hickerson

Julia B. Hammond

Early Hammond
Harvey Hammond
Nellie Hammond

James Hedges

Mary J. Hedges

Ulysses Hedges

Ollie Hedges
Edgar Hedges

John D. Huff

Blanche A. Huff

J.W. Hunter

Morgan Hunter
Nellie Hunter
Lulie Hunter
Ralph Hunter
Hinton Hunter
Orville Hill
Elmond Hill

James Hurst

Robert D. Hurst
Lida Hurst
Bessie Hurst

T.F. Hurst

Alice Hurst
Verna Hurst
Arthur Hurst
Clarence Hurst

W.J. James	Annie James
	Bertha James
	Clarence James
	Laura James
	William R. James
Samuel Knapp	Estella Knapp
	Nellie Knapp
	Rullie Knapp
Frank Littleton	Harley M. Littleton
	Chester Littleton
	Lula Littleton
Clay (Henry) Morrison	Eliza Maude Morrison
E S Morrison	Frankie J Morrison
	Nellie Steele Morrison
	Martha Lyons Morrison
Claude Reeves	Clifford J. Reeves
Elizabeth Reeves	Clarie Bratton
Charles Rickett, guardian	Charles Morton
Ulysses C. Royse	Estella Royse
	Lena A. Royse
William Royse	Erma L. Royse
	Omer F. Royse
	Ruth M. Royse
Clay Whisman	Anna Bessie Whisman
Samuel Williams	Flora Williams
	Ida Williams
	Stella Williams
Hiriam Yazell	Joseph Yazell
	Abby Yazell
	John Yazell
	Minnie Yazell
	Melvina Yazell

Oak Grove School Goddard
Number 53 1907

Parent Name	Child Name	Date of Birth	Age
William Bailey	Ella Bailey	August 17, 1898	8
	Frank Bailey	April 18, 1900	7
	James Bailey	January 5, 1893	14
Lizzie Byram	Nellie M. Byram	August 28, 1897	10
Charles Calvert	Dean Calvert	January 30, 1892	15
	Maude M. Calvert	January 10, 1894	13
	Lullie Calvert	December 1, 1896	10
	Anna G. Calvert	June 22, 1900	7
	Letcher Calvert	July 1, 1901	6
William Claypool	Millard Claypool	June 19, 1892	15
Leu Doyle	John Doyle	August 28, 1894	13
Leu Doyle, guardian	U.G. Hawkins	December 15, 1899	7
Sarah Evans, guardian	Chester Evans	October 16, 1893	13
Catherine Faris	Eunice Faris (grandchild)	December 20, 1890	16
	John R. Faris (grandchild)	April 15, 1892	15
James M. Faris	Estalla Faris	February 26, 1891	16
	Ransom Faris	June 19, 1892	15
	Mabel Faris	August 19, 1896	10
	Maud Faris	December 29, 1898	8
	Myrtle Faris	June 7, 1901	6
John W. Faris	Carl Faris	April 25, 1889	18
	James Gordon Faris	September 15, 1890	16
	Basil B. Faris	December 15, 1894	12
	Charley F. Faris	August 26, 1899	7
John W. Faris, Guardian	Curtis Yazell	November 25, 1890	16
	Riley Yazell	April 19, 1892	15

James Gooding	Estella Gooding	April 29, 1899	8
	Ethel Gooding	December 22, 1900	6
W. G. Hedges	Ollie Hedges	September 5, 1891	13
	Stanley E. Hedges	October 19, 1893	13
Bailey Huff, guardian	Lettie Huff	March 23, 1888	19
J.W. Hunter	Lucie Hunter	October 15, 1889	17
	Ralph Hunter	April 17, 1893	14
	Hinton Hunter	May 10, 1895	12
Guardian	Orville Hill	May 29, 1889	18
Guardian	Elmond Hill	June 25, 1893	14
James Hurst	Robert D. Hurst	September 21, 1887	19
	Lida F. Hurst	May 28, 1892	15
	Bessie Hurst	June 11, 1895	12
	Nellie Hurst	August 28, 1897	9
T.F. Hurst	Alice Hurst	March 4, 1889	18
	Verna Hurst	August 8, 1891	15
	Arthur Hurst	February 3, 1894	13
	Clarence Hurst	June 10, 1897	10
W.J. James	Bertha L. James	April 7, 1890	17
	Roscoe James	May 4, 1891	16
	Clarence James	February 28, 1893	14
	Lana C. James	October 9, 1894	12
	Annie G. James	August 8, 1899	7
J.S. Knapp	Estella Knapp	August 29, 1891	15
	Nellie Knapp	March 24, 1893	14
	Emma Knapp	January 21, 1899	8
Frank T. Littleton	Chester Littleton	December 27, 1891	15
	Lula Littleton	March 13, 1893	14
	Harley Littleton	September 29, 1895	11
	Emma Maude Littleton	January 30, 1892	6

J.W. McIntyre, guardian	Harry Hammond	February 7, 1891	16
E S Morrison	Frankie j Morrison	June 7, 1889	18
	Nellie Steele Morrison	December 8, 1893	13
	Martha Lyons Morrison	September 18, 1895	11
	Heiter Morrison	February 24, 1900	7
John Plummer	Donnie Plummer	July 14, 1891	15
	William Plummer	June 14, 1894	13
Riley Reed	Mary E. Reed	November 6, 1891	16
Claude Reeves	Clifford J. Reeves	May 25, 1897	19
Benjamin Rickert	Hattie Rickert	February 14, 1899	8
	George Rickert	December 26, 1901	6
Charles Ricket, guardian	Charles Morton	June 13, 1895	12
G.W. Royse, guardian	Lula Williams	March 6, 1896	11
Ulysses C. Royse	Estella Royse	February 28, 1891	16
	Lena Royse	November 13, 1896	10
	Russell Royse	September 8, 1898	8
Samuel Williams	Ida Williams	August 1, 1897	17
Samuel Williams, guardian	Golda Williams	November 8, 1899	8

1. The Fleming County, Kentucky School Board Ledger.
2. James R. Columbia. *Civil War Stories from the Buffalo Trace.* Northeastern Kentucky Genealogical Research Services, 2015, pgs. 121, 195, 243, 268.)
3. Maude Morrison Helphinstine. Letter to Christine Hurst.
4. Lewis, Alvin. *History of Higher Education in Kentucky.* (Washington, 1899, p. 31)
5. Maude Morrison Helphinstine, "Along the Buffalo Trail," c by Frances Helphinstine and Virginia Helphinstine Reeves)
6. Ibid.

Joseph Mahlon Plummer

Large landowner in the Goddard Community

**He sold the Fleming County Board of Education
the land for the Goddard School on
contract in 1909**

Photo courtesy of Jane Hinton Lands

Joseph Mahlon Plummer

Goddard School
Built in 1909
Closed in 1960
Photo courtesy of Marty Littleton

Marvin Evans and his Wife, Nell
Fleming County Superintendent of Schools
Mr. Evans developed the plan for building
Goddard School in 1909

Nell & Marvin Evans

Chapter 3

The New Goddard School 1909

In 1908, United States President Teddy Roosevelt established the Country Life Commission. The Country Life Movement sought to improve the living conditions of America's rural residents. The movement focused on preserving traditional rural lifestyles while addressing poor living conditions and social problems within rural America. (1)

During this period in the early 1900s, the normal school movement was being initiated in Fleming County, Elizaville, Hillsboro, and Flemingsburg all had High Schools. Consolidation was made of schools not having enough students in the census. Schools were being upgraded

Marvin N. Evans, county superintendent, developed a plan for building new schools in Fleming County. Goddard, Ewing, Muses Mills, Mt. Carmel, Hillsboro, and the new high school were all built as part of his building plan during his tenure. (2)

In the 1884 *Atlas of Bath and Fleming County, Kentucky*, Joseph Malin Plummer was the largest landowner in the Goddard area with 250 acres. (3)

In 1909, the Fleming County school board borrowed money on a note from Joseph M. Plummer for the land to build a new Goddard School next to the Goddard Church. The Goddard Church was a log structure and had been built around 1826. Money on the note to Mr. Plummer was paid in installments, with interest of $7.50 per month. N. J. Ferguson, local carpenter of the area, was employed to build the schoolhouse. He was paid in installments of $200.00 a month, and at the school board meeting on September 18, 1909, the balance for building the schoolhouse at Goddard was allowed, and a warrant for $486.72 was drawn to N.J. Ferguson. School board members on September 18, 1909, were Anna G. Six (chairman), Dr. J.B. O'Bannon, J.M. Ross, L.L. Emmons, W. J. Runyon, and J.W. Hunter (secretary). First, it was a one-room school.

H. C. Royse was paid $34.00 for painting on September 18, 1909; Thomas Plummer was paid $5.00 for painting on September 27, 1909 and R. B. Huff for painting on May 31, 1910. On April 5, 1910, J.J. Carpenter was paid $6.00 for hanging the shutters on the school. On July 11, 1909 and August 22, 1910, Marion Carpenter was paid $20.00 for hauling seats and chairs from the Fleming depot, where they had been shipped on the railroad to Goddard. H.C. Royse was paid for incidentals.

On February 19, 1910, H.B. Muse and Company was paid $15.80 for 113 locust posts for the building of fence. Wire, staples, and nails were purchased from O.L. Hinton. Thomas Plummer was paid for fencing October 1, 1910. On August 5, 1912, L.L. Emmons was paid for a cooler for the schools.

On August 13, 1912, the County School Board paid H. C. Royse $7.25 for floor oil for Goddard and Bluebank schools.

On February 5, 1910, the school board received $2,310.89 from J.W. Goddard for county taxation. He is the only person listed in the school board minutes for receiving taxes in the Goddard area.

At this time, students did not automatically graduate after attending for eight years. One must take a very difficult test.

The Kentucky Department of Education gave schools a master copy of the eighth-grade exam, and teachers could amend. Fleming County's test has not been found, but the master copy from the state, which would be similar for Fleming County, was found by Bullitt County schools, which follows.

Eighth Grade Examination for Bullitt County Schools
November, 1912

Spelling

Exaggerate, incentive, conscious, pennyweight, chandelier, patient, potential, creature, participate, authentic, bequest, diminish, genuine, vinegar, incident, monotony, hyphen, antecedent, autumn, hideous, relieve, conceive, control, symptom, rhinoceros, adjective, partial, musician, architect, exhaust, diagram, endeavor, scissors, associate, saucepan, benefit, masculine, synopsis, circulate, eccentric. 100

Reading

1. Reading and writing (given by the teacher)

Arithmetic

Write in words the following:
0.5764, 000003, 0.123416, 653.0965, 43.37   10

Solve: 35 minus 7 plus 4, 5 minus 8 plus 5, 14 minus 59.112 10   10

Find cost at 12 1/2 cents per square yard of kalsomining the walls of
a room 20 feet long, 16 feet wide and 9 feet high, deducting 1 door 8
feet by 4 feet 6 inches and 2 windows 5 feet by 3 feet 6 inches each   10

A man bought a farm for $2,400 and sold it for
$2,700. What percent did he gain?   10

A man sold a watch for $180 and lost 16 2/3.
What was the cost of the watch?   10

Find the amount of interest of $5,030 for 3 years,
3 months, and 3 days at 3 percent.   10

A school enrolled 120 pupils, and the number of boys was 2/3
of the number of girls. How many of each sex were enrolled?   10

How long a rope is required to reach from the top of a building 40
feet high to the ground 30 feet from the base of the building?   10

How many steps 2 feet 4 inches each will a
man take in walking 1 1/4 miles?   10

At $1.62 1/2 a cord, what will be the cost of a pile of wood
24 feet long, 4 feet wide and 6 feet 3 inches high?

                                                                        10

Grammar

How many parts of speech are there? Define each.   20

Define proper noun; common noun. Name the properties of a noun.   10

What is a Personal Pronoun? Decline I.   10

What properties have verbs?   10

"William struck James." Change the Voice of the verb.   10

Adjectives have how many Degrees of Comparison?

Compare good; wise; beautiful.   10

Diagram: The Lord loveth a cheerful giver.   10

Parse all the words is the following sentences: John ran over the bridge.
Helen's parents love you.

                                                                        20

Geography

Define longitude and latitude.   10

Name and give boundaries of the five zones.   10

Tell what you know of the Gulf Stream.   10

Locate Erie Canal; what waters does it connect, and why is it important?   10

Locate the following countries which border each other: Turkey, Greece,
Servia, Montenegro, Romania.   10

Name and give the capitals of States touching the Ohio River.   10

Locate these cities: Mobile, Quebec, Buenos Aires, Liverpool, Honolulu   10

Name in the order of their size three largest States in the United States.   10

Locate the following mountains: Blue Ridge, Himalaya, Andes, Alps,
Wasatch.   10

Through what waters would a vessel pass in going from England
through the Suez Canal to Manila?

                                                                        10

Physiology

How does the liver compare in size with other glands in the human body? Where is it located? What does it secrete?　10

Name the organs of circulation.　10

Describe the heart.　10

Compare arteries and veins as to function. Where is the blood carried to be purified?　10

Where is the chief nervous center of the body?　10

Define Cerebrum; Cerebellum.　10

What are the functions (or uses) of the spinal columns?　10

Why should we study Physiology?　10

Give at least five rules to be observed in maintaining good health.　20

Civil Government

Define the following forms of government: Democracy, Limited Monarchy, Absolute Monarchy, Republic. Give examples of each.　10

To what four governments are students in school subjected?　10

Name five county officers and the principal duties of each.　10

Name and define the three branches of the government of the United States.　10

Give three duties of the President. What is meant by the veto power?　10

Name three right given Congress by the Constitution and two rights denied Congress.　10

In the election of a president and vice-president, how many electoral votes in each state allowed?　10

Give the eligibility of President, vice president and Governor of Kentucky.　10

What is a copyright? Patent right?　10

Describe the manner in which the president and vice president of the United States are elected.

10

History

Who first discovered the following places: Florida, Pacific
Ocean, Mississippi River, St. Lawrence River?   10

Sketch briefly Sir Walter Rawleigh, Peter Stuyvesant.

By whom were the following settled: Ga., Md. Mass., R.I., Fla?   10

During what wars were the following battles fought; Brandywine,
Great Meadows, Lundy's Lane, Antietam, Buena Vista?   10

Describe the Battle of Quebec.

Give the cause of the war of 1812 and name an
important battle fought during that war.

Name two presidents who have died in office:
three who were assassinated.

Name the last battle of the Civil War; War of 1812; French
and Indian War and the commanders in each battle.

What president was impeached and on what charge?

Who invented the following—Magnetic Telegraph, Cotton
Gin, Sewing Machine, Telephone, Phonograph. (4).

1912 Common School Graduation Certificates
Goddard School
Division 3, Subdistrict 10

Date of Exam: January 26, 1912

Lena Royse Age 15, Average 87
Irene Staggs, Age 16, Average 87
Martha Morrison, Age 16, 87+
Basil Faris, Age 17, 85 average
Nell Gaines, Age 16, Average 86

Students graduating from the Goddard School and wishing to
attend high school were required to go to Hillsboro High School,
which was built in 1912. On May 15, 1913, the school board voted
that "all county common school graduates must attend the county
high school at Hillsboro in order to have free tuition. If the grade is

not sufficient, he may have free tuition at another school." Hillsboro High School was upgraded from second class to first class in 1913.

The students for Goddard School were from number 50 Goddard, number 52 Goddard, Goddard Oak Grove number 53, and number 54 Goddard one-room schools.

These four schools were moved to Goddard. The former buildings were in disrepair, and the census had declined. On August 22, 1909, Thomas Hammonds was paid three dollars for tearing down the old Goddard School at Oak Grove. Goddard was about equal distance from each school on a road that connected them.

The Swinging Bridge Across Sand Lick to Goddard School
Before the covered bridge was moved there
1920s

Creeks were often used to determine which school one attended. For example, those who lived across the creek where the Mt. Vernon church camp is now located went to Mt. Vernon. Those on the other side of the creek went to Goddard.

On the Wallingford Road, students who lived on the side toward Goddard went to Goddard. Those on the other side went to Wallingford. Changes were made after more bridges were built.

The location of Goddard School was ideal, with Sand Lick Creek running in front of it and the Goddard Methodist Church next to the school. The Sand Lick Creek provided an additional playground for students for fishing and skating. The school stood small but sedate surrounded by the Goddard Cemetery, a fence, and hilly pastures.

A small graveled road meandered past the school, which led to Horace Taylor's and Stuart McKee's homes. From early days to 1930, there was a swinging bridge that crossed the Sand Lick creek over to Goddard School. Little Ruby Hinton, daughter of Frank L. and Ellora Hinton, and Hazel Doyle lived across the road in 1919 and were afraid to cross the swinging bridge alone. Mrs. Vema Campbell was their teacher and punished the older boys for swinging the bridge. (5) The covered bridge was moved from a mile east of Goddard to replace the swinging bridge in 1930 when Route 32 was built. The school board was supportive of the covered bridge and had allowed ten dollars to W.R. Littleton on December 15, 1917, for repairs. The covered bridge was replaced with a two-lane concrete bridge. On October 3, 1929, the Fleming County school board made a motion to allow five dollars to assist with the movement of the bridge. This five dollars was paid to Hord Staggs on February 24, 1930. Schoolchildren were allowed to observe the bridge being moved to Goddard by mules and block and tackle. Bob Helphinstine was present as well as many others. Bob said as they put the bridge across Sand Lick Creek on the field stone abutment, the bridge fell in the creek because it was not long enough for the space. An apron was added to the bridge. When the bridge fell, observers started singing "London Bridge Is Falling Down."

The covered bridge provided a way to cross to the three country stores, Helen and Leo Cooper, Bessie and Curt Yazell, and Frank L. Hinton. Hord and Hattie Staggs purchased Frank L. Hinton's store. John Lewis and Lillian Staggs took over the Staggs' store when Hord was no longer able to operate it. In 1918, Frank L. Hinton's store handled everything from tobacco sticks, hickory nuts, and tobacco knives and spears to huckleberries, raspberries, and blackberries (anything the local people could use or produce) as well as a general store. In 1923, Frank and his family moved to Plummers Landing. He was known for his delicious country cured hams. (6) Mr. Hinton served as president of the People's Bank and served on the Fleming Rural Electric Board (REA).

In the early days of Bob Helphinstine's education (1920s), sanitation was not a priority. There was not even a privy, sometimes called an outhouse. The students obeyed the rules of the teacher, and when they wanted to leave the room for any purpose, they would hold up their right hand and would immediately get permission to leave the room for what they generally called the back woods. There was a clump of trees or vines covering the fence on each side of the schoolhouse, one for the girls and one for the boys. Bob said some boys would mess their pants on purpose to upset the teacher. In Frankie Nelle Hurst's end of the year teacher report in 1927 to 1928, she reported to Marvin Evans, superintendent, a need for outhouses.

A few years later, two outhouses were built. The boys' outhouse was in the back of the schoolyard near the cemetery fence. The girls' outhouse was on the other side of the yard near Horace Taylor's field. The school board member representing the Goddard district was responsible for having them cleaned. At the February 8, 1954, school board meeting, Uhlan Evans reported that he had not found anyone to clean them. In September of that year, Mr. and Mrs. Jones appeared at the school board meeting and requested that the outhouses be cleaned. They thought that Orville Gulley could be hired to clean them.

Students used the outhouses to pull pranks, especially at Halloween, when the outhouses may be turned over. The school board started hiring someone to be on guard during Halloween. In October 1942, Mr. Dickey and Charles Browning were hired to guard the outhouses.

Latches were on the inside and the outside of the outhouses. Many times, smoke would come through the cracks of the boys' outhouse as the older boys gathered to smoke. Little guys would not be able to get in to use the facility and would have accidents. This was especially true when no men were on the teaching staff.

The girls also pulled tricks on each other. Patsy Roberts and Maxine Gorman locked Margie Conley and Ruth Ann Porter in the outhouse and went to class. Mr. Barnett immediately noticed the girls were missing from class. Patsy and Maxine had to stay in at recess for a week.

The school students dabbled in the creek, fishing in the spring-time and skating on the ice in the winter, especially Mr. Barnett's and Mr. Robert's students during recess and on Friday afternoons. There was also a low place between the schoolhouse and cemetery fence where water gathered and students skated on a cold day. Joyce and Kenneth Muse were two of the good skaters.

Goddard School remained about the same for several years. Teacher Mrs. S.F. Planck, in 1925 to 1926, reports frame school was not in good condition with two classrooms and sixty seating capacity. Poor heating, no lights, no blackboards, and no library. The 1929 school report lists Goddard School still with only two rooms. In 1926 to 1927, eighty-three students were enrolled in the sixty seating capacity building, while 117 students were enrolled in 1929 to 1930. In the 1934 to 1935 school year, Mr. Howard B. Daulton, principal of Goddard School and teacher of grades four to eight, expressed the need for two more rooms. He also stated the need for a PTA. In July 1935, two rooms were added. M.O. McCall worked July, August, and September and was paid $100.00. Hord Staggs was paid $270.52 and Sam Fried $2.67. However, the interior of the building was not completed immediately as teachers Ruby Hunter and Howard B. Daulton on their year-end report in 1936 requested that the interior of the building be completed. James Cummins and George Plummer did some minor work in the summer of 1936. George Plummer was a dependable worker in the community with work from 1914 to the present, cleaning the house, mowing the schoolyard, hauling coal and wood, making repairs, and taking the school census several terms. On the same year in 1936, Beryl Glenn, teacher, requested that blackboards be installed and a chair to go with her desk. In 1937, teachers are still asking for blackboards. W. R. James did some work in April 1937.

The Goddard School was a frame building, with three class-rooms after 1935 and a lunchroom attached. There were two cloak-rooms, one in the middle room and one in the upper room, until the upper room cloak room was converted to a stage. A porch connected the rooms for grade three to five and six to eight. Posts were on the porch, and children like Evelyn Reeves and Crystal Plummer loved to swing around the posts. A large bell was in the belfry of the upper room with a rope hanging by the teacher's desk. Students knew it was time to head to class when they heard the bell. In September 1940, insurance on the Goddard School was paid to R. H. Glascock for $2.00. Ingram and Jones built steps for the Goddard School in November 1948. The fence in front of the school was replaced by Cooper and Company in 1954.

No well or cistern existed at Goddard School for many years. The students carried the water from Mr. and Mrs. Hord Staggs' home across the highway and creek. This was sulphur water and smelled. In the early 1940s, Evelyn Reeves contracted typhoid fever, and it was tracked to the well. A new drinking water source was found. When the students carried the water to the school, they put it in coolers on the porch for the students to drink and wash their hands. Students sometimes drank from the dipper, then they learned to make their own cone-shaped paper cups. In the early days, there was a water bucket and two pint tins with strings tied to them so they could not be removed. Then some teacher came up with the idea of having a dipper in the bucket and passing the bucket up and down the aisle at certain intervals.

Then many of the mothers came up with the tin collapsible cups. Danny Mattox said he still used the dipper to put the water in his cup. Later on August 1949, school board member Loright James reported at the school board meeting that he had secured a man to dig a cistern at Goddard. "He is to dig a cistern, twelve feet deep, twelve feet in diameter, furnish and install a lead trough, fur-nish and install two pumps, one inside and one outside and sealed so no surface water could enter at a cost of $575.00." G.T. Rice did the work. The cistern was located at the back of the school. This provided water for the students to drink and for the lunchroom, which had been built. The rocks from the digging of the cistern had fool's gold, and the students were fascinated and tried to dig out the gold. Some students kept their rocks for many years. Mr. Hunt was hired to supply water to the Goddard cistern in August 1957.

The fronts of the school rooms were covered with blackboards and half-worn erasers. It was a special privilege to get to clean the erasers. The flag on the blackboard was special to all the students as they said the pledge to the flag each morning. Monochrome portraits of George Washington and Abraham Lincoln and the Ten Commandments were displayed above the blackboard in Mr. Barnett's room. One morning, Imogene Littleton remembers that when she arrived at school, a large bat was sitting on the Ten Commandments, not far from the belfry. The teacher's desk was a standard four-legged oak table. Not all teachers had a chair to go with the desk. One teacher requested on her formal sheet for the superintendent that she would like a chair.

Some desks were single, and some were double with a hole in the right hand corner, a place for an inkwell that was no longer used. Miss Mary Faris, teacher of grades one to three in 1935, when the two rooms were added, requested single seat desks, the proper height for pupils. Miss Mary had a Standard Life certificate and seventy-nine college hours that year.

One must be quiet and prepared on the recitation bench in grades one to two as John Acie Mattox and Ginny Helphinstine soon learned. Mrs. Jessie Hall swatted them with a ruler for talking.

In the schoolyard, a large grassy area surrounded by a wire fence kept the children in and the cattle out. The school had trees around the fence and a large sycamore tree in the front, which provided shade on a hot fall day. Most of the time, parents mowed the grass. However, in war years, not many men were available. In October 1941, Horace Taylor was paid $1.50 for mowing. On October 24, 1942, Jim Gardner was paid $2.00 to mow the schoolyard.

Schools were heated by wood or coal potbellied stoves, which were comfortable when the weather was mild in autumn, but not warm enough during extremely cold weather. Then the students would move their seats nearer the stove to keep warm. Dorothy Reeves Conley remembers the rooms were so cold in winter. If one sat very far away from the stove, she about froze, and if one set close to the stove, you about burned up, especially in Mrs. Moore's room.

School board members were responsible for getting the coal, having it weighed on a scale approved by the school board and delivered. Bids were let at a later date. Students carried the coal in the schoolhouse. Eugene Hall said he loved to do this chore, especially when he got out of class to do so.

Local farmers sold wood and kindling to the school. Wells Campbell, C.L. Mattox, George Mattox, and Ransom Plummer sold kindling for fires. Sometimes, the students gathered kindling by the creek. J.R. Hurst, Charlie McKee, George Wayne Littleton, John Lewis Staggs, and Glen Lewis sold cords of wood to the school. Goddard School had no electricity in the early days. It was difficult on dark days for the students to do their work because they needed more light. Teachers asked for either more windows to be added or artificial lights installed. Globes were ordered by the case by the school board for the oil lamps. In 1941, the F & N Railroad was paid $1.63 freight for shipping the globes. Electricity was added in 1947. At a school board meeting on February 8, 1947, on motion by Roy Gray seconded by Kidwell, it was unanimously voted to wire the Goddard School for electricity provided the school buy the fixtures. The fee of $15.00 was paid to the Fleming RECC in April, and in June, Amos Harmon wired the school for a cost of $68.05. Amos Harmon was the pastor of the Goddard Methodist Church.

On September 10, 1949, the school board discussed the condition of the Goddard School roof and gave Loright James the authority to find someone to put on a 5V 28 gauge roof. G.T. Rice did the work. The school board also allowed Loright James to purchase rock for the school.

In the 1950s, the building needed repairs. Thurl Pendland did some minor repairs. Uhlan Evans, school board member, reported on February 8, 1954, that the ceiling in Mrs. Wentz's room needed fixing. The board granted permission for Cooper and Company to fix it for $148.79. Helen Barnett remembers a large hole in the door between her room and Lois Moore's. Both rooms could hear the instruction that was taking place.

In March and April 1956, repairs were made to Goddard School. Lumber was purchased at H.B. Hinton and Son and supplies at E.L. Palmer, the store across the road from the school. Clifford Reeves and Henry Back did the labor. Ben Johnson repaired the door.

1. web.stanford.edu/group/rural west)
2. "Project Receives Approval," *Fleming Gazette*, December 9, 1937, No. 6.
3. *Atlas of Bath and Fleming County, Kentucky.* D.J. Lake and Company, 1884, p. 59.
4. www.huffpost.com/entry/1912-eighth-grade-exam
5. Letter to the editor, Ruby Hinton Spradling. *Flemingsburg Times Democrat,* From scrapbook, Jane Hinton Lands
6. Story's Stories, *Flemingsburg Times Democrat,* March 12, 1970.

(Board minutes were used and interviews.)

Chapter 4

Subdistrict Trustees and Compliance with Laws

Subdistrict trustees were elected to serve on the County School Board for three years in the late 1800s and then two years after 1903, and they were responsible for helping hire teachers and provide other needs of Goddard School. Note that Goddard was once called Sanford.

Trustees were officially sworn in as illustrated by Superintendent L.N. Hull on June 27, 1898.

"Then being a vacancy in the Board of Trustees for District No. 53 by reason of the expiration of E.S. Morrison's time, H. C. Morrison personally appeared before me this day and after appointed was duly sworn in as Trustee for said District for a term of three years. L.N. Hull, Superintendent."

Year 1898

Sanford School Number 50
Trustees: Russ Hinton, Lee Arnold, and Wat Carpenter. Wat
    Carpenter was removed from the District and replaced with
    J.H. Mattheos.
Teacher: Mollie Waltz, paid $36.70 per month

Sanford School Number 52
Trustees: Joseph Plummer, H. P. Staggs, and W. Ham
Teacher: T. F. Hurst, $38.30 per month
Sanford School Number 53
Trustees: E. S. Morrison (Morrison taught at Poplar Plains the same
    year), U.C. Royse, and J.S. Knapp
Teacher: J. F. Littleton $42.56 month
Sanford Number 54
Trustees: John Zomes, J. P. James, G. T. Thacker
Teacher: Sudie Reeves, paid $32.83 per month and $164.16 for the year

Year 1899

Sanford School Number 50
Trustees: J. H. Mathews, James Ham and Wes Gooding
Teacher: Mollie Waltz, paid $36.70 per month
Census: 21 Males, 30 Females Total 51
Sanford School Number 52
Trustees: James Staggs, O.S. James and C. W. Staggs
Teacher: T. F. Hurst, $38.30 per month
Census: 36 Males, 32 Females Total 68
Sanford School Number 53
Trustees: U. G. Hedges, U.C. Royse, and J.S. Knapp
Teacher: J. F. Littleton $42.56 month
Census: 42 Males, 33 Females Total 75
Sanford School Number 54
Trustees: George W. McKee, J. P. James, G. T. Thacker
Teacher: Sudie Reeves, paid $32.83 per month and $164.16 for the year
Census: 46 Males, 26 Females, 72 Total

Year 1900

Sanford School Number 50
Trustees: J. H. Mathews, James Ham and Wes Gooding
Teacher: Mollie Waltz, paid $36.70 per month
Census: 30 Males, 39 Females, 69 Total

Sanford School Number 52
Trustees: Edgar Jordan, O.S. James and C. W. Staggs
Teacher: Amanda Evans
Census: 41 Males, 31 Females, 72 Total
Sanford School Number 53
Trustees: U. G. Hedges, J. F. Plummer, and J.S. Knapp
Teacher: T. F. Hurst, $49.44 per month
Census: 44 Males, 36 Females, 80 Total
Sanford Number 54
Trustees: George W. McKee, George James, G. T. Thacker
Teacher: Dora McKee, paid $32.83 per month and $164.16 for the year
Census: 49 Males, 31 Females, 80 Total

Year 1901

Sanford School Number 50
Trustees: Russ Hinton, James Ham and Wesley Gooding
Teacher: Mollie Waltz, paid $36.26 per month
Census: 36 Males, 38 Females, 74 Total
Sanford School Number 52
Trustees: Edgar Jordan, Charles Ham
Teacher: Emma Lewman
Census: 41 Males, 32 Females, 73 Total
Sanford School Number 53
Trustees: U. G. Hedges, J. F. Plummer, and J. W. Faris
Teacher: T. F. Hurst, $41.16 per month
Census: 56 Males, 47 Females, 103 Total
Sanford Number 54
Trustees: George W. McKee, George James, George Wheat
Teacher: Sudie Reeves, paid $38.71 per month

Census: 50 Males, 26 Females, 76 Total

Year 1902

Note: The name of Sanford has been changed to Goddard. School Number 54 is no longer in operation.
Goddard School Number 50
Trustees: J.H. Mathews, C. A. Jordan and Wesley Gooding
Teacher: Mattie Evans
Census: 31 Males, 43 Females, 74 Total
Goddard School Number 52
Trustees: Lewis Staggs, Charles Ham
Teacher: Alice Staggs, paid $28.60 per month
Census: 36 Males, 34 Females, 70 Total
Goddard School Number 53
Trustees: U. G. Hedges, J. S. Knapp, and J. W. Faris
Teacher: T. F. Hurst, $39.49 per month
Census: 43 Males, 41 Females, 84 Total

Year 1903 is missing on the Trustees, but gives the Census.

1903 Census

Goddard School Number 50
Census: 40 Males, 35 Females, 75 Total
Goddard School Number 52
Census: 34 Males, 29 Females, 63 Total
Goddard School Number 53
Census: 42 Males, 45 Females, 87 Total

Year 1904

Goddard School Number 50
Trustees: Charles Goodan, Foster Vize, and R.R. Hinton
Teacher: Mrs. Mollie Porter, paid $38.26

Census: 43 Males, 37 Females, 80 Total

Goddard School Number 52
Trustees: Lewis Staggs, W.K. Ham, and C.W. Staggs
Teacher: T. F. Hurst at $30.13 per month
Census: 32 Males, 31 Females, 63 Total

Goddard School Number 53
Trustees: U. G. Hedges, J. S. Knapp, and J. W. Faris
Teacher: E. S. Morrison, $43.52 per month
Census: 41 Males, 50 Females, 91 Total

Elisha S. Morrison, educational division number three of Goddard, was elected 1908 to serve until 1910. J.W. Hunter, Subdistrict 10, Goddard, was elected in 1909 and served until 1911. In 1911, John Sorrell, Divisions 3 and 4, and Reck Carpenter, subdivision 10, were elected for subdivision 3 and served until 1913. D. C. Colgan was elected November 1925 and served from January 1926 to January 1930.

Ben A. Royse served for eighteen and a half years and resigned on June 8, 1946, to become the deputy county tax commissioner. During his eighteen years, he assisted with consolidation, bus routes, building programs, mergers, changes of personnel, and tax levies. Roy C. Gray was elected to take his position.

On June 19, 1940, the Fleming County school board complied with the act of the legislature requiring the county to be divided in five divisions for the purpose of electing members of the Board of Education. Goddard was placed in Division No. 2 with the following communities:

Goddard	9
Poplar Plains	23
Wallingford	10
Mt. Carmel	16
Mt. Carmel	26
Clerks Office	12

In March 1942, Superintendent Marvin Evans attended a conference to learn to implement Ky. Statute Section 4384-16 on the sugar rationing program incidental to wartime operations.

In June 1942, the school board required all teachers to take the TB tests at the health department.

Chapter 5

Moonlight Schools

Fleming County Schools participated in the moonlight schools movement, where country schools were used at night for adult education. This idea originated with Cora Wilson Stewart, the superintendent of schools in Rowan County, Kentucky, in 1911. She was dismayed that 7.7 percent of adults could neither read nor write. (1) The schools taught adults between the ages of eighteen and eighty-six how to read their Bibles, write letters to their children, and sign their names with more than just their mark. Ms. Stewart had larger goals of more than to just read and write—better schools, improved roads, sounder nutrition, better health, and cleaner homes with indoor plumbing. (2) Attendees were farmers, their wives, former school teachers who wanted a refresher, the postmaster, the country merchant, and the mill owner. (3)

Moonlight schools met Monday to Thursday evenings from 7:00 to 9:00 p.m. for six weeks. (4) Graduation ceremonies were held complete with diplomas and a Bible for each and cookies and lemonade. Fleming County schools paid a premium for teaching in the moonlight schools on December 21, 1918, to teachers Bess Ross (ten dollars), Lula Evans (five dollars), Anna Hawkins (twenty dollars), and others. (5)

1. Yvonne Honeycutt Baldwin. *Cora Wilson Stewart and Kentucky's Moonlight Schools: Fighting for Literacy in America.*

Lexington, Kentucky: University Press of Kentucky, 2006, p.51.
2. Stewart, p.84.
3. Gulliford, Andrew. *America's Country Schools.* National Trust for Historic Preservation, 1984, p. 88.
4. Ibid, p.44.
5. School Board Records, 1918.

Chapter 6

School Census

The state required a census each year to determine if the schools had the required number to meet standards. J. W. Hunter, teacher and school board member, was paid to take the census for several years. This was no small job. If the schools had decreased in census and did not have a sufficient number, new boundaries may be taken with a nearby school. If this was done, a boundaries change report had to be completed and sent to the State Board of Education, complete with the legal description. The school may also be closed and combined with another school.

In 1922, Fleming County had the following county schools. Note that Ewing, Elizaville, and Flemingsburg do not have a number. They were independent schools and not part of the county common school system. The independent schools had electricity, water, indoor plumbing, janitorial services, and the first pick of the teachers. However, it was very different in the county schools. Parents, teachers, and community members did much of the work and had outdoor toilets, no janitorial services, no electricity, no water for many years, and no telephones, library books, or teaching supplies. The school board bought only chalk, coal, wood, brooms, fly spray, locks, and oil for the floor. Teachers had to work with people in the community to paint the buildings, build fences, and fix pumps.

Names of County Schools in 1922

Sherburne **Number** 1	Concord **Number** 2
Olive Branch **Number** 3	Peck's Ridge **Number** 4
Hilltop **Number** 5	Battle Run **Number** 6
Tea Run **Number** 7	Tilton **Number** 8
Locust **Number** 9	Lytle **Number** 10
Bald Hill **Number** 11	Barbee view **Number** 12
(no 13 listed) Hillsboro 14	Sunset **Number** 15
Edens Chapel **Number** 16	Grange City **Number** 17
Colfax **Number** 18	Arnold's Chapel **Number** 19
Stone Lick **Number** 20	Rock Lick **Number** 21
Johnson **Number** 22	Plummers Mill **Number** 23
Plummers Landing **Number** 24	Crain Creek **Number** 25
McGregor **Number** 26	Poplar Plains **Number** 27
Emmons **Number** 28	Bluebank **Number** 29
Muses Mill **Number** 30	Ryan **Number** 31
Sugar Tree **Number** 32	Anderson Branch **Number** 33
Pea Ridge **Number** 34	Goddard **Number** 35
Big Run **Number** 36	Mt. Carmel **Number** 37
FoxPort **Number** 38	Cold Springs **Number** 39
Pleasant Valley **Number** 40	Long Knob **Number** 41
DeBell **Number** 42	Poston **Number** 43
Wallingford **Number** 44	Turners **Number** 45
Poplar Grove **Number** 46	Woodlawn **Number** 47
Sutton **Number** 48	Washington **Number** 49
Strode **Number** 50	Crains **Number** 51
Bethel **Number** 52	Cowan **Number** 53
Wayside **Number** 54	Sunnyside **Number** 55
Fairview **Number** 56	Oakwood **Number** 57
Poplar Run **Number** 58	Snow Hill **Number** 59
Deer Lick **Number** 60	Tunnel Hill **Number** 61

Nepton **Number** 62	Mt. Vernon **Number** 63
Ewing (122 Students)	Flemingsburg (295 Students)
Elizaville (108 Students)	Sherburne Colored School (45 Students)
Nepton Colored School (45 students)	Subdistrict A Colored School (235 Students)

* List from Fleming County school board records, 1922

At the May 21, 1932 school board meeting, "Woodlawn School District, having only 21 pupils in school censuses was ordered to be combined with Goddard District and so reported to State Board."

Students were still given the State exam after finishing the eight years of school in order to graduate.

In 1932 the graduates after the exam date of February 1932 were:

Floyd Faris
Eugene Gooding, age 15
Robert Lee Helphinstine, age 14
Emory Littleton, age 13
Ruth Muse, age 16

In 1933 the graduates after the February 1933 exam were:

Flora McRoberts, age 14
Samuel McRoberts, age 16
Anna Mary McKee, age 14
Phillip Oney, age 13
Mildred Royse, age 15
Mary Frances Saunders, age 13

At that time, the graduates of Goddard School were combined with other graduates in the common schools in Fleming County for a graduation ceremony. A speaker and special music were given. In 1911, a commencement was held for all eighth graders of the common schools in Fleming County. Lutie Palmer Williams, county school treasurer, was paid $10.63 for expenses for the event. Mrs. M. Andrews was paid $2.00 for providing the music.

Robert (Bobby Lee) Helphinstine
Eighth Grade, Goddard School
1932

    To graduate from the eighth grade at that time was a big event. Many students may not go on to high school. In the early days, many students did not finish the eighth grade.

    In 1936, the Fleming County Public School Corporation was formed. Hillsboro, Ewing, and Mt. Carmel conveyed their remaining funds on June 5, 1936, and Elizaville Independent System on November 23, 1936. Plans for a new high school were discussed in 1937.

Community Use of Goddard School Grounds

At the May 8, 1948, school board meeting, Mr. Carpenter of Goddard requested that the people of the community be permitted to pass the school ground and that they be permitted to put a gate in the school fence for purpose of ingress and egress to a lot there to be used as an extension to the cemetery. This was granted with the understanding that Goddard people need to bear the expense and the grounds were not to be altered so as to interfere with their use as a playground.

The American Legion requested on March 21, 1949, to use the Goddard school grounds as a baseball field on Sunday afternoons. Allen Hall represented American Legion number 1, and L.S. Bower, Herd Shrout, and Kenneth Fern, represented American Legion number 2. The board granted permission with the understanding that the American Legion was responsible for the care of the property and the conduct of the crowd.

Chapter 7

Goddard School Lunchroom

Fixing lunch was very difficult before the lunchroom was built. Many items that can now be purchased were not available in the country stores. Before the lunchroom was built, sometimes potatoes were laid on the potbellied stoves. Students would carry their lunch in a tin lard pail or paper bag and place them in the cloak room. Some would have only a cold biscuit and jam. Some students would be ashamed and get under the schoolhouse to eat their lunch. Hilda Mattox remembers joining friends under the shade tree over by the church fence to eat the lunch she brought from home in the 1930s. Crystal Plummer walked home for lunch in Goddard. Louise Yazell, daughter of Curt and Bessie Yazell, who operated the country store across the highway from the school, also went home for lunch. Students and teachers gave her a list of things to purchase. Mrs. Bessie made bologna sandwiches from a large roll of bologna and crackers. The students loved the candy brown cows and sugar daddies. A large bag of loose candy or a bag of cookies could be bought for five cents.

No lunchroom existed until 1947. The school board responded to President Harry S. Truman's National School Lunch Program, which began in 1946. It is a law to provide nutritious low-cost or free lunch to qualified students. President Truman began the National School Lunch Program in 1946 as a measure of national security. He initiated this act after reading a study that revealed many young men failed to pass the test for armed forces because of medical conditions caused by childhood malnutrition. The Fleming County school board voted to participate in the National School Lunch Program. At the August 10, 1946 school board meeting, Mr. Roy Gray, school board member, was advised to go ahead with both interior and exterior repair on the Goddard School to prepare for a lunchroom.

The school board voted to have the building wired for electricity in February 1947.

Several parents in the PTA worked to build the lunchroom, along with some work by the school board.

At that time, the room that was the original room of the school and later became Mr. Barnett's room, which was in terrible repair. One could see the ground through the cracks in the floor. It was very cold. Cooper and Company were paid $198.38 to do some work.

Cooks

Eva Littleton
Virginia James
Ruby McKee
Hattie Staggs
Dewey Wagoner
Nancy Staggs
(Individual picture) **

Some of the parents approached Mr. Noah Fried of Fried's Department Store in Flemingsburg and asked for funds for flooring, wallboard, and paint. This Mr. Fried provided, and several men in the PTA installed it. Bob Helphinstine, John Mattox, George Mattox, Loright James, and others helped with this. This room became the sixth, seventh, and eighth grade classroom, and the former room for those students became the lunchroom since it was larger and had a large cloakroom. The work was completed in 1947. The Goddard School immediately qualified for the government school lunch program. At the December 13, 1947, school board meeting, the superintendent asked for four organizations to pay twenty-five dollars each for a fee to form membership in the North Central surplus army disposal organization, which allowed Fleming County schools to participate in the purchasing process. These donating organizations would be allowed to use the gymnasiums at the high school twice without the usual fees.

The school board purchased a large water tank for the lunchroom from the army surplus organization, but it was too large to get through the school door. The school board borrowed a smaller tank from Jack Grannis and used it for two years. G.M. Campbell was hired to haul water to fill the tank. In March 1949, Loright James and Mr. Dorsey, school board members, were appointed to negotiate with Mr. Grannis for a trade of the tanks.

In February 1949, the school board required each school lunchroom to pay their own fuel, gas, and electric bills.

In August 1949, when Nora Meade became principal and Loright James became school board member, a large cistern was built at the back of the school. A hand pump was put on the kitchen sink, and water was carried and put in the coolers in the classrooms each day. In warm weather, the cooler sat on the porch. Eventually, a pump was put on the cistern. The army surplus membership allowed the Goddard School to purchase large segmented aluminum serving trays and cookware. The older female students washed the trays after lunch each day. Large cookers of water were boiled on the stove and used to wash the dishes, being careful to not spill the boiling water on the students. The smell of bleach was prominent for disinfecting.

Ed Gilliam's mother, who was married to Horace Taylor for a short time, was one of the first cooks. Hattie Staggs (Mrs. Hord) was one of the early cooks in 1947 to 1948 and 1949 to 1950, along with Dewey Wagoner from 1947 to 1948, Eva Littleton from 1947 to 1948, Virgie Rogers and 1948 to 1949. Virginia James replaced her on 1950 to 1951, 1951 to 52, and 1952 to 1953. Eva Littleton did not drive, and she rode the school bus to Goddard to cook. While she was cooking that year, she delivered her son, Ronnie. She brought him to school and kept him in the lunchroom. Eva Littleton quit after that year, and Ruby McKee took her place and cooked in 1949 1950 and 1952 to 1953. The food they had to cook was government commodities. Gail Claypool remembers when the lunchroom opened. Hot food, instead of leftovers from breakfast, was a real treat. Mrs. Hattie Staggs made wonderful desserts, and the commodity cans of peaches were made into delicious peach cobblers with a clear sauce. Yummy! She also cooked vegetables, mashed potatoes, buttered com, and crusty com bread. George Littleton liked the raisin pudding best. One of the favorite dishes with the children was the old-fashioned potato candy. It did not require any baking. Leftover mashed potatoes could be used. The recipe on a smaller version to serve twenty-four pieces is as follows:

Old Fashioned Potato Candy

1 small potato, peeled and chopped
6 to 7 cups powdered sugar
1 teaspoon vanilla extract
2/3 cup peanut butter

In a small pan of boiling water, cook the potato until tender. Drain. Put in a bowl and mash until smooth. (Remember at the time the cooks were making this, there were no electric mixers.) Keep warm but not hot. You'll need 1/2 cup of mashed potatoes.

In a large bowl, blend the potatoes and 2 cups of the powdered sugar. Add the vanilla flavor. Continue to add the powdered sugar, one cup at a time, until it makes a mound of dough.

Put the dough on an 18 x 12 sheet of wax paper sprinkled with powdered sugar. Sprinkle the top with a little powdered sugar. Roll out with a rolling pin to approximately 1/4 inch thick.

Spread the peanut butter over the top. Slowly roll the candy from the long end to the other. Wrap with wax paper. Cut in half. Chill for one hour.

Slice the rolled candy into 3/4 inch pieces and enjoy, just as the children did.

When Virginia James was the cook. George Littleton was a little guy. He did not see Virginia carrying a bowl of soup to someone else and jumped up from his seat, causing Virginia to dump the soup on his head. Soup beans were served often, and George said he had them at home and got very tired of them. However, he did love ice cream. One day, when the students were allowed to go to John and Lillian Staggs' store, George had a quarter. He asked for an ice cream cone with five dips as each dip was five cents each. What a treat!

Nancy Staggs, Noted Cook
Photo courtesy of Patsy Roberts Stacy

In 1950, the superintendent asked the school board to purchase a jeep from the government surplus cooperative. Mr. Scott used the jeep in bad weather to bring commodities to Goddard School and the other country schools. In the superintendent's report in June 1951, he reported that he delivered food four times by jeep last winter to the county schools at a cost of forty dollars for 400 miles.

Miss Nancy Staggs, Cook
1953 to 1958

Goddard School was fortunate to have innovative cooks. They knew how to cook and improvise. Miss Nancy was known throughout Fleming County as being able to add items to make good food. Miss Nancy started cooking in the fall of 1953 and cooked until 1958. Mrs. Fannin cooked in 1959. The school lunches continued to be made from government commodities: big cans of peanut butter, large drums of Swiss and cheddar cheese, crackers, large bags of potatoes, twenty-five-pound bags of rice, white beans, flour, meal, gallon cans of grapefruit and peaches, large blocks of hamburger, and gallon cans of canned meat. The canned meat had tallow on the top, which Miss Nancy scraped off, then she added ketchup, chopped onions, and other ingredients to make a delicious barbecue for the students. Other cooks in the other county schools did not know how to make this delicious barbecue and did not want the canned meat. Mr. Roberts and Mr. Barnett requested the school superintendent to send the unwanted canned meat to Goddard because the children loved the barbecue sandwiches. Mr. Barnett assigned Frances Helphinstine the job of recording the commodities used each day and the number of lunches served and making a list of items needed for the future.

The girls in the sixth, seventh, and eighth grades helped cook, clean tables, wash dishes, and serve. Louise Yazell helped wash dishes, even though she went home for lunch each day. Louise enjoyed washing dishes with her friends.

The eighth grade girls helped peel potatoes and finish the lunch each day. Elsie Hardy, Bernice Muse Plummer, and Frances

Helphinstine were among those who helped Miss Nancy Staggs cook. Bernice and Frances remember peeling canners full of potatoes. They would use the new french fry cutter to make french fries. This cutter was also used for cutting onions. When Mr. Barnett had to go to Flemingsburg during school hours, James Rogers and other boys would ask Miss Nancy to make french fries for them! Mashed potatoes were mashed with a hand potato masher as no electric mixers were available at that time. Instant potatoes or french fries were not available to purchase until the last three years of school operation. At that time, Miss Nancy received bags of instant potatoes. The recipe said to add water, but not for Miss Nancy! She added butter and milk, and the kids loved them. Miss Nancy sent Frances to the edge of the school property on the Plummer property to pick up the Goddard apples. Miss Nancy then had her peel and slice them very thin, and she put them in Jell-O for lunch. Frances also trimmed the hamburger from the large blocks of meat to fix for chili. Miss Nancy made a delicious pimento cheese sandwich to go with the chili. Other days, peanut butter sandwiches were served. Miss Nancy made everything from scratch. Mr. Roberts and Mr. Barnett bought raisins from their own funds to make rice pudding. The white beans were cooked in large cookers and served with com bread. Danny Mattox loved Miss Nancy's com bread. However, he remembers thinking there were raisins in the com bread one day. This turned out to be flies as there were no screens on the windows in the lunchroom at that time. The school board bought fly spray to assist with this problem. George Cooper remembers Miss Nancy giving him extra portions as other children had. Garnett Bays remembers her delicious peach cobbler!

Children got Meadow Gold glass bottles of milk for lunch. Sometimes, they got orange sherbet push-ups. Junior Prater was the milk man, and he gave the boys who helped unload a chocolate milk or an ice cream.

At the November 13, 1954, school board meeting, the board asked the superintendent to explore the new school Special Milk Program, where the Eighty-Third Congress authorized use of Commodity Credit Corporation funds for fiscal years 1954 to 1955 and 1955 to 1956 to reimburse schools for milk served over and above the amounts they normally used. In the following year, the Eighty-Fourth Congress extended the program two more years. Children who could not pay were given the milk at Goddard. (1)

On Fridays, one of the teachers gave the students an ice cream, such as chocolate fudge bars or orange push-ups, or chocolate milk. This was a real treat. Mr. Roberts and Mr. Barnett got some small cartons of chocolate milk! Several children came to school without breakfast. Miss Nancy cooked rice and put milk on it. Those children were brought to the back door of the lunchroom and brought in for breakfast to protect their identity so the other children would not make fun of them.

Some children did not eat in the lunchroom. Several children brought their lunch in ten-pound lard buckets and would gather under the schoolhouse to eat. The lunch buckets had big biscuits with blackberry jam, fried chicken, and other leftovers. In the fall at hog-killing time, the smell of breakfasts of side meat hung heavy in the classroom. However, country ham was rarely smelled as the fathers sold their country hams to the Bon Ton Restaurant in Flemingsburg. Some students traded food from time to time. Elizabeth Sloas Wagner recalls trading biscuits with Frances McKee's daughters. She said, "It was one of the best biscuits I had ever eaten. It had sugar in it." Jeri Sloas remembers the delicious brown beans and corn bread that she traded from another one of Frances' daughters.

Miss Nancy took several of the eighth grade girls home with her overnight, usually in groups of three. Imogene Littleton, Dorothy Reeves, Ruth Ann Porter, and Ginny Helphinstine were some of the students. Miss Nancy took them to Frisch's drive-in restaurant with drive-up speakers at Aberdeen, Ohio, and the drive-in theatre on Maysville hill. It's the first time the girls had experienced a drive-in theatre! She usually requested a boyfriend to ride along. The girls were surprised when Miss Nancy ordered a cup of buttermilk to drink at Frisch's.

Miss Nancy gave Imogene Littleton a coloring book and a box of crayons for Christmas. Imogene's mother, Doshia, enjoyed coloring the men and women in the pictures, while Imogene colored the rest of the picture.

In the last years of the school, Helen Barnett helped plan the menus for lunch when Mr. Barnett was the head teacher, which the children enjoyed.

Occasionally, the school would be broken into, and food would be taken from the lunchroom. Students would see a large hole in the doorknob upon arrival at school, and the door would have to be fixed. On December 8, 1951, the school board talked with Mr. Lloyd McDonald in regard to the theft of food from the Goddard lunchroom.

Students looked forward to lunch each day with Miss Nancy!

1. P.L. 690, 83rd Congress, August 28, 1954, 68 Stat. 900. www.fns. usda.gov/nslp/history 11.

Chapter 8

Reflections on Attendance and Discipline

Attendance at Goddard School was poor compared to the number eligible on the census. For some students such as Irvin Whitten and Mary Lucy Conn, it was an eight-mile walk each way. Teacher records in the 1930s recorded the number of miles for students to walk. Students would walk to the top of Pea Ridge mountain or Mt. Vernon Road. Hilda Mattox walked from Pea Ridge, which was four miles each way. Sometimes, she and her siblings would cut down the side of the mountain, holding on to trees to keep from sliding. Hilda, who was eight years old when she started first grade, left school at the end of the day as soon as it was over so she could get home before dark. Eugene Ellington, Archie Gardner, Sadie Gardner, Bruce Gardner, and Floyd Jesse walked seven miles a day. Many students walked five miles a day. Some students may not enroll until older. In the 1920s, before Route 32 was built, it was not uncommon for some parents to not enroll a child when they were six years but wait until the next child was old enough to go to school. This could result in large classes for first and second grade. Mrs. Jesse Hall had fifty-six students in 1949 to 1950. The school district had a different starting date for schools in the county to assist with students walking in bad weather. At the July 25, 1942, and again in July 1943 and 1944 school board meetings, the school board ordered that the rural schools on bad roads begin as soon as possible, not later than the middle of August, and Mr. Evans, superintendent, was instructed to secure teachers for the same. The Flemingsburg schools would not start until September 14 and September 18 in 1944. This was changed on July 13, 1946, as all schools in the county opened on September 9, 1946

John K. Ryan was added as an attendance officer for the county schools in 1936. New school laws had been enacted in 1934 and gave the truant officer's position the new name of attendance officer. Charley Cooper had previously served as the truant officer. Mr. Ryan's role was to convince parents that their children should be in school and to round up the hooky players. Included in the work was that of setting up for the first time a card system on every child in the county and following their progress through school. It was a brand new idea and was used to replace the truant officer of previous days. Mr. Ryan served until 1942 when he resigned when he purchased the *Flemingsburg Times-Democrat* paper.

Mrs. Owen B. Story succeeded Mr. Ryan and worked for a few years. Mary Rice was hired in 1946 to replace Mrs. Story.

Usually, school was not closed for bad weather. The Goddard School was only closed three times in the history of the school for bad weather: January 28 to 29, 1943; December 11 to 20, 1944; and December 2 to 3, 1950. On January 28, 1943, it snowed over twenty inches. On December 11 to 20, 1944, the National Weather Service reported that Kentucky experienced one of the worst snowstorms in history. Temperatures dropped below zero, and massive snow and ice storms with over twenty inches of snow and three inches of ice occurred. (1)

On December 2 and 3, 1950, the National Weather Service reported one of the most damaging and meteorologically unique winter storms to strike the eastern United States, which occurred on Thanksgiving weekend 1950. Damaging wind events and drastic temperature drops created a foot of snow with drifts up to ten feet in Fleming County. Old sleighs, which had been stored in the haylofts, were resurrected and used once again.

Crystal Sapp and Donald Bays remember the snow being over the fence posts in the fields near Goddard. Ice was on top of that. Children skated on top of the packed ice. The grader could not remove the snow from the roads, and a bulldozer had to be used.

The health department closed the school for scarlet fever on October 10 to 13, 1941, and outbreaks of flu on January 13 to 24, 1941, and March 24 to 28, 1947.

School was also closed for registration day for Selective Service on February 17, 1942, and April 27, 1942, during the war years. A county festival was held on October 10, 1941, when servicemen were honored. On November 20, 1942, school was closed because of gas rationing.

In February 1949, the school board required the teachers to do home visitations to improve attendance. Teachers were given two days, March 3 and 4, to visit the homes, whether they had children or not. They were to collect information of how many children were of school age and invite the children to attend. If the teacher's work was not satisfactory, they would not be paid for the two days. Jesse Hall made home visits when the oldest child of the family was ready to start school. Woodie Reeves remembers when Mrs. Hall visited their home when he was ready to start school and explained what was expected to his parents.

Reflections on Discipline

In the 1920s, Chester Emmons threw a forty penny nail at teacher Owen Story and just missed his head, but the nail stuck in the blackboard behind him. Willie McRoberts shot Owen Story's hat off with a slingshot. His twin brother got the whipping for it. The boys pulled numerous tricks on Owen Story. Bob Helphinstine put mice in Mr. Owen Story's coat pocket while hanging in the cloak room in the upper grades classroom. Others put tacks in his chair and turned over the outhouse on Halloween. Considerable damage might be done on Halloween, until the school board hired guards to watch not only Goddard School but other schools in the county.

The boys put skunk oil in Mr. Caywood's coat pocket and made him sick.

Wendell Staggs, Donnie Wright, and B. C. Emmons attended Goddard School from 1939 to 1948. Wendell remembered Jack Williams had tied a string with a can and rocks around a dog's tail. He then rubbed the dog's tail with turpentine. The dog ran under the schoolhouse and made a loud noise. Mrs. Brooks Duncan, head teacher, was not happy with Jack.

One day, several tombstones were turned over in the cemetery adjoining the school. George Littleton had to help set them back up, but he didn't do it. He also had to stay in at recess with the boys that did do it. Brooks Duncan was a strict disciplinarian! Some of the older boys did other mean tricks. They removed weatherboarding from the back of the school and whittled out pistols to threaten other students.

Another year, George Littleton did get in trouble when he was in Mrs. Hall's room. When Mrs. Hall was going to paddle him, Birdie Littleton took off her scarf from around her head and gave it to George. He put the scarf in the seat of his pants to soften the blow.

Bob Helphinstine may not be paying attention at all times. Bob shares his favorite memory as a grade school student at Goddard. "I loved to sit and look out the window at the droves of hogs, sheep, and cattle being brought along the pike from Virginia through Goddard to court day in Flemingsburg or Maysville. These lines were a mile long. This was before Route 32 was built."

In the 1940s, a student stole a bicycle at Western Auto in Flemingsburg and rode it to Goddard School before being apprehended.

At the January 10, 1948, meeting, the school board discussed the theft of coal from Goddard School.

In the 1940s, several moonshine stills operated in the area. Gatewood Back reported some older students to the sheriff's department saying his sisters had to walk past the stills that were located in the woods. There was a question if the moonshine was offered to the girls.

In the early 1950s, when Nora Meade was principal, and Miss Cay wood taught there. Some of the older boys liked to hide out in the outhouse and smoke. One boy was reporting them to the principal. One day, the older boys decided they had had enough and put a rope around the boy and tied him up in the tree. Mr. Frank Scott, superintendent, drove out from Flemingsburg and cut him down.

Faris Viars created some problems, and Mrs. Meade was going to whip him. Faris said "No way," jumped out the window, and ran and hid in the covered bridge the remainder of the day. Faris's brother, Raymond, liked to draw attention to the other boys. His dog followed him to school one day. Raymond had a cookie and would take a bite then give the dog a bite. This continued until the cookie was gone.

At the February 7, 1953, school board meeting, the board discussed the discipline problems at Goddard. At the following meeting, Mrs Martha Royse, Mrs. Nora Meade, Mrs. Jesse Hall (teachers at Goddard), and Mr. George Viars (a patron at Goddard School) were present. Mrs. Meade discussed the discipline problem created by George Jr. and Faris Viars. The other two teachers agreed. George Viars offered his apologies and offered assistance to help keep the boys under control to the extent of coming to school if needed. The board thanked him and gave the boys another chance.

Mrs. Meade also discussed discipline problems with Joe Brabant. The board voted to send a letter to Mr. O.N. Routt, the grandfather, advising him that Mrs. Meade is authorized to dismiss the pupil from school should his conduct not improve and asking for his cooperation.

When Mr. Roberts was principal, Billy Jones had a pin in his shoe and was sticking people with it. He stuck James Rogers, and he yelled. Mr. Roberts wanted to know what was going on and had Billy come up to get a paddling. James, not wanting him to be paddled, said it didn't hurt real bad. Mr. Roberts then had James come up front to be paddled and said, "If it didn't hurt so bad, then you should not have yelled and disturbed the class."

Mr. Myron Barnett used the belt instead of the paddle, which the students feared more. He did not allow students to sass or talk back to him. One day, Margie Conley talked back to Mr. Barnett about extra play time. She had been used to talking back at home. She almost got the belt but got a lecture instead. From then on, Margie watched her mouth.

Eugene Hall recalls getting in trouble when several of the girls gave him a dime to go across the covered bridge to Mrs. Bessie's to buy a bag of candy. He went but got caught!

In the 1950s, several students were waiting for the school bus over in front of the church. They started throwing rocks at Mollie Henderson's house near the bridge. Miss Mollie reported them to Mr. Barnett. He called all of them in and removed his belt. Imogene Littleton was the only girl among fifteen boys to get the whipping.

On another day, a ball game was being played in the rear of the school. Sherley Taylor had brought his bike to school. Imogene Littleton had been wanting to learn to ride, so she asked Sherley if she could ride his bike. He said, "Sure." While the ball game was in session, Imogene was riding the bike up and down the road by Conley's house at Goddard Road.

1. National Weather Service, "The Great Appalachian Storm of 1950," weather.gov/jkl/events

Chapter 9

Curriculum and Textbooks

Fleming County schools complied with state regulations for teaching needs.

In 1893, Kentucky Section number 61 suggested lists of textbooks to purchase. Examiners were to be appointed for the county.

On June 18, 1898, L.N. Hull, superintendent, appointed J.W. Hunter and William Conley as examiners. They submitted the following lists of books for adoption for a five-year period.

McGuffey's Revised Speller
McGuffey's Revised Primer
McGuffey's Revised Readers
Ray's New Arithmetic and Algebra
Long's New Language Exercises Parts 1 and 2
Harveys Revised Grammar
Swinton's School Composition
Long's Home Geography
New Eclectic Geographies, Kentucky edition
Spencerian Vertical Penmanship
Eclectic Primary History of the United States
Barnes Brief History of the United States
The House I Live In (Primary Physiology)
Overton's Intermediate Physiology
Overton's Advanced Physiology

Townsend's Shorter Course in Civics
Webster's New Primary Dictionary
Webster's New Common School Dictionary
Kincaid's History of Kentucky

Supplementary Reading:

Easy Steps for Little Feet
Golden Book of Choice Reading
Stories of Great Americans for Little America
Book of Tales
Readings in Nature's Book
Seven American Classics
Carpenter's Geographical Reader—Asia

Five years later in 1903, examiners J.W. Hunter and R. J. Sousley presented a similar list with the exception of reading and arithmetic. It was more comprehensive.

McGuffey Speller
McGuffey Primer Reader
McGuffey 1st Reader
McGuffey 2nd Reader
McGuffey 3rd Reader
McGuffey 4th Reader
McGuffey 5th Reader
Ray's New Primary Arithmetic
Ray's Intelect Arithmetic
Ray's Elementary Arithmetic
Ray's Practical Arithmetic
Ray's Elementary Algebra
Ray's Higher Algebra

At the May 1904 school board meeting, a county school book commission was established and met on May 28, 1904. "We the county commission provided for in an account passed by the legislature, which became a law on February 18 without the approval of the governor, to create a state school book commission and a county school book commission to procure for the schools of Kentucky a uniform system of textbooks met in the superintendent's office on May 28, 1904, and adjourned until June 11, 1904, and adopted books."

Students were exposed to difficult material at an early age. From the preface of Ray's *Intellect Arithmetic Book* in 1860, for second graders, it states, "By its study, learners are taught to reason, to analyze, to think for themselves; while it imparts confidence in their own reasoning powers, and strengthens the mental faculties." "The pupil should be required to furnish a similar explanation to each of the succeeding questions, and to give, not only a correct answer, but also, the reason for the method by which he obtained it." A method of solving questions in mental arithmetic is the following called the four-step method.

"Illustrations—*First Step*, James gave 7 cents for apples and 8 cents for peaches; how many cents did he spend? *Second step*, as many as the sum of 7 cents and 8 cents. *Third step*, 7 cents and 8 cents are 15 cents. *Fourth step*, hence, if James gave 7 cents for apples and 8 cents for peaches, he spent 15 cents. (1)

By 1918, the Fleming County school board distributed lists of textbooks for the parents to buy. One such list is on display at the Fleming County Museum.

Twenty-Ninth Session
Opens Monday, September 2, 1918
Textbooks 1918 to 1919

Elementary Department

First Grade
First Term
Palmer's Writing Lessons for Primary Grades. (In hands of teachers only)
Easy Road to Reading, Primer
Free and Treadwell Primer

Second Term
(Additional books)
Baldwin and Bender First Reader
Free and Treadwell, First Reader

Second Grade
First Term
Palmer's Writing Lessons for Primary Grades
Baldwin and Bender Second Reader
Hamilton's Primary Arithmetic
Practical Drawing Part 2
Second Term
Free and Treadwell, Second Reader

Third Grade
First Term
Potter's Common School Spelling Book
Palmer's Writing Lessons for Primary Grades
Baldwin and Bender Third Reader
Hamilton's Primary Arithmetic
Practical Drawing Part 3
Aldine First Language Book
Second Term
Free and Treadwell, Third Reader

Fourth Grade
First Term
Potter's Common School Spelling Book
Practical Drawing Part 4
Hamilton's Primary Arithmetic
Aldine First Language Book
Graded Classics Fourth Reader
Palmer's Method of Business Writing
Fairbanks Home Geography
Second Term
Free and Treadwell, Fourth Reader

Fifth Grade
First Term
Potter's Common School Spelling Book
Practical Drawing Part 5
Graded Classics Fifth Reader
Palmer's Method of Business Writing
Modem Elementary Arithmetic
The Mother Tongue, Book 1
Natural Primary Geography
Gullick's Good Health
Second Term
Evan's First Lessons in American History
Elson Grammar School Reader, Book 1

Sixth Grade
First Term
Potter's Common School Spelling Book
Practical Drawing Part Six
Free and Treadwell, Fifth Reader
Modem Advanced Arithmetic
Palmer's Method of Business Writing
The Mother Tongue, Book 1
Natural Primary Geography
Gullick's Emergencies

Sixth Grade
Second Term
Kinkead's History of Kentucky

Seventh Grade
First Term
Potter's Common School Spelling Book
Palmer's Method of Business Writing
Elson Grammar School Reader
Practical Drawing Part Seven
Modem Advanced Arithmetic

The Mother Tongue, Book 2
Natural Complete Geography
Gullick's The Body and Its Defenses
Dickson's Grammar School History

Eighth Grade
First Term
Payne's Common Words Commonly Misspelled
Palmer's Method of Business Writing
Elson Grammar School Reader
Practical Drawing Part Seven
Modem Advanced Arithmetic
The Mother Tongue, Book 2
Natural Complete Geography
Dickson's Grammar School History
Ritchie's Human Physiology
Second Term
Forman's Essentials in Civil Government

Attention: It is very important that every child be fully supplied with books before the opening of school. Regular work should start the first day. It is too great a waste of time to delay and create a general state of haphazardness in the beginning of a term. Come and bring your books with you on the first day. Lessons will be assigned for the next day's work, and you want to start right in the beginning. Do not buy secondhand books unless they are in good condition.

The school board authorized a business in different areas of the county for parents to buy textbooks. On June 16, 1930, the school board appointed Frank L. Hinton, Plummers Landing, to be the textbook dealer for the eastern part of the county that would serve Goddard parents and students.

It was not until April 1937 that the school board authorized free textbooks.

Teachers learned new ideas from their students. Faye Taylor was left-handed. Teachers tried to change her to be right-handed until

Faye's mother came to school and insisted that Faye continue in her left-handed learning. Faye succeeded and was an excellent student.

Many techniques over the years supported the curriculum. Some techniques included **religious and moral instruction.**

The Common School Ordinance 1869 and the Common School Amendment Ordinance 1870 had specific requirements for religious instruction:

"With a view to secure the Divine blessing, and to impress upon the pupils the importance of religious duties, and their entire dependence on their Maker, it is recommended that the daily exercises of each Common School be opened and closed by reading a portion of Scripture and by Prayer. The Lord's Prayer alone, or the Forms of Prayer hereto annexed may be used or any other Prayer preferred by the Local Board and Master of each School; but the Lord's Prayer should form part of the opening exercises, and the Ten Commandments be taught to all the pupils, and be repeated at least once a week; but no pupil shall be compelled to be present at these exercises against the wish of his parent or guardian expressed in writing to the Master of the School."

"The Clergy of any persuasion shall have the right to give religious instruction to the pupils of their own Church in each Common School at least once a week, at the hour of half-past three in the afternoon, or such days as shall be agreed upon by them and the Inspector General."

"It shall be the duty of the Teacher to maintain proper order and discipline, according to the authorized forms and regulations; punctually to observe the hours for opening and dismissing the School; to see that the exercises of the School are opened and closed each morning and evening, as hereinbefore recommended; and daily exert his best endeavors, by example and precept, to impress upon the mind of the pupils the principles and morals of the Christian Religion, especially those virtues of piety, truth, patriotism and humanity, which are the basis of law and freedom, and the cement and ornament of society." (2)

Instruction in values and ethics was part of the daily class schedule at Goddard School. The importance of truthfulness, purity, public spirit, patriotism, work ethic, and obedience to parents was stressed.

The Ten Commandments were posted in front of each room. A Bible was on the teachers' desks, and the flag was on the blackboard. Goddard was blessed to have many Christian teachers and principals. Mr. Earl Roberts and Myron Barnett were ministers. Lois Moore and Helen Barnett were wives of ministers. Mrs. Nora Meade was a Goddard Sunday school teacher, and Brooks Carpenter Duncan was the daughter of Marion Carpenter, Goddard Sunday school superintendent for many years. Most of the teachers read directly from the King James Version of the *Holy Bible*, and students stood and said the pledge of allegiance to the flag in unison with their eyes fixed on the flag since many of their fathers had fought for what it represented, and many of the students would someday do the same. Parents in the community had served in World War I and World War II, such as Woodrow Reeves, who had been a prisoner of war twice. Crystal Plummer's father, Clyde Plummer, was sent to Pennsylvania to train to wire warships during World War II. The family moved to Pennsylvania in 1940 then moved back to Goddard while Clyde was serving his country.

In addition, Lois Moore, in her fourth and fifth grade classes, had construction paper fishes with Bible questions on them. Paper clips were attached. Students used a magnet to fish, and if one could answer the question, his/her name was written down. At the end of the year, the student who answered the most questions got a prize. Ginny Helphinstine won a plaque that read "God is our refuge and strength."

Arithmetic

Arithmetic was one of the most practical subjects taught at Goddard School. Parents and their children used mathematics to solve problems on the farm. Farmers may want to know the tonnage of hay in a haystack, given the dimensions of the stack, or how much corn to expect from the number of com shocks in the field. Bob

Helphinstine, in the 1920s, learned how to assess the weight of a cow and could come within a few pounds of the actual weight. As he grew older, the pen hookers at the Farmers Stockyards in Flemingsburg appreciated his knowledge as it was usually an accurate assessment.

All students learned the multiplication tables from the 2s to the 12s, and baseball multiplication was held as a game to reinforce skills.

The most proficient students could figure huge sums in their heads. Bob Helphinstine knew the rules and could work problems in his head faster than the modern-day calculators or computers.

Different games were used to support the use of arithmetic. Charles Emmons enjoyed the math tricks. One such math trick that Charles used is shown below:

1. Choose a number from 1 to 9.
2. Multiply your number by 2.
3. Add 5 to your result.
4. Multiply the result by 50
5. If you've had a birthday this year, add 1767. If you haven't, add 1766.
6. Subtract the year of your birth from the result.
7. You should get a three-figure number. The first figure is the number you chose initially, and the other two are your age.

In grades one and two, Jessie Hall, teacher in 1950 to1951, listed in her lesson plans that she worked orally and had seatwork with numbers.

Grammar

Grammar was taught by exercises in diagramming. Proper sentence structure and the correct use of adverbs, adjectives, and prepositional phrases were emphasized in the diagramming.

Reading

Students were taught mainly by sight reading. Teacher lesson plans reflect reading silently and orally and choral reading by groups.

No phonics were taught in the 1950s. Students were not passed on to the next grade if they could not read. Helen Barnett was the first teacher in the 1950s to level the reading groups to A, B, and C so that students that could read could move on.

In Owen Story's lesson plans in 1933 to 1934, he described his reading lessons as the following: "Oral expression is making sentences about pets, play, and things of general interest to the pupils. These are placed on the board or charts for the children to read. Literature activities means storytelling, dramatization, and poetry. Reading drill is reading from old charts and word drill on blackboard and finding words in stories already read."

In 1938, Mary Faris requested supplementary readers for her primary students.

Spelling

Spelling was the cornerstone of education. Spelling tests were given every Friday, and near the end of the day, the entire room from grades six to eight participated in an oral spelling bee or spelling match. In the spelling bee, students had two teams and gave out spelling words. If the opposing student didn't spell the word correctly, he/she would have to sit down. Whoever was still standing at the end was the spelling champion of the week. In the spelling match, two teams were formed. A student on the opposing team would spell a word, then the student across him/her had to spell a word that began with the last letter in the word. Many of the students tried to spell a word that ended in *x* or *y*. If the student could not think of a word beginning in the letter, he had to sit down. Sometimes, the large unabridged dictionary would be consulted to settle a dispute on the spelling.

Mr. Barnett made games on how to spell difficult words, such as substituting a word for each letter or using mnemonic spelling devices. For example, *geography*: Georgie's old granny rode a pony home yesterday. I There is also *Mississippi*: Mi crooked letter, crooked letter I, crooked letter, crooked letter I, humpback, humpback, I. Students were given gold stars on a chart if they got all words right on their tests. In Mr. Barnett's class, students also had to write misspelled words twenty times each. Ginny Helphinstine and Shirley Gulley studied hard to try not miss any.

Writing and Penmanship

Students were taught printing in the first grade with each letter individually formed. Letters were above the blackboard for students to copy.

In the second grade, Mrs. Jesse Hall taught the Palmer Method of penmanship, developed by A.N. Palmer in his book *Palmer's Guide to Business Writing*, which was written in 1894. The Palmer Method combined the clarity of manuscript letters with the ease of cursive writing. The Palmer Method replaced what students used before 1894, which was the famous Spencerian copybook the *Spencerian Key to Practical Penmanship* (1866), developed by Platt Rogers Spencer, featuring elaborate flourishes and intricate designs within the enclosed spaces of capital letters, such as *P* and *S*. Spencer's style required a great deal of time to ensure the correct number of flourishes and filigrees for words that began and ended paragraphs and sentences.

Mrs. Jesse Hall was very strict that penmanship be neat, clean, and legible.

Poetry

Students were encouraged to memorize poetry and also write poetry.

Four Eyes

Author Garry Barker went to Goddard School with Fran Helphinstine. Many years later, he became a noted Kentucky author and editor of the *Flemingsburg Gazette*, and Fran became a college professor. Garry was influenced by Jim Wayne Miller in the approach of allowing laughter to be a part of serious writing. Garry's first attempt along those lines was a poem about Fran Helphinstine called "Four Eyes," written the morning after he was fitted with his first pair of bifocal eyeglass.

On the playground of the Goddard School
We taunted Frannie Whitt
Sent her hiding to the outhouse
In tears behind thick glasses.
We called her "four eyes."

Arrogant with perfect vision,
Sharpshooter with rifle or basketball,
Unsmudged by corrective ugliness,
I flaunted 20/20 eyesight,
Hid my college roommate's lenses
And laughed as he blundered,
Searching blind.

Then it happened to me.
Myopia. Astigmatism.
Tiny bookworm lenses.
In tortoise shell frames
That slid down my nose when I sweated.
Four eyes.
Forever doomed.
Sore ears, sore nose. Dirty lenses.
Bent frames, broken hinges.
Fog and frost.
Couldn't swim anymore.
Couldn't shoot pool.
Couldn't wear contact lenses.
Four-eyed agony
Made worse by memory.

Twenty years pass.
Fashion and technology attack the issue.
Invent lightweight, designer-signed frames,
Plastic lenses, and sexy advertisements
To prove that men do make passes at girls who wear glasses.
And vice versa, thanks to Woody Allen.

I adjust, accept,
Wear bulletproof two owner glasses
Designed in Italy
And Manufactured
By NASA, I think.

Then the unthinkable, unacceptable comes to pass.
Over forty, pre-senile, unbelieving,
I can no longer read my watch
Or anything else close to me.

Bifocals.
Funny little thumbprint smudges
On both lenses.
Tilted head, in the wrong direction,
Can't focus on my toes.

Little Frannie Whitt outgrew her thick glasses,
Got a Ph.D.
And teaches lit at the University.
I saw her last week.
Frannie looked me over, grinned.
And called me "Six eyes."
(3)–Garry Barker, *Humor Is as Humor Does.* Pp. 125 to 126.

(Permission granted by Danetta Barker)

Composition

The upper grades wrote compositions. A composition written by a student in the late 1800s at Goddard's common school with the theme "The Teacher's Influence" is as follows:

The Teacher's Influence

The teacher's influence are the acts which follow it. He had perhaps in mind the influence that every teacher can exert upon her pupils either for good or for evil. Without doubt, no person in any vocation has greater responsibilities resting upon her than the teacher in our common schools. It is during the plastic period of youth that the children are under the care of the teacher. It is then that character is shaped and habits formed. To no other person, not excepting even the parents, will pupils look more than to the teacher to give them proper directions and set the right kind of example. The result of the teacher's work more than that of anyone else, is not seen at once, but on the contrary, it may be years before the seed sown in times past will bring forth fruit. The work of the teacher is sure to be a blessing or a curse to the pupil in after years. Imparting knowledge, while very important in its self, is far less than building of character. The teacher, who after faithful toiling in the schoolroom has succeeded to be instrumental in making out of his pupils strong men and women, will, when life with all its toils is ended, be sure to hear the most welcome of all words: "Well done, thou good and faithful servant.

Very respectfully,
(the student's name is not signed)

Art

Art was taught in the earlier days. It was encouraged in later days, depending on the teacher's training. Johnny Jett of the famed *Barnwood Builders* television show was a student at Goddard School and did many sketches as a student. He later did prized paintings and sketches of the Goddard community and one of the Goddard School, Goddard Church, and the Goddard Bridge.

Singing School at Goddard Around 1911
Picture in Goddard Cemetery

Seated: Oscar Helphinstine, Walter Jones, William Staggs, Pearl McCall, Brook Hammond (McIntyre),

Standing behind them: Maggie Hiner (Gray)

Standing in back: Harvey Hiner, Jesse Hiner, Marion Helphinstine, Ed Helphinstine, and George Muse (father of Owen Muse)

Music

Singing played an important role in the Goddard School education. Music served as the great socializer. Music was often used to open officially the school day or to begin and end community programs. In the early days of Goddard School (1911), singing schools were popular. The Singing School was a joint effort with the Goddard Methodist Church next door and Goddard School. The Singing School was an informal program in which students were taught to sight-read vocal music. It was associated with the Sacred Harp movement, whose music is religious in character but sung outside the context of church music. (4) The music taught in the singing schools used shape note or buck-wheat notation, in which the notes are assigned particular shapes to indicate their pitch. Sacred Harp music used the four-note system. Singing school teachers used the shape notes as an aid in learning to sing by sight. Many young men and women saw the singing schools as important to their courtship traditions. At Goddard, Oscar Helphinstine, Walter Jones, William Staggs, Pearl McCall, Brooks Hammond McIntyre, Maggie Hiner Gray, Harvey Hiner, Jesse Hiner, Marion Helphinstine, Ed Helphinstine, and George Muse were among the students at the Singing School. Oscar's mother, Mary Bell Helphinstine (Mrs. Robert Lewis Helphinstine), bought him a dulcimer to learn the sounds. This dulcimer is currently owned by Mrs. Helphinstine's great-granddaughter, Fran Helphinstine.

In the 1920s, Emory Littleton played many different instruments. In the Claude Reeves family, most family members played an instrument—Kelly, the fiddle; Woodrow, the banjo; Eck, the guitar; and Onie, the guitar.

In the early 1950s, Betty Claypool learned to play the accordion and piano. She and Faye Taylor developed a duet. With the school being next door to the church, often funerals were held while classes were in session. When there was no one to sing at the funeral, the pastor would send word for Betty and Faye to come and sing. Mrs. Verna Campbell would accompany them on the organ.

The Kentucky Travelers appeared at a music program one night at Goddard School. Tom T. Hall was one of the singers and players. He listened to Betty Claypool sing and accompanied her with his guitar. He invited Betty to sing on his radio show the following day, and she entertained many.

During recess, Betty and Faye practiced singing, and sometimes, Nellie Kirk would sing with them for a trio. She had a beautiful alto voice, and it was fun to have a trio. Betty and Faye sang not only for the school but also for revivals in Kentucky and West Virginia. Betty met her future husband in West Virginia while singing at a revival.

In the 1950s, Goddard students were enjoying the rock 'n' roll era. Elvis Presley was the dream of every girl. For the few that had the newly invented television, students watched Dick Clark and the

American Bandstand. The rest listened to WAKY radio station from Louisville, Kentucky. The sixth, seventh, and eighth grade girls in 1957 to 1959 could sing all the words to songs by Elvis, Ricky Nelson, The Big Bopper, Paul Anka, and others. Bill Littleton remembers the first transistor radio he saw at school a year after transistor radios were invented. Music at school on a radio was a wonderful surprise!

A musical concert with fiddles, guitars, and accordions was often the highlight of a wintry evening. The PTA sponsored several musical events to make money for the school. Tom T. Hall, before he became a star, was one of the entertainment venues. Dunbar Faris and Miss Caroline, Hershell Fields and daughter, Freda, were among other concerts.

Teachers who had musical background put that as a skill on their teaching applications. Naomi Clary, a young fourth grade teacher in the 1940s from Mt. Carmel at Goddard, taught music in her classroom. Noreen Staggs gave piano lessons. In the 1950s, Lois Moore, fourth and fifth grade teacher, played the piano, the accordion, and the guitar. Helen Barnett, first and second grade teacher in the 1950s, played the piano and often accompanied students for graduation. Helen's grandmother had taught her the notes, and she played for several ceremonies.

In August 1955, Mrs. Alberta Atkinson, high school music teacher, asked the school board for the development of a county-wide music program. Anna Lou McNeill was hired as a part-time music teacher that year.

Helen Fern was hired as the county music teacher on July 14, 1956. When she came to Goddard, the students loved her. She banged out many tunes on the old dusty piano in the lunchroom. Danny Mattox and Bill Littleton would request to sing "The Marines' Hymn" every week. Students like to sing "Way Down Yonder in the Pawpaw Patch" and "Froggie Went a Courting," among others. Mrs. Fern practiced with the eighth grade singers for graduation.

1.   Joseph Ray, M.D., *Intellectual Arithmetic by Induction and Analysis.* Cincinnati: Sargent, Wilson, & Hinkle, 1860, pp. 7 to 8.

2. E. Graham Alston, Inspector General. "Rules and Regulations for the Management and Government of Common Schools." *The Government Gazette.* May 28th, 1870, pp. 2 to 3, www. 1870 Rules and Regulations of Common Schools, s.web.uiv.ca/homeroom/content/topics
3. Garry Barker, *Humor Is as Humor Does.* pp. 125 to 126.
4. Sacred Harp Music.wikipedia.org

Teachers
Lois Moore and her husband, Kermit. Lois was known for her musical ability at school and in the community.

Chapter 10

Goddard School Teachers

Many of the early teachers were women who taught for a few years until they married. Others took courses at Morehead State College, and when they had completed several courses, they would move to a better school in the county with more pay, running water, and teaching supplies.

Before the desegregation law was passed, the white teachers' and colored teachers' exams were held on different days and labeled that way.

Colored Exams held May 22 to 23, 1903; May 27 to 28, 1904, June 24 to 25, 1905

White Exams held May 20 to 21, 1903; June 17 to 18, 1904; July 15 to 16, 1905

Teachers were tested in spelling, reading, writing, arithmetic, grammar, English composition, geography, physiology, civil government, history, and theory. If average was eighty-five to one hundred, they had first-class certification that lasted four years. If average was seventy-five to eighty-four, they had second-class certification that lasted two years. Below seventy-five, one failed and was not allowed to teach.

1911 to 1913 Fleming County Record of Teachers

Emma Morrison

E.S. Morrison

Mabel Davis

John Waltz

H.P. Hurst

Lula Evans

Charlie Gilmore

T F Hurst

Nannie Staggs

Wilson Hams

S.F. Filson

Hattie Johns

H. L. McGregor

B.H. Story

Alice Hurst

C. H. Evans

Ida Evans

Gertrude Mason

Goddard Applications to Teach
May 1911 to 1913

E S Morrison, age 52, 87 average on Exam, 1st class certificate; had 99 pupils; average attendance, 47 plus fifty dollars a month, School began August 12, 1913

Harley G. Campbell, 1911, average 80, 2nd class certificate, expires 1913. (Institute fee paid)

Alice and Verna Hurst
Students at Oak Grove (First Goddard School)
Daughters of Tom Hurst, Teacher
Alice and Verna were also teachers at Goddard School

C. B. James, age 20, 87 average on Teacher Exam, 1st class certificate, May 1913, expires 1917

W.R. James, age 22; 85 average, 1st class certificate

W.R. Littleton, 86 average, First Class, expired August 30, 1916

Two Early Teachers at Goddard School

Alice Hurst and Verna Hurst, daughters of Professor T. F. Hurst and Mary O. Hurst, and both graduates of Oak Grove Common School at Goddard, taught at the new Goddard School. In those days, one could teach if she passed the teacher test. Verna Hurst was first certified for 1909 to 1912 and then recertified. Her first test scores are as follows: Spelling, 93; Reading 80; Writing 95; Arithmetic 53; English Grammar 61; English Composition 77; Geography 80; Physiology 72; Civil Government 80; History 75; Theory 75; General Average 76; Received 2nd Class Certification.

Alice Hurst was first certified for 1910 to 1914 with a First Class Certification. Her scores were: Spelling, 90; Reading 92; Writing 85; Arithmetic 82; English Grammar 90; English Composition 96; Geography 82; Physiology 95; civil Government 90; History 95; Theory 90; General Average 89. She was paid $33.85 per month for her first years of teaching at Goddard.

Biographies of Goddard Teachers
Mr. Elisha Smith Morrison

Mr. Morrison was chosen to teach at Goddard the first year it opened. The other applicants were assigned to other county common schools.

Elisha Smith Morrison was the teacher who taught the longest at Goddard, with several years at the first Goddard School, Oak Grove Number 53. He also taught at Poplar Plains (1898), Hillsboro (1899), Wallingford (1902), the Emmons School (1930), Big Run (1933), and Woodlawn (1931). In 1928 to 1929, E. S. Morrison completed his fiftieth year of teaching, many of those years at Goddard. He had a life certificate and graduated from the Flemingsburg Commercial School in 1893.

Elisha Smith Morrison was born August 26, 1860, to William Heyter Morrison and Mary Ann Lyons Morrison. He married Jennie Wadsworth Morrison in 1882, and they were the parents of Mary Lena Morrison and Frankie Morrison. Teacher salaries were low; Mr. Morrison earned 67.48 per month for a total of $337.44 for the five months of 1898 to 1899 school term. He received a raise for the 1899 to 1900 term with $71.28 per month with $356.44 for the five-month school year. Even though all had low salaries, women received even less. Mr. Morrison's half-sister, Emma, received only

$23.94 per month with $119.70 for the 1899 to 1900 year near Plummers Mill. Even though teacher salaries were limited, Elisha and his wife lived on a farm and raised much of their food. After he retired, he is listed in the 1930 census as a farmer.

Mr. Morrison was noted for his discipline techniques and could control the ninety-nine students he had in his grades one to eight classroom at Goddard and probably moved to other one-room schools that needed discipline.

Bob Helphinstine attended Goddard School from 1925 to 1933. His classmates were Emory Littleton, Calvin Mattox, Estill Gardner, and others. Bob related how strict teachers were on attendance and being prompt. One morning, when Mr. Elisha Morrison was his teacher, Bob was late for school. There had been a bad storm the evening before, and his mother asked him to walk the telephone lines, installed by Ernest Rogers, to see if a tree had fallen across and knocked out their service. She had given Bob a note for the teacher. As Bob walked in the school, Mr. Morrison, in a loud voice, asked him, "Why are you late?" Bob started to tell him, and Mr. Morrison shook him and said, "Don't you talk back to me, young man!"

Elisha Smith Morrison could take care of issues in the building as they arose. From the 1910 ledger page two, E. S. Morrison was paid $13.95 for pump and incidentals.

He was a teacher that asked for very little. On his year-end reports, he rarely stated any problems.

Elisha Smith Morrison also served as the subdistrict trustee (elected in 1908 and expired in 1910), draft registrar for Fleming County in 1917, and the census taker for the Poplar Plains area in 1900, 1910, and 1920.

Mr. Morrison died February 5, 1933, of pneumonia.

Some other early teachers were the following:

Waltz Hunter, Himmer McGregor, Morton Davis, May Zimmerman, Clyde Flannery, Mike Littleton, Maggie Campbell, Myrtle Hickerson, Nell Davis, and Rosco James. Sometimes these teachers may have one hundred pupils at a time.

Other teachers at Goddard were Clarence Caywood, Nellie Caywood, Brooks Duncan, Willie Littleton, Thomas Hurst, Alice

Hurst, Verna Hurst Campbell, Kay Reynolds, Howard Daulton, Owen Story, Ethel Story, Rena Lee, Ruby Watson, Earleen Saunders, Flora Botkins, Lillian Carpenter Planck, Frankie Hurst, Mrs. Cropper, Mary Faris Ward, Ersil Ward, Miss Marshall, Beryl Glenn, Lucile Gray, Mary Allison, Elsie James, Christine Teagarden, Emma Morrison, Helen Tackett, Andrew Porter, Martha Harlan Royse, Nora Meade, Jessie Hall, Mrs. Maude Caywood, Mr. Caywood, Alta Wentz, Mabel Hellard, Rev. Earl Roberts, Rev. Myron Barnett, Helen Barnett, and Lois Owens Moore. Leota Jett substituted for Lois Moore for six weeks while she was ill.

In 1929 to 1933, teacher records were kept of experience, when the certificate expired, the type of certificate, the number of high school units, and college hours.

For Goddard, teacher records were as follows:

Mary Faris, L.E. 1929 and 1931, expired June 1933, sixteen high school units, forty-three and a half college hours.

Owen B. Story, L.E. expired 1932, seven years experience, sixteen high school units, thirty-five college hours.

Ethel Story, C. E. expired 1933, three years experience, sixteen high school units, twenty-four college hours.

Goddard School Teachers

1910 to 1911

E. S. Morrison

1911 to 1912

E. S. Morrison
C. B. James

1912 to 1913

E.S. Morrison (eighty-eight students)
T. F. Hurst

1913 to 1914

Alice Hurst
E. S. Morrison

1915 to 1916

E. S. Morrison

1916 to 1917

E. S. Morrison, Verna Hurst

1917 to 1918

E. S. Morrison

1918 to 1919

E. S. Morrison

1919 to 1920

E.S. Morrison, Verna Hurst

1920 to 1921

E.S. Morrison, Verna Hurst

Teacher records were missing for 1921 to 1922, 1922 to 1923, 1923 to 1924, and 1924 to 1925.

1925 to 1926

Alma Muse Carpenter and Mrs. S. F. Planck

1926 to 1927

Frankie Nell Hurst and E.S. Morrison

1927 to 1928

Frankie Nell Hurst and E.S. Morrison

1928 to 1929

Frankie Nell Hurst and Flora Botkin

1929 to 1930
E. S. Morrison and Frankie N. Hurst

1930 to 1931
Owen Story, Ethel Moore Story, and Beryl Glenn

1931 to 1932
E. S. Morrison (Woodlawn), Owen Story, Brooks Carpenter

1932 to 1933
Owen B. Story, Lucille Gray, Mary Faris, Brooks Carpenter (Woodlawn), Mae Andrews

1933 to 1934
Owen B. Story, Mary Faris, and Beryl Glenn

1934 to 1935
Howard B. Daulton (principal), Beryl Glenn, Mary Faris

1935 to 1936
Mary Faris, Beryl Glenn, Ruby Hunter, Howard Daulton

1936 to 1937
C.P. Caywood (principal), Beryl Glenn, Mary Faris, and Ruby Hunter

(In November, Mr. Caywood asked for a sub due to illness.)

Teachers in 1935 to 1936
Howard Daulton, Beryl Glenn, Ruby Hunter, and Mary Faris
Photo courtesy of Patsy Watson Bumgardner

1937 to 1938

Andrew Porter, Principal, Mary Faris and Beryl Glenn, Mary Allison–
in November, Ruby Hunter replaced Ms. Allison.

1940 to 1941

Earlyne Saunders, Principal, Ruby Hunter, Beryl Glenn and Mary
Faris

1941 to 1942

Hazel Perkins, Mary Faris, Christine Teegarden, Ersil Ward

**On March 22, 1941, C.D. Blair, Fleming County High School
was inducted into service and Ruby Hunter of Goddard School
was elected to fill his position. Ersil Ward filled Ruby's position at
Goddard.

1942 to 1943

Hazel Perkins, Christine Teegarden, Elizabeth Gooding and Mary
Ward

1943 to 1944
Elizabeth Gooding and Mary Ward

1944 to 1945
Brooks Duncan, Maude Caywood and Lillian Tackett

1945 to 1946
Brooks Duncan, Maude Caywood and Grace Middleton

1946 to 1947
Brooks Duncan, Helen Tackett and Jessie Hall
Substitutes Catherine Burke and Nelva Hayes

1947 to 1948
Brooks Duncan, Maude Caywood and Jessie Hall

1948 to 1949
Brooks Duncan, Maude Caywood and Jessie Hall

1949 to 1950
Nora Meade, Maude Caywood, Jessie Hall

Teacher
Nora Meade

1950 to 1951
Nora Meade, Naomi Clary, Jessie Hall

Teacher
Naomi Clary

1951 to 1952
Nora Meade, Martha Royse, Jessie Hall

1952 to 1953
Nora Meade, Jesse Hall, Martha Royse

1953 to 1954
Earl Roberts, Alta Wentz, Mabel Hellard

1954 to 1955
Myron Barnett, Alta Wentz, Norman Kizer, Carmie Cooper, Lois Moore,

1955 to 1956
Myron Barnett, Carmie Cooper, Lois Moore

1956 to 1957
Mr. Myron Barnett, Mrs. Lois Moore and Mrs. Helen Johnson

1957 to 1958
Myron Barnett, Lois Moore, Helen Barnett

1958 to 1959
Myron Barnett, Lois Moore, Helen Barnett

1959 to 1960
Myron Barnett, Lois Moore, Helen Barnett

Helen Tackett

Helen Tackett's first year of teaching was in 1946 to 1947. She taught first and second grades. Faye Taylor still remembers her kindness to the students in the first grade. Faye received her perfect attendance certificate in the summer from Miss Tackett, the first mail she had ever received. She felt so proud.

Ruby Hunter Watson

Ruby Watson taught at Goddard from 1935 to 1936 to 1940 to 1941. There was no lunchroom at that time. When World War II started, there was a shortage of men teachers. Ruby then went to the high school and replaced CD Blair, who had been drafted to the service, to teach math, where she finished her career.

Naomi Clary

Naomi Clary was a young teacher from Mt. Carmel. She stayed with Wells and Verna Campbell on Wilder Loop and walked to Goddard School.

While she was teaching, some boys were under the schoolhouse rearranging the kindling, putting them in designs of rooms and making different things. One of the boys decided he wanted a fire in his living room and lit the kindling. Slowly, the smoke came in Miss Clary's room, but the fire was put out before any major damage was done.

Tom Thumb Wedding
Frances Helphinstine, bride, James Lloyd Rogers, groom
Jimmy Jones, minister
Picture taken on top of the new cistern

Mary Faris Ward

Bob Helphinstine said Miss Mary was his girlfriend when he was a first grader. However, Wendell Staggs said she slapped him on the arm for talking, which he said, looking back, he probably deserved. Ervin Gardner remembers Miss Mary being very strict. She pecked him on the head with a ruler numerous times for talking and once a paddling. Miss Mary was talented in teaching children to read. She took courses at Morehead State College and finished her degree.

Mrs. Maude Caywood

Mrs. Caywood taught third grade. She was known for her excellent plays. At the end of the year, she produced the Tom Thumb wedding. Fran Helphinstine played the bride and James Lloyd Rogers the groom, and Jimmy Jones was the minister. Fran wore a lace piece of curtain from her mother's sewing basket as her wedding gown. This wedding was part of the May Day Celebration, complete with the maypole. Anna Lee Preston was crowned the queen.

Mrs. Caywood kept a disciplined classroom. Fran Helphinstine finished her lessons early, had problems sitting in her seat, and liked to roam around to see what others were doing. Mrs. Caywood threw erasers at her when she was up on the floor, trying to get her to sit in her seat (around 1950).

Brooks Carpenter Duncan

Brooks Duncan was the head teacher in the 1940s. Wendell Staggs gave a great tribute to her. He said she instilled the love of math and taught him a good foundation. He was hired at Cincinnati Milicron and could do many things for the company because of his math background. He said Mrs. Duncan taught it to him. In the eighth grade, Wendell and Charles Edward Johnson got in a fight, and Wendell got a D in conduct. He said he still had the highest regards for Mrs. Duncan. Ervin Gardner agreed that Mrs. Duncan was an excellent math teacher.

Nora Meade

Nora Meade was a true lady who has had a profound influence on former students, parents, community members, church members, and family. She gave unselfishly of her time and served as a role model for others.

When Ginny Reeves was a first grader, Nora Meade was the head teacher or principal and taught grades five through eight at Goddard Grade School. She was Fran Helphinstine's teacher. Mrs. Meade operated by the Golden Rule, and was an example, emphasized by the Ten Commandments that were displayed over her desk. In her first year at Goddard, she invited several students to attend a revival at the Goddard Methodist Church. At that service, Mrs. Meade, Louise Yazell, Gail Claypoole, Betty Claypoole, and Faye Taylor all accepted Christ. They were baptized at the same service at Plummers Landing in the creek. Mrs. Meade's influence is still with us today. Her love and concern have motivated many along life's pathway.

Mrs. Meade was a graduate of Alice Lloyd College. In her first year at Goddard, she contacted teachers at Alice Lloyd, and they sent Christmas gifts for her students.

She was not afraid to tackle anything. She was a problem solver. At Goddard School, her room was the large room on the end, which was later switched to be the lunchroom. Her room had a large cloak room but no stage. Mrs. Meade removed the cloak room and replaced the space with a stage, with the assistance of some of the older boys. She taught the boys how to use hammers and saws. The boys also built new shutters for the school. She asked the school board for a partition in the lunchroom to have a private area for piano lessons, but they did not approve.

The years of Nora Meade's supervision were the beginning of Ginny Helphinstine's lifelong pursuit of the love of reading. The school did not have a library; however, that did not stop them from getting books. Mrs. Meade ordered trunks of books to be sent from the State Library at Frankfort. Ginny can still remember her anticipation for the new trunk of books each month. It was like opening a treasure chest to see what new adventures would lie ahead. Those adventures inspired Ginny to be a certified librarian, a career she worked for forty-four years.

Dr. Fran Helphinstine was equally inspired by Mrs. Meade. Mrs. Meade had a new rule: that one must hold up her hand before answering a question. One day, Fran was reading *The Davenports and Cherry Pie* by Alice Dalgliesh under her desk during class time. She was engrossed in the story. "If anyone had told the Davenports that they were going to have a poodle, they wouldn't have believed it. Not that winter when so much was happening. Certainly not while, on account of the housing shortage, they were living in the cramped quarters of a made-over bam. And certainly not a poodle called Cherry Pie." About that time, the student behind Fran poked her and said Mrs. Meade was asking her a question. Fran blurted out the answer, but forgot to raise her hand first. She promptly got a spanking!

Henry David Thoreau, Longfellow, Tennyson, and other great writers were shared by Mrs. Meade as the students memorized poems of the great authors. Fran Helphinstine studied literature as she received her Doctorate of English from Indiana University and then served as dean of the Graduate English Department at Morehead State University. She retired as a professor of English at Morehead State University after fifty-two years.

Mrs. Meade was an innovator in education. Today, we beg for parents to be involved in their children's education. At Goddard School, Mrs. Meade found creative ways to involve the parents. The children on Pea Ridge did not have a way to school in bad weather. They had to walk to school. Times were tough, and the graveled road up the mountain was muddy and almost impassible in inclement weather. Mrs. Meade purchased an old army jeep and brought the children to school. Many times, mothers would ride with her to catch the bus at Goddard to go to Flemingsburg to take care of business. Mrs. Meade also took parents and children to area church services.

Mrs. Meade had running water installed at Goddard School with the building of the cistern instead of having to haul water.

Mrs. Meade organized a very active parent-teacher association (PTA). Dixie Helphinstine served as president of the PTA and learned many organizational and leadership skills from Mrs. Meade. Numerous fund raising events were held to buy school supplies and have special events for the children: box suppers, pie suppers, ice cream suppers, chili suppers, country music shows, to name a few. A hectograph, which consisted of a gelatin base for the stencil copy to do duplicating, was purchased to make copies of the lessons for children. This was many years before duplicators, copiers, and computers were invented!

Mrs. Meade wanted all children to feel that they were a part of school, that they were important and could learn. She would encourage the other two teachers to have children make valentines for the big valentine box so that every child would receive some. No one was left out because they couldn't afford it. Nora operated from the heart. She would take children home with her who were experiencing a loss in the home. Last year, a former student named Faris Viars came from another state to the Goddard School reunion especially to see Mrs. Meade.

He related how Mrs. Meade had taken him under her wing at a difficult time in his life when he lost his mother.

Boys will be boys, and when Mrs. Meade would step out of the room, Charles Reeves would be on the lookout. When Mrs. Meade was returning, Charles would alert the others, "Here comes Nora!"

Mrs. Meade worked with the Lions Club to furnish glasses for needy children.

Mrs. Meade organized the only yearbook that was ever made at Goddard School. This was before scanners, copiers, and other technical means were available, and this was no easy feat. Today, former students are still sharing this yearbook with their children, grandchildren, and great-grandchildren. This is the only pictorial account that documents the existence of Goddard School.

When Ginny Helphinstine was a third grader, Mrs. Meade's husband, James Meade, got a job in Dayton, Ohio, and Mrs. Meade moved there and taught until she retired in 1970.

Martha Harlan Royse

Frances Helphinstine remembers another special teacher, Mrs. Martha Harlan Royse (Mrs. Leo).

"Martha Royse really inspired us to learn. She was instrumental in our having *World Book Encyclopedia* for our room-grade 5. She then assigned us topics to research and share with the class. She always was finding ways to take us beyond the little textbooks into more exciting realms. Even though she went elsewhere to teach, she remained loyal to all of us in her class. She looked after us. She was concerned that the Viars boys lived in the woods with no mother and a long walk to the school bus. When I was ready to start to high school, she came to our home in the summer to help me plan what she knew was a good pre-college curriculum, pointing out why I needed to take as algebra, etc. When I was ready to finish high school, she and Mrs. Norean Staggs, the piano teacher, also went to groups as the Women's club to promote their granting their college scholarship to me. She was determined that I get to share her love for teaching by having the opportunity to go to college. She wanted the Viars boys to have a better life than their Dad; she wanted all of us to have better lives."

Fran continues about **Rev. Earl Roberts**

Mr. Earl Roberts, a Methodist minister at Tilton, was Fran Helphinstine's seventh grade teacher. Although he was a short, stocky man, he came to Goddard because there were some problems with boys and families who liked to fight. On February 3, 1954, Mr. Roberts had disciplined Isaac Route's granddaughter, Patricia Braybrant, and Bobby Sloas for arguing and asked them to enter the schoolroom and seat themselves. Hearing of the disciplinary action, brothers Isaac Routt, aged sixty, and Sam Routt, fifty-five, both of Goddard, came to the school and called Mr. Roberts into the yard from the building. During an exchange of words, the Routt brothers told the principal to remove his glasses. After which, they struck Rev. Roberts and cut his shirt with a knife. Mr. Roberts bloodied Mr. Route's nose as he had boxing in the army. Rev. Roberts received only minor injuries. Sheriff Clarke was summoned to the scene via a phone call from a nearby store and arrested Isaac Routt, who was later released under fifty-dollar bond. Sam Routt left the scene and was not found. Assisting Sheriff Clarke in the arrest were deputies Lloyd Compton and Robert Saunders. (1) Eighth grade students who saw the fight were summoned to court and testified to what they saw. Louise Yazell recalls how frightened she was when she was on the witness stand.

On February 8, 1954, Mr. Roberts reported his account at the school board meeting. Joe Brabant, fifteen, has consistently been a problem in Goddard School for several years. Mr. Roberts tried every way to appeal to the boy and get him to take an interest in school-work to no avail. On the occasion of the attack on Mr. Roberts by the Routt brothers on February 3, 1954, Joe Braybant came on the school grounds with two big rocks to take part in the fight after being forbidden by Mr. Roberts. The motion was made to expel Joe Brabant from school for willful disobedience and defiance.

James Lloyd Rogers observed the fight from inside the building. Many years later, Mr. Roberts apologized to James Lloyd.

On another occasion, student Eddie Guy refused to be paddled and drew a pop bottle on Mr. Roberts. Mr. Roberts tackled him, and while sitting on him, he had someone else bring the paddle and paddled him on the scene.

Mr. Roberts also looked out for us. When he saw that Fran Helphinstine had learned sixth, seventh, and eighth grade lessons the year before by listening, he tried to get Miss Rice, the attendance officer, to let her break the rules and go on to Flemingsburg to school. He was unsuccessful. He also wanted Fran to be more humble. He was delighted that George Mattox made a higher grade than her on one test, so he could tell the whole class.

When Mr. Roberts was principal, he organized some of the parents to build the first swing set for the children. It was made with heavy boards and rope and put in the large sycamore tree at the side of the schoolhouse. Another swing was made from an old tire.

Teacher
Jesse Hall

Hall
First and Second grades

Royse
Third, Fourth and Eighth grades

Frank Scott
Superintendent

Nancy Hart
Supervisor

Lois Cannon
Secretary

Rice
attendance officer

Meade
Fifth, Sixth and Seventh grades

Attendance Officer
Mary Rice

Teachers
Myron Barnett, Mabel Hellard, and Lois Moore

A great tragedy caused Mr. Roberts to leave. His son committed suicide in the spring, which caused Mr. Roberts and us, his students, great emotional and mental anguish. None of us had even thought a child capable of such a thing or of imitating a Western movie scene. Only a few weeks before, the child had purchased Ginny Helphinstine's box at the box supper.

Mrs. Jesse Hall

Mrs. Jesse Hall taught first and second grade.

Attendance was an issue in the first and second grade since many students had long distances to walk. The students would be retained in the first grade when they missed many days and could not read the primer. Mrs. Hall would have fifty to sixty students in her room on most years.

Mrs. Hall was Frances and Ginny Helphinstine's first and second grade teacher. Mrs. Hall let Fran help the other children with their assignments. After school, while waiting on the bus, Mrs. Hall worked with Fran Helphinstine on another project. Mrs. Hall was working on her degree at the time at Morehead State College. She was taking up School Art with Mrs. Naomi Claypool. Mrs. Hall wanted to see if the techniques she was being taught in art class worked. She coached Fran Helphinstine to draw animals using letters such as *o*'s and *c*'s. Mrs. Hall was thrilled when Fran drew the animals, just like Mrs. Claypool had taught Mrs. Hall. Right then, Fran knew she wanted to be a teacher to see how she could teach others.

Mrs. Hall had students compile a portfolio of their work to give to their parents on the last day of school. Students decorated it with yellow construction paper and the picture of a school bus. Ginny Helphinstine remembers that Mrs. Hall kept telling her that she did not write like her sister. She needed to work harder at her handwriting. Ginny received her only spanking in school that year. She was up on the floor talking to her neighbor while the teacher was out of the room. On a positive note, Mrs. Hall involved students in plays. Ginny remembers that when they were in second grade, Mrs. Hall dressed the class in crepe paper outfits for a performance of nursery rhymes for the school. Ginny still remembers part of her recitation. "Little Miss Muffet sat on a tuffet, eating her curds and whey. A spider sat down beside her and frightened Miss Muffet away."

Mrs. Hall had a clock in her room that she used to teach students to tell time. There was one problem—it ran backwards.

Teachers
Lois Moore

Mrs. Hall's husband, Allen Hall, visited the school on occasion and demonstrated his magic tricks. He would raise his arms, and a quarter would come from the air. He said the money came from a child's ear. He would have a 50-cent piece fly through the air and catch it with his hat, as students watched while he told a story. Mr. Hall was quite an entertainer! The students were fascinated with him.

Bernice Muse Plummer recalls that in 1953, Mrs. Jesse Hall had left Goddard School to teach at Flemingsburg Elementary. However, she only taught there until November when she resigned. Mrs. Carmie Cooper took Jesse Hall's place at Goddard and taught first and second grades in 1954 and 1955 to 56. Her husband was a minister, and after two years, Mrs. Cooper went with her husband to be a missionary in Brazil. She left and was replaced by Mrs. Mabel Warren. Elizabeth Sloas Wagner said she loved her, but she became ill and was replaced by Mrs. Helen Barnett.

Mrs. Alta Wentz

Mrs. Alta Wentz was Ginny Helphinstine's third grade teacher. Mrs. Wentz only taught at Goddard School two years. Mrs. Wentz taught comprehension skills with the joy of reading every afternoon. Mrs. Wentz spent time after lunch each day for each student to share information about the exciting books they were reading. Mrs. Meade had trunks of books delivered from the state library in Frankfort, and Mrs. Wentz told the students she would give a prize to the student who read the most books and told the other students about them. On the last day of school, she presented Ginny Helphinstine with *Old Mother West Wind* by Thornton Burgess. Ginny still has the book, which she has read numerous times. Mrs. Wentz, along with Mrs. Meade, influenced Ginny Helphinstine to be a library media specialist, a job she enjoyed for forty-four years.

Mrs. Wentz was strict. She slapped Imogene Littleton with a yardstick for talking. On the last day of school, she gave the students their school pictures if they had not purchased them.

Mrs. Lois Owens Moore

Mrs. Lois Moore taught third, fourth, and fifth grades. Several students remember her wonderful Bible flannel board stories. She could make those characters step off the flannel board and cross the Red Sea. Edith Plummer said she learned about the Bible from Mrs. Moore as she wrote "Jesus" on the Board each morning and discussed a new Bible story.

Valentine's Day was special to the students.

This Valentine was sent in 1911. Valentines could be purchased at John Lewis Staggs' store and Mrs. Bessie Yazell's across the road from the Goddard School.

Bill Littleton said he looked forward to the Bible stories each morning. Mrs. Moore had written in her lesson plans to have devotions in the morning and to pray before lunch.

Ginny Helphinstine and Dorothy Reeves looked forward to the stories Mrs. Moore read aloud after lunch each day. A favorite was *The Five Little Peppers and How They Grew*. We loved that book!

Years before computers and copiers, Mrs. Moore used the pur-ple hectograph, which was very messy, to make copies. She made art copies for students to color to decorate the blackboard and windows, especially at Christmastime. Students exchanged names. Mrs. Moore gave each student a box with three pencils that had the student's name on them.

Elizabeth Sloas remembers that they played cowboys and Indians when she was in Mrs. Moore's room. She also remembers when Mrs. Moore read the fairy tale "Hans, Who Made the Princess Laugh" from *Stories Around the World*. In this story, the princess is very sad and would not smile. The king said he would give half his kingdom to get his princess to smile. Mrs. Moore had Elizabeth Sloas sit on the edge of the desk and see how many students could get her to laugh. Elizabeth could hold a frown like no other and never laugh. Kenny Roberts tried hard to get Elizabeth to smile, as did the other classmates, but to no avail. The principal, Mr. Barnett, heard of the challenge. He filed his sixth, seventh, and eighth grade students past the little girl. Finally, one boy pretended to sit on an imaginary chair then fell over in the floor. It wasn't a laugh, but a smile did come across that face.

On Valentine's Day, students decorated a big box for valentines. Mrs. Moore had each student make a valentine for everyone in the room so that every child received several valentines. Some students made comic valentines, which were popular at the time.

Kenny Roberts related that fifth grade was his favorite year of all years when he was in Mrs. Moore's room. One of the reasons was his deep friendship with Harold Bays. Kenny and Harold had been best friends since third grade and continued to ninth grade in high school. Kenny said, "He was to me a Fonzie, the toughest guy around." However, Harold surprised Kenny one day when Denzil Conley challenged Harold to a fight. Harold had the courage to walk away from the bully as his parents had taught him to do. In later years, Kenny realized that it takes a bigger person to walk away than to stand and fight.

That same year, Harold Bays had a childhood sweetheart that he had liked since third grade. She apparently liked him as well, until one day, three of the fifth grade girls decided to drop their current boyfriends and claim guys in the sixth or seventh grades. Harold's girlfriend was one of the three. The green-eyed monster raised its ugly head! Harold took a pair of scissors and carved a big X in both sides of his girlfriend's favorite loose leaf binder. That was not bad enough, but then he took the binder under the schoolhouse floor and buried it under a big rock. Kenny Roberts hated to see Harold's girlfriend cry, so he dug the notebook up from the ground and gave it to Mrs. Moore, the teacher. Eventually, Harold and his girlfriend got back together, but she was jealous of Harold and Kenny's friendship. She whispered to Kenny in his ear, "I hate your guts." What a surprise! Kenny was expecting a "thank you" for finding her notebook.

Sometimes the boys grew noisy, and Mrs. Moore said she needed a paddle. Donald Bays and Larry Swim were eager to please Mrs. Moore and volunteered to make one and fixed the paddle just right, complete with holes bored in it. Guess who the first ones were to be paddled. Donald and Larry. The names were written on the paddle with a mark for every paddling.

Mrs. Moore paid Imogene Littleton ten cents per day to sweep her floors. Imogene was excited and went to Mrs. Bessie's store and purchased a Sugar Daddy, a brown cow or a five-cent bag of candy.

Some accidents happened those early years with Mrs. Moore. Billy Jett fell out the window and broke his elbow. Donna McKee did not want to get out of the swing on another day, and when someone tried to make her, she got her finger caught in the chain link and injured it. Mr. Barnett quickly took the children to Flemingsburg to the doctor.

Another day, Roy Plummer came running across the porch, breathless, and ran in Mrs. Moore's room, escaping three dogs that had chased him to school. Mrs. Moore quickly closed the door.

In the springtime, students looked forward to the annual field trip walk up Pea Ridge mountain. On a beautiful sunny day, the outdoor classroom exhibited nature's paradise as birds sang like angels, the green moss provided a bed for hopping frogs, and the lush fern moved gently in the breeze. Birds of all kinds were migrating north and singing to find the perfect mate. Mrs. Moore helped identify many of the beautiful birds. Students rushed to pick fragrant sweet Williams, honeysuckle, and bluebells for their teacher while she explained the names of the native redbuds, dogwoods, and century-old oak trees. Jack-in-the-pulpits, mayapples, and violets decorated the pathway as the students were winding around the cliffs. Some imagined a woodland fairyland was made with the intricate spiderwebs. The boys searched for wild grapevines on which to swing. A special treat awaited at Price Mattox's home: He let the students climb the fire watchtower. A breathtaking view of the valley below awaited the excited students at the top of the mountain. Tomorrow's worries were forgotten. As Thoreau wrote, "Let us spend one day as deliberately as nature and not be thrown off the track by every nutshell and mosquito's wing that falls on the rails." Nature became the subtle teacher for all.

Mrs. Moore worked hard to make sure every student enjoyed school. Kenny Roberts worked hard to please her and didn't miss one day in her fifth grade class! Mrs. Moore gave Kenny a paint by number portrait she painted herself, signed and dated for Kenny's award, a treasure which he still has to this day.

Mrs. Moore took several of the girl's home with her for the night for a slumber party. Ginny Helphinstine and the other girls loved taking a bath in a real tub as they used the wash tub at home with no running water.

Mrs. Moore, who became Mrs. Phillips, kept in contact with her students as long as she was able. She died on February 25, 2020, at Pioneer Trace nursing home in Flemingsburg.

Kenny Roberts

Awarded Perfect Attendance Award by Lois Moore
Photo courtesy of Patsy Roberts Stacy

Teacher
Helen Barnett

Helen Barnett

Helen Barnett taught the first and second grade. Goddard was her first teaching assignment. She started teaching at Goddard when she had two years of college and came in November to replace Mrs. Mabel Warren, who became ill. Mr. Barnett was her mentor and taught her many things about teaching. Helen was innovative and passed on children that were much older to the next grade. She started the leveled groups of reading so bright children could move on to increase their skills and others would get the help they needed. One day, when Diane Gulley, Alvin Gulley's daughter, was reading aloud, she fainted. Mrs. Barnett put her on the reading table, and then Mr. Barnett took her home. Elizabeth Sloas was a big help to Mrs. Barnett. She worked with students at the reading table while Mrs. Barnett helped other students. Another day, Mrs. Barnett left Elizabeth Sloas in charge when she took the lunch count to the lunchroom. Several tall boys were in the second grade. When Mrs. Barnett returned, Elizabeth had drawn circles on the board and had boys who had been talking, standing with their noses in a ring on the blackboard. Everything was in control.

Helen was so compassionate with the children. On very cold days, Helen warmed water in a pan on the coal stove and warmed children's cold feet from the frigid walk. She also put newspapers on the oiled floor around the stove on cold days, and children did their reading lesson around the stove. Elizabeth Sloas was in the third grade, and her little sister, Jerri, was in the first grade. Every afternoon, Jeri would start crying, afraid she was going to miss the bus. Helen would hold her on her lap and have Elizabeth come to the room, then Jerri would be okay. Jeri learned the first day what was expected in Mrs. Barnett's room. Only one person was allowed on the floor at a time to sharpen one's pencil. Jeri did not look to see who was at the pencil sharpener. She just got up and got the reward of staying in at recess. Later, Jeri decided she wanted to be Lynn that day (her middle name). Mrs. Barnett called out Lynn to get her paper. By this time, Jeri had forgotten that she had used her middle name, Lynn.

While teaching at Goddard, Helen Barnett became pregnant with her son, David. Elizabeth Sloas (Wagner) remembers that when she came home from the hospital, she came by school to show the children the new baby. The children lovingly called him Davey Crockett. When Helen came back to work, she brought David with her for a short period and put him in a playpen in the lunchroom. Miss Nancy Staggs, the cook, watched him. Many years later, Miss Nancy wanted David to come spend the night. She was very attached to him. Bernice Muse stayed with the Barnetts' for a while and babysat David and Brenda. She also helped with washing, ironing, and cleaning.

Helen had a child run away one day at recess across to the country store. Mr. Barnett went after him. When asked why he did it, he replied that he was hungry. Mr. and Mrs. Barnett brought food many mornings to feed hungry children. They also supplied crayons, scissors, paper, and other supplies from their own funds to children who could not afford what they needed.

Helen and Myron enjoyed their years at Goddard and looked forward to going to school each morning. The children were so appreciative of everything they did for them.

Teacher
Myron Barnett

Rev. Myron Barnett

Mr. Barnett, a Christian church minister, taught the sixth, seventh, and eighth grades. Ginny Helphinstine was in his class for all three grades. He was clothed with compassion, kindness, humility, and patience. He started the day with the Pledge of Allegiance, the reading of a Bible verse, and the Lord's Prayer.

Ginny Helphinstine remembers many things about those three years. Shirley Gulley, Dorothy Reeves, Danny Mattox, Bill and Imogene Littleton (twins), Oscar Mathison, Betty Jones, and Linda James were classmates. Mr. Barnett assigned memorization of many things: "The Village Blacksmith," by Longfellow, the Gettysburg Address, preamble to the Constitution, and other famous poems. Oscar loved to memorize poetry and would encourage Mr. Barnett to make this assignment. Mr. Barnett was noted for his ability to teach literary selections that referred to farm living, such as "When the Frost Is on the Punkin" by James Whitcomb Riley, "The Old Hay-Mow" by Robert Louis Stevenson, "The Hayloft" by Holmes, "The Deacon's Masterpiece" or Shelley, "To a Skylark," *The Hoosier Schoolmaster* by Edward Eggleston, and *Huckleberry Finn* by Samuel L. Clemens.

In the seventh grade, Mr. Barnett taught many things about Kentucky history. Students toured Blue Licks Battlefield State Park, enjoying the wonderful museum, and Daniel Boone came to life in the student's imagination. Bill Littleton loved the hike down to the Licking River and the roasting of hot dogs and marshmallows. It was a fun day!

Students had to memorize all one hundred twenty counties and their county seats, as well as the states and all their capitals. When Bernice Muse was in Mr. Barnett's class, he had her write the tests on the blackboard because she had beautiful writing. Bernice also took excellent notes and wrote her history notes in the textbook. The following year, Mr. Barnett borrowed her notes to add to his lesson plans. Students also went to Joyland Park in Lexington, Kentucky, and Coney Island near Cincinnati, Ohio, on school trips on Saturdays.

Mr. Barnett would have someone write numbers on the black-board and see who could give the sum of the numbers the quickest. Woodie Reeves usually won this contest in his grade. Mr. Barnett also had students figure the batting average of their favorite ball player.

Mr. Barnett taught the students to enjoy their environment. Students were taught to use the blue clay mud to make clay dishes. Dishes would be decorated with dandelions on top. Clover blooms were tied together to make necklaces and bracelets. The schoolhouse was built off the ground on one end, and students would make the clay items under the schoolhouse. The boys liked to play under the schoolhouse. Some boys built a large fort. One boy thought the fort needed a fire and built a fire, which caused much concern. The fire was quickly extinguished. On rainy days, Wes Adkins and Eugene Hall played marbles in the dirt under the schoolhouse.

Mr. Barnett played with the students! My, could he run fast, especially in tag! Recess was a special time, and on Friday afternoons, if students had their work finished, they would have a ball game or some other activity. The boys loved to play baseball. If Johnny Bays, parent, was at one of the country stores, he came over and joined the game. He coached the boys on Sunday afternoons, and some good players developed. Eugene Hall enjoyed the days they got to go fishing in the springtime. He borrowed safety pins from the girls and used them for fishing hooks. Sitting in the peppermint weeds on the creek bank made one feel that this was a little bit of heaven. Students also saw how they could excel in "Pop! Goes the Weasel" and drop the handkerchief. Mr. Barnett and other teachers worked hard at making all students feel they were part of a big family. Students who entered Goddard School said other schools where they attended did not have the same atmosphere. Some had been bullied.

Mr. Barnett taught many students to spell *procrastination*. If they were talking or acting up when he left the room, he came back and had everyone write "Procrastination is a thief of time!" five hundred times. Ginny Helphinstine remembers getting caught talking one time and had to write the sentence five hundred times. She was sneaking upstairs at home to write it so her mother would not catch her. She knew the spanking she would get if her mother knew!

When Mr. Barnett brought his small child, David, into the classroom, the boys liked to play tricks. Someone gave David the rope from the window, and David pulled the rope down the aisle, not knowing what this caused with the window.

Mr. Barnett gave ice cream to whomever swept and cleaned the room each day. The last week of school, someone pulled the plug on the ice cream freezer, and Mr. Barnett gave each student a free ice cream. Mysteriously, the same thing happened the following year.

The school board bought oil to put on the floors to help keep down the dust. Ginny Helphinstine remembers sweeping the floors. If the floors were freshly oiled, she would get black oil on her socks. Ginny's mother gave Ginny a lecture to be more careful as the oil was next to impossible to remove.

The boys carried in kindling from under the schoolhouse floor and coal from the coal pile out front for all the stoves. Kelly Bruce Reeves carried kindling and took out ashes. Sometimes the students gathered kindling from the banks of the creek. Emerson Plummer helped build fires. Miss Nancy Staggs, after she was hired to cook, came early and built the fires in all four rooms.

Mr. Barnett loved to tease. One day a student found a small green snake at lunch and gave it to Mr. Barnett. Mr. Barnett hid the snake in Mrs. Moore's teacher desk drawer. Imagine the scene as she leaped from her chair when she opened her drawer!

Mrs. Ann Mosely and Mrs. Nettie Honea Cooper, County Nurses

On August 12, 1944, Mrs. Ann Mosely was elected the school nurse at an annual salary of $500.00.

Mrs. Nettie Cooper replaced Mrs. Mosely for the county nurse and came occasionally to Goddard School. She gave needed shots and talked to girls about their monthly issues. She also talked about hygiene and the importance of brushing your teeth. She gave students a chart with stickers to put on each morning if they brushed their teeth. This was a real motivator for Ginny Helphinstine. When the floods came, Mrs. Cooper came with the needles to give everyone shots. It was time to line up to get a shot, a dreaded day for many!

She also brought sugar cubes for polio vaccine. Students had to have the smallpox vaccine before entering school. This would make a large place on your arm, especially if the scab got knocked off before it had completely healed. Mrs. Cooper checked to see if the arm was healing properly.

Mrs. Mary Elizabeth Rice, Attendance Officer

Mrs. Mary Rice, a former teacher, was a kind lady that visited and collected attendance reports, which were part of her attendance reports to the school board. She was the first director of pupil personnel, which removed the stigma of an attendance officer from the position and which set it on a steady and very important course. Students got a gold star on a chart in the front of the room for perfect attendance each week. She did so much more for students. She worked with the Lions Club to obtain glasses for needy children as well as other organizations for clothing.

Mrs. Nancy B. Hart and Mrs. Wanda Maxey, Elementary Supervisors

Nancy B. Hart was employed as the elementary supervisor on June 14, 1947. The following year, she submitted a supplementary elementary textbook list to the school board, which was approved. In February 1949, Mrs. Hart reported to the school board that she was coordinating the curriculum in the county schools. Wanda Maxey was employed for this position for the 1958 to 1959 school year.

Mrs. Noreen Staggs, Piano Teacher

Mrs. Noreen Staggs came to Goddard School and gave piano lessons. She also had chapel for the students and sang with them. "God Bless America" was the most requested song. James Lloyd Rogers and Gerald James were two of her students. After a few weeks, she gave up on Gerald since he had learned to play by ear. Mrs. Staggs said she could not teach him because he did not want to learn the notes. Frances Helphinstine was another one of her piano students. She continued to give Frances lessons when she went on to high school. Frances left high school in her study hall, and Mrs. Staggs met her at the Baptist church for her lessons.

Teacher Salary Schedules and Retirement

At the September 4, 1940, school board meeting, the superintendent announced that the State Board of Education was requiring the districts to make salary schedules. Frank Scott, superintendent, updated the salary schedule for the 1948 to 1949 school year as follows: $105.00 base salary, $0.55 per college semester hour, $2.00 per year experience up to five years, $5.00 per teacher for supervision.

Elizaville High School, Hillsboro High School, and Flemingsburg High School were merged into one high school. Mr. Scott, superintendent, said the main reason for the merger was so Fleming County could have one good high school. The Southern Association was about to drop Fleming County from membership because of low teachers' salaries.

The October 26, 1940, minutes recorded that the school district was now paying teacher retirement. For the month of October 1940, $173.82 was paid to the state treasurer. Teacher contracts were developed and issued beginning July 12, 1947.

1. "Goddard School Principal Assaulted by Two Men in School Yard Wednesday." *Times Democrat.* February 4, 1954.

Chapter 11

Student and Teacher Dress

Farm families did not have the funds for designer clothes. Very few families had enough money to buy many new clothes at a store. Many mothers sewed for their children.

Clothing in the 1913 period was very different from today. Most of the clothes were handmade. Most of the body was covered regardless of the outside temperature. Female teachers usually wore long dark skirts, white long-sleeved blouse, long dark stockings, lace handkerchief tucked in the sleeve, and a straw or felt hat for outside. Men teachers wore three-piece suit, long sleeves, shirt with collar, suspenders, dark plain tie, and dark shoes.

During the Great Depression, farm mothers repaired, reused, made do, and didn't throw anything away. Mothers mended socks and sewed patches over holes in clothes. Clothes were handed down to younger children. Before the Depression until well after World War II, farmers brought home big cotton sacks of chicken feed. The chicken feed sacks usually came in a patterned material, and many ladies sewed at the time. Farm women used the sacks as material to sew everything from girls' dresses to boys' shirts and even underpants. A one-hundred-pound bag of chicken feed became a thirty-six inches by forty-four inches piece of cloth. One feed sack could have easily made a child's dress, boy's shirt, underwear, a bonnet, and apron. Three identical sacks were needed to make a woman's dress. By the 1940s, the bag manufacturers sold bags in bright col-

GINNY REEVES

ors and printed designs. Magazine and pattern companies published patterns to make feed sack outfits. Some ladies just cut out a pattern from newspapers. Louise Yazell remembers Dora Claypoole making several dresses for her from feed sacks. Ruby Riickert and Ella Hughes were seamstresses who sewed for local people. Ginny and Fran Helphinstine remembers their mother showing their father the print she needed to match to complete a dress when he was going to the store to purchase feed. She then washed the sack, starched it, ironed it, and sent it to her sister to make dresses for Fran and Ginny. Aunt Beulah Hampton added different details to each dress. Some had little puffy sleeves, some with self-collars, some with contrasting solid colors, and some with ruffles. The feed sacks were so popular that John Lewis Staggs added a room to his store at Goddard for additional feed sales. When a new feed shipment arrived, one could notice children with new dresses with a different print. On Saturday nights at the country stores, ladies traded prints to get enough to make what they wanted. Ginny used a feed sack material, blue and rose flowers on white, to make her first 4-H apron. She won a blue ribbon. Many of the little boys wore bib overalls with their feed sack shirts. Dorothy Reeves made shirts for her sons.

Many of the students wore overshoes, especially those that walked to school.

In the 1940s, Dorothy Plummer (Briggs) remembers her grandmother made her and her sisters wear black cotton stockings under their dresses. The students made fun of them at school so they removed the stockings on their way to school each morning and put them on as they returned from school.

If families had money after the Burley tobacco crop sold in the winter, students may get to select a dress or trousers from one of the mail order catalogs, such as Montgomery Wards, Sears Roebuck, Aldens, or Spiegel. Ginny Helphinstine remembers her favorite: the 1950s charcoal poodle skirt with matching pink sweater she got from Sears one year.

In the 1950s, the girls wore oxford shoes or penny loafers and cancan slips with their full skirts. This was the rage. The slips were starched stiff to make the skirt full. The only problem was that when

160

one stepped on the school bus, the aisles were narrow and the slips flipped the skirts above a level that was not proper for young ladies. The same was true in the aisles of the school. Pretty collars that could be attached to a sweater with a spoon pin dressed up any outfit. Girls could not wear jeans or slacks unless the weather was extremely cold.

Chapter 12

School Programs and School Trips

Easter egg hunts were held on beautiful sunny days in the spring-time. Sammy Reeves remembers when Horace Taylor hid the eggs and Sammy was a little guy. Horace told Sammy to look up on the window ledge. Three eggs were laying in the school window.

The school board set the date each year for the Halloween pro-grams. A Halloween program was held in the 1950s at Goddard. The stage was dark as students moved across and felt the spaghetti for the human insides and grapes for the eyeballs. Imogene Littleton (Wheeler) was perched overhead the stage and poured water on stu-dents as they made their way across the stage.

Mrs. Moore had Halloween programs in her room. Student ghosts wore sheets over them with only their eyes exposed. Mrs. Moore tried to guess who the child was by only looking in their eyes.

First grade students of Ms. Jesse Hall recited nursery rhymes for the parents decked out in crepe paper outfits. "Mary, Mary, quite contrary, how does your garden grow?" Mrs. Hall made crepe paper outfits for many programs. She taught the girls in several grades to make crepe paper flowers with pipe cleaners for their homes and the cemetery. The following years, most graves in the Goddard Cemetery were decorated with crepe paper flowers, since few flowers were avail-able for purchase. Mrs. Meade also taught the girls to make flow-ers from different materials. They dyed nylon stockings in different colors and cutout leaves, flowers, and other designs and put wire to make shapes for decorations. Peonies were made from different colored tissues.

In one of the last years at Goddard, Mr. Barnett had a program with "Lazy Bones" lyrics, written by Louis Armstrong. Joe Roberts played "Lazy Bones." All he had to do was wear a straw hat and lie on a lunchroom table like a country bumpkin with no shoes, while the class surrounded him and sang the song.

"Lazy bones sleepin' in the sun
How you think you gonna get your day work done
You'll never get your day work done
Sleepin' in the noonday sun.

Lazy bones sleepin' in the shade
How you gonna get your com meal made
You'll never gonna get your com meal made
Sleepin' in the noonday shade.

**Joe Roberts
Played "Lazy Bones" in the play given
by Mr. Myron Barnett, 1960
Photo courtesy of Patsy Roberts Stacy**

When taters need sprayin'
I bet you keep prayin the bugs fall off of the vine
And when you go fishin'
I bet you keep wishin' the fish won't grab at your line.

Lazy bones loafin' through the day
How you 'spect you gonna make a dime that way
You'll never make a dime that way
Sleepin' in the noonday shade."

Christmas programs were always a highlight of the year. Older boys went to Curt and Bessie Yazell's field across the highway and cut a large cedar tree for each room and one for the stage. Students spent much time making paper chains and wrapping sycamore balls from the tree in the schoolyard with the aluminum foil from their chewing gum wrappers.

Before the stage was built, Christmas programs were conducted in the Goddard Methodist Church next door, as well as some other years. The students worked for weeks learning poems, songs, and lines to a play. Wires were strung across the stage, and sheets were used for curtains. One year, a student was so excited that he pulled the sheet down on the floor trying to close the curtain just as the play started! Students' parents always attended, and that made for a large crowd.

Terry Hurst recalls a Christmas program conducted by Nora Meade when he was a student. Goble and Charles Reeves sang "We Three Kings," and it was the highlight. They did a fabulous job. In later years, Charles sang and recorded gospel music.

The year the stage was built, the eighth grade boys had carefully chosen a large cedar tree at Curt and Bessie Yazell's for the stage lit by the new bubble lights! What excitement as this was the first time most students had seen bubble lights. The strand had eight small glass cylinders that were filled with different color liquids, and when plugged in to electricity, the cylinders would light up, and as they warmed up, bubbles began to light up the liquid. Aluminum icicles were placed strategically on the branches of the tree. A cardboard star, covered with aluminum foil, was placed on the very top. The fragrance of the cedar and the lights from the tree set the mood for the excited children. John Mattox played Santa and had peppermint stick candy, Wrigley's chewing gum, and oranges for everyone! A Christmas program followed, and Mrs. Hall made crepe paper outfits for the characters. Fran Helphinstine was an angel and carried a wand. Gene Littleton was baby Jesus that year. In previous years, Louise Yazell's large doll was used for baby Jesus. This big boy doll was lifelike with two front teeth and ceramic arms and legs and cried like a baby. Louise's mother, Mrs. Bessie Yazell, had won the doll for selling the most cookies in a country store. Mrs. Bessie also won a large Santa Claus, which she displayed at the store. She let students touch him when they visited from school.

Christmas programs and carols were conducted other years. Anna Florence Jones recalls that when she was in Mrs. Martha Royse's room in the third grade, they were supposed to memorize poems. Her poem was "O Christmas Tree." Anna Florence had a cheat sheet to help her remember.

Kenny Roberts remembers the Christmas program on the last year of Goddard School. The program was held at the Goddard Church to allow room for parents and neighbors to come. The Nativity scene was reenacted with some students playing roles of Joseph, Mary, and wise men. Larry Swim was a shepherd and wore a burlap coffee sack. Kenny remembers his part was small. He held a small cardboard cutout of a donkey and recited these words: "If I was the donkey and Mary rode on me, I'd be so proud and filled with joy. I'd bray lustily." After the Nativity scene, students in grades three through eight sang the following song:

> "It was on one Christmas evening
> When a thousand different toys were displayed
> upon the counter of the stores.
> You could hear the shouts and laughter of the
> happy girls and boys
> As the Christmas lights were flashing ore and ore.

When suddenly a whistle gave a loud and shrill-
ing blast.
An officer came running down the way
A man had been caught stealing.
It was just a china doll
As they tore it from his grasp
I heard him say:
Chorus
It was for my little baby
How I long to bring her joy
She's been writing notes to Santa
Asking for a little toy
Oh I'd rather go to prison
Bear the load of shame and scorn
Than to see her stocking empty
When she wakes on Christmas morn.
Now isn't that a likely story
Said the officer aloud
As they tried to drag the broken man away
When a fine and wealthy gentleman
Stepped up from the crowd
And he said, "Let's hear what more he had to say"
And when they heard the story
Of a man without a job
His little daughter sick in bed
He said I'll pay the damage
And I see that he gets work
For it broke my heart with pity when he said
(Repeat chorus)

After the song was finished, Kenny noticed that one of the
grandmothers had broken into tears.

James Rogers treated all his classmates in his room with paddles
with rubber balls attached. The students enjoyed them.

The school trip was the highlight of the year. When Nora Meade
was head teacher, she was taking the seventh and eighth graders to see

the Breaks of the Big Sandy. This was the time when the Kentucky transportation department was building a new road through the Eastern Kentucky Mountains and the bus got stuck. After the bus got out of the mud, the students had a picnic and went to a movie in Pikeville, then came home.

The school board had to approve the school trip and would not allow a trip that was not educational to be taken. They would not allow Joyland or Coney Island on a school day.

Patsy Roberts
Queen of Hot Jump Rope
Photo courtesy of Patsy Roberts Stacy

Chapter 13

Clubs and Activities

Students entertained themselves in numerous ways during recess and lunch hour. The large schoolyard provided a playground for individual and group activities.

In the early days, students played games such as marbles, thimble, running games, or singing games. Handy over, horseshoes with real horseshoes, fence tag, stoplight game, hot jump rope, and drop the handkerchief were some of the activities. The stoplight game engaged students to run as fast as they could until the leader called them to stop. Those that kept running were out of the game. Louise Yazell still has a scar on her leg from where she fell in the coal pile trying to stop. Hot jump rope was when one could jump real fast and sing the song "Down in the valley, where the green grass grows, along came Patsy, sweet as a rose. She sang, she sang, she sang so sweet. Along came Sherley and kissed her on the cheek. How many kisses did he give her? One, two, three, four, five…" Patsy Roberts and Sherley Taylor got married when Patsy was only fourteen years old. Any name could be substituted.

Some students became tight rope walkers when they developed their acrobatic skills by walking on the top of the Goddard Church board fence.

On cold days, competitive snowball fights were held if there was snow. Otherwise, the children played with Chinese checkers, checkers, and dominos, and they made pot holders with pot holder looms.

Children brought some toys from home. Louise Yazell brought her tea set, silverware, and doll to school. This was her prized doll, and no one had one like it. Diane Swim wanted to play with it but didn't want to give it back. A disagreement developed, and Louise pulled Diane's hair to retrieve the doll.

When Mr. Roberts was principal, some of the parents made a swing with rough boards and put on a large limb of the large sycamore tree on the side of the schoolyard.

Under the schoolhouse was another playground. The schoolhouse was built on rock columns, with the lower columns three and one-half to four feet high up to the floor of the school, plenty of room for fourth grade boys to scratch dirt roads. Creative boys played cars and trucks under the floor of the school in the dirt. Clear medicine bottles represented plain Chevrolets or Fords. Kenny Roberts had an amber-colored Lavoris mouthwash bottle with a pink lid; it had to be a Lincoln Continental!

Sand Lick Creek, which ran in front of the school, provided another playground for students. When Mr. Roberts and Mr. Barnett were teachers, students slipped off to the creek. Hobart Muse fell through the thin ice one day. However, when the creek froze over, Mr. Roberts and Mr. Barnett would take their classes to the creek at recess to ice-skate. Eugene Hall remembers his new engineer boots with hard soles that were perfect for skating on the ice. Mr. Barnett skated up beside students to teach new tricks. He laughed when he heard the ice cracking. Of course, the water was not that deep. Donald Bays has a scar to remind him as he fell on the ice and cut a large gash in his face. It took six stitches to sew it.

Fifth graders Kenny Roberts, Harold Bays, Tommy Gorman, Sammy Reeves, and Johnny and Billy Jett found a way to go fishing one day. They were not allowed to go down to the creek in front of the school with Mr. Barnett and his upper-grade class, so they fished in the schoolyard. When the ground was very dry, there were small holes in the ground about the size of a pencil made by cutworms. If a broom straw was dropped in one of the holes and the straw started to move, one of the cutworms was trying to clean out his hole. He grabbed the straw with his pinchers and pushed up on the straw. If the boys pulled up on the straw quickly, they could pull the worm out of the hole before the worm had a chance to let go.

Later they began playing baseball and basketball. There was friendly competition among the schools to be the winner.

Jim Meade, Nora's husband, installed the first basketball goal, but it had no net. The basketball was used more for keep-away than actual basketball games. This was late 1940s and early 1950s.

On Friday afternoons in warm weather, students went on a bus to other schools in the eastern part of the county where the boys would play baseball with the boys at the other schools. Boys from the other schools came to Goddard also. Great competition existed between butler at Plummers Mill. The boys also played Tilton and Muses Mill. Sometimes players would be taken on a wagon to Pea Ridge while Muses Mill did the same. They played in a large field on Pea Ridge owned by Price Mattox. Billy Conley could get a good hit and run fast around the bases. He was later killed in the Vietnam War and is buried in the Goddard Cemetery. The 1956 class at Goddard was all boys, and all nine made up the team that year. Carl Bays was one of the excellent players. Avery Curtis was quite tall and could hit the ball well. These boys played on a community team on Sunday afternoon and played against the noted Woodie Fryman. Harold Bays and Donald Bays had uniforms, but many others did not.

In the 1950s, autograph books were popular. In Shirley Gulley's autograph book, below is written by classmate Oscar L. Mathison:

When your work on earth is ended and your path of duty trod,
May your name in gold be written in the autograph of God.
With lots of luck to a swell girl.

Shirley had autographs of teachers as well. Myron Barnett, teacher, wrote, "Shirley, you are a very good student. I am sure you will succeed in whatever you do."

The two main clubs were 4-H and conservation clubs. Most students belonged to at least one club.

Junior Conservation Club

Jim Meade, Nora's husband, started the Junior Conservation Club. He served as the conservation officer for the Fleming County area at the time. He held a shooting match with clay pigeons on Pea Ridge. He taught many students how to shoot a gun. Terry Hurst remembers going to Conservation Camp (not Dale Hollow). He was prepared with a box of fishing worms. This was the first time he had been in a boat and the boys tried some new sports. On the way home, they stopped at a restaurant that served fried chicken, another first for the students.

Later, Pete McNeill helped with the Conservation Club. The students looked forward to Mr. McNeill's weekly visits and activities.

Pete took Woodie Reeves and others and planted trees behind D.A. Watson's store, near Plummers Landing. Pete secured funds for children to have life experiences. Woodie Reeves, the oldest of nine children, was selected to attend Dale Hollow for a week. This was the first time Woodie had been away from home without his family and one of the few times he had been out of Fleming County at that young age. What an exciting week this was! Woodie learned to cast a rod and reel, quite an experience for a twelve-year-old child who loved to fish but had only fished with a cane pole! Swimming in a swimming pool instead of Trace Run creek was another new adventure. Woodie made new friends by playing ping-pong and learned new things to do in nature, which made memories to last a lifetime.

4-H Club

Christine Hurst and Mamie Morrison were 4-H leaders. They were patient ladies. Ginny Helphinstine won the prize for beginning sewing for Fleming County with Mrs. Mamie with her feed sack apron. Mrs. Mamie reminded the girls to keep the stitches small.

Christine took the girls to her house to do cooking. Can you imagine sixth, seventh, and eighth grade girls cooking in your kitchen? Students made fruit milkshakes, banana milkshakes, and cocoa. They also baked cookies like butterscotch fingers, peanut butter, oatmeal, and brownies. They learned to stir up a busy day yellow cake, which Ginny Helphinstine made numerous times for her family. The recipe is from the University of Kentucky, 4-H 1008 booklet.

Busy Day Cake

1 2/3 cup sifted flour
1 cup sugar
1/4 t salt
2 1/2 t baking powder
1/3 c shortening or margarine
2/3 c milk
1 egg
1 t vanilla or other flavoring

The egg and milk should not be real cold; the shortening should be soft but not melted. Sift flour once before measuring, then sift flour, sugar, salt and baking powder together in a mixing bowl. Add shortening, milk, unbeaten egg and flavoring all at once to the flour mixture. Beat all ingredients together with a spoon, rotary egg beater or electric mixer for two minutes. Pour into a well-greased pan which has been lightly dusted with flour. Use a pan 9 inches square and about 1 1/2 inches deep. Bake 35 minutes at 350 degrees.

When the cake is still warm, make the jiffy icing for the Busy-Day Cake:

3 T melted butter
1/3 cup brown sugar
2 T cream
1/2 cup shredded coconut or chopped nuts

Mix all ingredients and spread on cake while cake is still in the pan and still warm. Put cake back in over (350 degrees) until it bubbles all over the surface and becomes brown but does not bum. Remove from oven. When cake is cool, cut from pan and serve.

Faye Taylor remembers her 4-H group went to Pea Ridge to see how sugar maple syrup was collected in 1952.

Fran Helphinstine recalls her 4-H experience at Goddard School. "Kathryn Sebree (a beautiful lady) was the county home demonstration agent. Lovell Gooding and Christine Hurst helped us with 4-H. Our first year we made an apron, a pin cushion, a pot holder and a dish towel. I did not properly knot my thread when hemming the apron, so at the county judging, they pulled on it and showed that it comes undone without a knot—that white ribbon impressed me. The second year I got a blue ribbon for a yellow with tiny dark pink roses print dress and a white slip. The third year Wanda Littleton, Thelma Faye Littleton and I made solid color short house coats and the fourth year matching print pajamas. We won the county 4-H award as a team demonstrating our housecoat and pajamas ensemble that fourth year. We even had the button holes where one sews in the little lining on the house coats. Mine was wine and the pajamas were white with wine print. John and Lillian Staggs' store sold all these cotton percales we used. During the sixth grade, Nora Meade lived behind Mrs. Hattie Staggs at Goddard and we did sewing there. She had a hem measuring stand so we could put pins all around the big circle skirts that were in style then so our hems would turn out even. I made a blue dress with red and green dots with that big wide skirt tail. I left my hem too wide so that it did not iron down smoothly so I got a red ribbon. The next year I made a green Indian Head jumper and the final year a red linen jumper (had to learn to work with those more tedious fabrics).

Fran even had a project to mow the yard. That was tough with that old mower we had. Even the wheels on ours were steel. No rubber, or at least none left."

In 1958, the eighth grade 4-H Club, Danny Mattox, Shirley Gulley, Dorothy Reeves, Ginny Helphinstine, Betty Jones, and others decided to participate in the county 4-H musical competition at Flemingsburg. It was held at the Fleming County High School auditorium, quite different from what the students were used to with performing in the lunchroom at Goddard School. They sang "He's Got the Whole World in His Hands." Danny Mattox and Ginny Helphinstine had solo parts on the verses. The club won the county competition.

The Goddard Methodist Church
Graduations were held here.
Around 1950
Photo courtesy of Patsy Roberts Stacy

8th Grade Graduation
1955
Frances Helphinstine

Chapter 14

Eighth Grade Graduations

To graduate from the eighth grade at that time was a big event. Many students may not go on to high school.

In 1947, George Littleton drove his dad's new tractor to school on the last day of school. He took several students for a ride up the Pea Ridge Road and back.

In 1948 there were four students in the eighth grade: Wendell Staggs, Donnie Wright, James Farrow, and Jimmy Conley. For the 1949 to 1950 graduation, Nora Meade, head teacher, organized a nice graduation ceremony at the Goddard Methodist Church next door. Five students graduated that evening. Gail Claypool was valedictorian. Other members of the class were Violet Mattox, Billy Doyle, Glennis Sloas, and Lewis Yazell. On the week of graduation, Mrs. Meade gave the five some free time. The students went up in the back of the schoolyard, and Glennis Sloas dared the others to bite a fishing worm (earthworm) in half. Since no one would, Glennis showed everyone how brave he was and bit the worm in half.

Dixie Helphinstine and other mothers organized the neighborhood boys to climb the ladders to wash the church windows and move the pews to wax the floors, while the rest of the students used the tall red bottles of furniture polish to shine the pews and provided food and fun in the process.

1953 graduates were Emma Keaton, Sherley Helphenstine, and Libby Wagoner.

1954 graduates were Frank Littleton, Edward Plummer, Wanda Littleton, Bobby Taylor, James Jones, Kenneth Reed, Lillian Mattox, and Louise Yazell.

In 1955, graduation was held on May 19 at the Goddard Methodist Church. The class roll included Patricia Braybant, Ronnie Gooding, Elsie Hardy, Frances Helphinstine, Joy Ann Keaton, Thelma Littleton, and George Mattox. Rev. Amos Harmon, pastor at the time of Goddard Church, gave the invocation and benediction. Patricia Braybant presented the welcome. The school trio sang two songs. Joy Ann Keaton gave the class prophesy while Thelma Littleton presented the salutatorian address, and Frances Helphinstine gave the valedictorian address. Elsie Hardy gave the will. Mrs. Lois Moore was the accompanist on the piano.

Eighth Grade Graduation
1957
Bernice Muse
Photo courtesy of Bernice Muse Plummer

177

1956 Goddard School Graduation

Bobby Sloas, James Rogers, James Littleton, Muse, Donnie Porter, Billy Jones, Carl Bays, and J.C. McKee were members of this class. In 1956, silver class rings were purchased. Carl Bays donated his ring to the Fleming County Covered Bridge Museum, where it may be seen. At the **May 23, 1957,** graduation, the class roll included Anna Florence Jones, Vernice Muse, Wanda Mattox, Diane Swim, Sherley Taylor, Kelly Bruce Reeves, Eugene Littleton, and Frank Back. Gene Littleton gave the welcome, Anna Florence Jones the class prophecy, and Diane Swim the class will. Wanda Mattox and Vemice Muse were co-valedictorians. Mrs. Moore and Mrs. Barnett sang two duets, and the sixth grade trio, composed of Ginny Helphinstine, Shirley Jean Gulley, and Dorothy Reeves, sang a song accompanied by Mrs. Helen Barnett. On the day of graduation, the class went up to Mrs. Lucy McKee and got roses for decorating and corsages. Roses were put in tin cans and covered with crepe paper and made a beautiful arrangement at the front of Goddard Church. Miss Nancy Staggs, the cook, made the corsages.

In the year 1958, there were only three boys in the eighth grade: Ronnie Littleton, Billy Conley, and Ray Curtis. They were too shy to do the program for graduation so Mr. Barnett had some of the seventh graders help with the ceremony. Wills were part of the ceremony. The following is the will of 1958:

"The last will and testament of the Class of 1958, of the Goddard School.

The members of said class, being of sane mind well stored with knowledge, do hereby decree and bestow our legacies in full and unconditionally, to wit as follows:

To our beloved teacher, Mr. Barnett, we bequeath the memory of our class brilliancy, our remarkable recitations, our industrious habits, our proper deportment, our sunny dispositions, and our wit. May this memory ever remain bright and be a comfort in lonely hours of the future.

To the classes who have been associated with us we leave our wonderful example as a modem class. May they imitate but never equal us.

To next year's Eighth Grade Class we leave a large supply of sympathy because its members will not be able to maintain our high standard of wit, wisdom, gush and gab.

To James Lowell we leave Ronnie's gift of chewing gum in school without getting caught.

To Danny we leave Billy's ability of keeping his hair neatly combed.

We leave John Acie, Ray's huge success in entertaining the girls.

To Joe, we leave Ronnie's place sitting with Ruth going to ball games.

To Willie Gene, Billy leaves his best girl friend, Margie.

To Woodie, we leave Ray's job of walking Maxine home from the P.T.A. meetings.

To the 6th and 7th grade boys we leave the 8th grade's ability of being the stars of the baseball team."

1959 Eighth Grade Class
In front of Goddard School

Mr. Myron Barnett, teacher, Dorothy Reeves, Ginny Helphinstine, Shirley Gulley, Betty Jones, Imogene Littleton

Boys: Danny Mattox, Willie Gene Littleton, Oscar Mathison

The theme for the graduation in **1959** was "The Wheel of Destiny." Graduation was held at the Goddard Methodist Church. Much time was spent decorating that afternoon. Students made a large wheel and decorated it with roses from Mrs. Lucy McKee's yard. Each spoke represented an important event for students' lives. Ginny Helphinstine, Danny Mattox, Shirley Gulley, Dorothy Reeves, Betty Jones, Willie Gene Littleton, Imogene Littleton, and Linda James were classmates. Shirley Gulley was the valedictorian. Mrs. Fern had worked with the students on the music, and Danny Mattox had a special part. Students dressed up in the best they could afford. Ginny wore her sister's fancy dress, which she had purchased for class night and then decided to not wear. Fran Helphinstine was graduating from high school. The class members sat in the front of the church facing the audience. The church house was full as many members of the community attended.

The last class to graduate from Goddard School in **1959 to 1960** were Marjorie Conley, Maxine Gorman, James Lowell Hall, Bobby Mattox, John Acie Mattox, Ruth Ann Porter, Woodie Reeves, and Joe Roberts.

Horace Taylor

Parent, active in the PTA and school, auctioneer for Pie, Box, and Ice Cream Suppers

Photo courtesy of Patsy Roberts Taylor Stacy

Chapter 15

The Goddard School PTA (Parent-Teacher Association)

Dixie Helphinstine, as PTA president, supported Goddard teachers Nora Meade, Mr. Barnett, Mr. Roberts, and Noryean Staggs by organizing box and pie suppers, chili suppers, bake sales, or a good night of entertainment with Tom "Pee Wee" T. Hall and his group from Olive Hill. The typical box supper or pie supper began with Horace Taylor auctioning off dozens of well-wrapped boxes (usually decorated shoe boxes) filled with grapes, country ham or pork sandwiches, transparent pies, Dixie Helphinstine's fudge, and other goodies. Many times, the boys would bid on Dixie's daughters' boxes when they learned the boxes had Dixie's fudge. Dixie made her fudge for several decades for Halloween, youth group activities, and school activities, and everyone loved it.

Dixie's Peanut Butter Fudge

5 cups white sugar   1 large can evaporated milk
2 sticks margarine   2 tablespoons white syrup

Mix and bring this to a boil. Boil 8 minutes after it starts to bubble.

Add:

1 pint marshmallow cream	18 oz. peanut butter OR
	1 lb. chocolate chips (for chocolate fudge)

Stir and then beat with mixer until it thickens. Pour into 9 x 12 buttered pan. Cool. Cut into squares.

Most boxes brought less than a dollar, or maybe a few dollars if some guy really wanted to eat with some young lady. One night, a visitor named Jack Frost, who was a friend of Bye Williams, came to the pie supper. He saw a cute young lady that he wanted to eat with and paid fifteen dollars for the pie. This was unheard of in those days. Mr. Frost spent his check from the week of work in the nursery near Cincinnati.

The cake walk was a fun time as all cakes were baked from scratch, and guys enjoyed eating with their girlfriends so that may win the cake walk. Mrs. Hattie Staggs baked her prized fruitcake, and Dixie Helphinstine her large angel food cake. Other ladies donated their specialty as well. A broom was dropped when it was determined who would win the cake. Garnett Bays still has a scar on her nose when the broom was dropped on her. She enjoyed her delicious cake, however. Several contests were held, such as the husband calling contest, where women would see who could call the loudest, the ugly man contest, and the pretty woman contest.

The money may be used to apply wallboard over the cracks to keep out the chilly winter wind or to pay for those wonderful boxes of books to establish a reference bookshelf.

Dixie Helphinstine turned her house and yard into the neighborhood playground, whether for racing around the bases in softball with neighborhood children waiting on the school bus, building a Native American igloo on snowy days, or engaging teenagers in weekend volleyball.

Chapter 16

Goddard School Bus Drivers

In the early days of Goddard School, students either walked or rode horseback with a parent. If the parents picked up children, you would see many children on the horse. Most students walked. Roads were limited, many had not been built yet, and students walked through major mud through pasture fields or dirt roads for many miles. Teachers recorded that some children walked as far as eight miles, while several others walked five miles each way.

As motorized vehicles became available, transportation was provided for grade one through grade eight. On September 16, 1929, John Zornes was paid fifty dollars for transporting students. Also in 1930 and 1931. Another route was driven by Owen Muse on 1930 and 1931 and Wells Campbell in November 1929 and 1930. On July 23, 1932, Owen Muse and Aaron Royse were elected truck drivers for the Goddard School at a salary of forty-five dollars a month each. In 1933, Owen Muse transported the Mt. Vernon children to Goddard, and in 1939, he transported students to Goddard and Plummers Mill. In 1939, Dan Wagner had part of Logan Pike on his route. He exchanged that route with G. W. Edmon to have the Poplar Plains route instead at a salary of ninety dollars per month. On June 24, 1933, the superintendent was instructed to advertise for the Goddard School route.

Owen Muse drove the bus when Bob Helphinstine was a child. When Bob was twelve years old (1928), Owen Muse and Mary, his wife, took the students to Coney Island in Cincinnati. What an exciting experience! The students rode across the Ohio River on the ferry at Maysville to get there. Coney Island had girls in bathing suits, a sight to behold! Bob said this was the first time several of the boys had seen a girl in a bathing suit. Owen took the students to other exciting adventures. He took the children to Plummers Landing to the circus. Bob was in awe with the elephants, tigers, lions, and bears brought by boat to Maysville and then drove on foot to Plummers Landing. Frank Hinton also had a Wild West show with roping contests of bulls, and Bob developed aspirations of becoming a cowboy out west. He would practice on the cattle in his pasture field until the bull got so mean he could not enter the field without being chased!

High school students had to pay a fee to ride the bus. Leo Royse provided a bus from the Hillsboro-Poplar Plains area. A year later, Enos Hinton of Goddard provided a service from Goddard. Bobby Lee Helphinstine walked from where they lived on the historic Morrison-Conrod farm across the hill to Poplar Plains. This was a very long walk of seven miles a day one way. He checked the sheep and animals on the Parkersburg side of the farm. Mr. Hinton charged a dollar a week more than Leo, so Bob continued the long walk. If Bob was a little early, he could catch Leo's bus on his way to Hillsboro and not have such a long walk. Leo was very good to Bob, and he enjoyed talking with him. Leo was the husband of Mrs. Martha Harlan Royse, who later taught at Goddard. On one particular day, it snowed several inches while the students were at school. Bob remembers that the students would get out and push the bus. The winds howled, and the snow was beating down. The students would shovel a few feet and then push the bus. These students really wanted to go to school. Shortly after that, Bob started riding with Enos Hinton to high school and did not have such a long walk.

Another noted bus driver was Mrs. Dewey (Myrtle) Royse Wagoner, working with her husband, Dan Wagoner. Miss Dewey drove on the west side of Goddard during the 1930s and 1940s. Sometimes her husband, Dan, drove. Her students and neighbors loved her because she was so sweet and kind. Buses did not run when the weather was bad. However, sometimes it would snow while the

185

students were at school. Mrs. Dewey stopped at Hord Staggs' store (where the Goddard Craft Mall was) and got men to shovel the snowdrifts so she could take the children home.

She was a beautiful, classy lady who promoted education. She would often say "You are never too old or too young to learn." She was a role model for Ginny and Frances Helphinstine. Since television had not been invented, Miss Dewey was their example of what a fashion model looked like. She wore her beautiful suits, matching hats, and lovely accessories to the Goddard Church and looked like a movie star. When Frances and Ginny were young, they thought college was for rich people, but Miss Dewey quickly told them that she was sending her son, Charles, to dental school. "Honey," she would say, "where there is a will, there is a way. Set your goals now to attend college someday." That they did. Miss Dewey was a loving neighbor and friend. John Lewis Staggs took over driving the bus when Mrs. Dewey quit.

Helen Cooper and her husband, Cleo Cooper, drove the bus east from the school toward Morehead. Helen and Leo ran the upper grocery store and the post office. Helen too was wonderful to children. Frances Helphinstine had started to school, but Ginny had not when she was driving. Ginny wanted to go so badly that Helen would stop on her way down and let Ginny and Fran ride to the county line and back many mornings. Louise Yazell, daughter of Curt and Bessie Yazell, who lived at Goddard, rode with Helen on her route. This was a real treat since she lived in sight of the school. Oh, what a great time! Cleo drove the bus in the afternoons. Cleo was a wonderful man. Cleo died, and Helen decided to not drive the bus anymore. She then married Bud Palmer, and they moved to Sharkey, then to Flemingsburg.

Anna Lee Preston drove for a little while.

In August 1940, Herschel Daniels and Henry Hunt were employed to transport children from Pea Ridge to Goddard and Rock Lick to Sharkey Road.

In August 1940, school superintendent Marvin Evans presented a plan by which all the school bus drivers could be placed on an equal basis. The plan called for payment of ten cents per mile on paved highway, eleven cents per mile on gravel roads, and twelve cents per mile on all other roads. The mileage actually traveled while transporting children being counted for two trips per day for twenty days per month. It also called for the payment of a salary of a dollar and fifty cents per day or thirty dollars per month beside the mileage. The plan was adopted. Dan Wagoner would receive eighty-four dollars per month and Owen Muse would receive sixty-nine dollars and sixty cents.

In July 1941, small bus routes were consolidated. First-class, steel-bodied buses were placed on main routes. Goddard bus drivers were still employed. Owen Muse number 25, Dan Wagoner, number 29, Herschel Daniels, number 30, and Henry Hunt number 31. On July 25, 1942, the school board voted that bus drivers who own their own buses with standard manufactured steel bodies, meeting state requirements, would be allowed fifteen dollars per month bonus above the salary schedule. Several of the county schools had free transportation to the high school in 1942. Goddard was not listed. In 1944, Owen Muse and Louie Flannery exchanged routes, Muse number 26 and Flannery number 25. Muse agreed to furnish a new bus for the route. In 1945, Cleo Cooper was hired as a bus driver and also Glenn McRoberts. In December 1946, Owen Muse asked for Leo Royse' route, using his bus. This was approved. In January 1950, there was a change in bus operators. Erma Sloas took over the route driven by Dan Wagoner and Glenn McRoberts for the route previously driven by Cleo Cooper. In September, Erma Sloas' route was extended on the road between Bluebank and the home of Loright James. In August 1951, Erma Sloas sold his bus route to Elkin Brown. In 1948, Jim Meade was awarded the route from Pea Ridge to Goddard. The road had been graded so a four-wheel drive could get over it. In 1951, Jim Meade's route was given to his wife, Nora, when he obtained a job in Ohio. Nora Meade, principal, drove an army jeep off Pea Ridge. In the winter, when the roads were slick, she prepared students if she needed to hit the ditch instead of going over the hill. Sometimes, she asked the children to pray.

John Mattox took over Nora Meade's route when she moved to Ohio. He drove a small yellow panel truck with benches attached to the floor around the sides inside. Crates were turned upside down in the middle that could be moved. Mr. Mattox made three trips in the morning and in the afternoon. Elizabeth Sloas (Wagner) remembers riding home with her friend Kathy Adkins and then back down the hill to the school to catch her bus home. Elizabeth and her niece, Cathy Sloas, would ride with Erma Sloas, Elizabeth's father, when he drove his route, and get out at John and Lillian Staggs' store. They would purchase the five-cent bag of candy, which would last most of the day. They would then walk across the covered bridge to the school. Cathy dropped her lunch money one day through the cracks in the bridge. She was afraid of the rushing water. Sometimes, Erma would stop and build fires for the teachers. Alvin Gulley replaced John Mattox for the Pea Ridge route.

Some children walked a long way, and in the winter, their feet would almost freeze. Even though bus drivers were available for the main roads, no buses operated on the back roads. For example, on the Justice Road, some students would walk two miles to Bob and Dixie Helphinstine's home and catch the bus there. The teachers would warm water on the potbellied stove and warm the children's feet in the wash pans. Mittens were hung by the stove to dry.

Floods also created a problem. Mary Lucy Conn (Emmons) recalled that before the Fox Valley Lake was built, Sand Lick Creek would flood, and the bus could not get to the school to pick up the children. Sometimes, students would have to wait until dark to go home. One day, there was a flash flood during school hours. The water got up to the porch boards but did not run in the school. Students were not allowed to go outside until the water receded. Anna Florence Jones was afraid to cross the bridge that evening because she was afraid of the high water. Jimmy Jones dreaded the visit of the county nurse, who lined everyone up for a shot after a flood.

Loright James, then John Staggs, later drove the bus. As did Gene Austin McRoberts. Gene Austin transported the students on to high school. The bus drivers gave kids a candy bar on the last day of school. Bennie Richmond drove on school trips.

Chapter 17

Consolidation and the Closing of Goddard School

At the March 13, 1954, school board meeting, a sizeable delegation from Plummers Mill was present to talk about their needs with the school board. Mrs. Frank (Maxine) Hinton was spokesperson for the group. They wanted a new consolidated school building in the eastern part of the county to replace smaller schools that were virtually obsolete. The board agreed but thought a bond issue would fail. The delegates thought it could be done. At the same meeting, the board voted to put shelves in the kitchen at Plummers Mill and authorized Frank Hinton to supervise the installation.

At the April 10, 1954, school board meeting, the superintendent reported he had talked with Mr. Young and Dr. Martin in the state office concerning a consolidation of schools in the eastern part of the county.

On April 9, 1955, the superintendent reported he had met with Mr. Gordie Young, assistant state superintendent, and that they drove around the eastern part of Fleming County and discussed requirements for a new building. Mr. Young suggested they have a special election before the site was purchased.

On June 4, 1955, Mr. William Crawford was hired as the architect for the project.

On July 9, 1955, fifty members of PTA members in the area were present at the public hearing for a new school. Attendees were asked for suggestions.

A called meeting of the school board was held September 30, 1955, to discuss the building program with Mr. Emery Eyler of Charles A. Hinsch Co., Inc, Cincinnati, Ohio, and Mr. William Crawford, architect, of Louisville.

Various phases of the school building program were discussed. Members of the board felt that advice from the two visitors was helpful in their approach to the problem. No time for the vote was set, and no committees were appointed. However, the members of the board felt it might be wise to have a citizens advisory committee to help with plans for the building program.

On October 8, 1955, the school building was discussed. The following names were discussed as a nucleus for a citizens committee to present the school building needs to the people of Fleming County:

Mrs. Frank Hinton, Jr. (Maxine), Kenneth Fern, Kirk Owens, Harold Gaines, Charles Cowan, Noel Walton, Harlan Watson, Mrs. Marvin McDonald, Mrs. Richard Hinton, Jack Dye, and Mrs. Ashton (Maxine Denton). The board requested the committee meet with them on October 22, 1955, at 7:30 p.m.

On October 22, 1955, the following people attended: Mrs. Frank Hinton, Jr. (Maxine), Kenneth Fern, Kirk Owens, Harlan Watson, Jack Dye and Mrs. Ashton (Maxine Denton) and Board members, Charles Barnett, C.D. Blair, Lowell Lee Emmons, Uhlan Evans, and Leo Royse. Jack Dye was selected as temporary chair. Mr. Ernest Rogers and Mrs. Emery Hunt's names were added to the list. Various phase of proposed building plans were discussed. The board approved for the superintendent to provide information cards for the use of the school building committee.

On January 3, 1956, upon recommendation of the citizens committee and motions by Mr. Blair and Mr. Emmons, the board requested in accordance with H.R.S. 160.477 to give the voters of Fleming County the opportunity to vote for the revenue needed.

The board respectfully urged that February 7, 1956, be the date set as recommended by the citizens committee.

On February 8, 1956, the board met and discussed the failure to carry a vote for school buildings at length.

For the next year, the school board devoted their time purchasing the land for a new elementary school in Flemingsburg, buying and remodeling the hatchery across the high school and adding an addition to the high school vocational department. They also discussed reworking the high school gym. No plans were made for a new school in the eastern part of the county.

On February 9, 1957, the elementary building program was discussed at length. It is believed that buildings located in Flemingsburg, one out on Highway 32 and one at Tilton, would be approved by the state office in the order named.

On March 9, 1957, Estill Flora, Johnny Vice, and the superintendent were appointed as a committee to investigate the possible school sites along Highway 32.

On April 13, 1957, the plans for Flemingsburg were studied and approved. The superintendent was to call Architect Crawford and the State Department of Education to study the sites on Highway 32 and at Tilton.

On September 9, 1957, E.L. Cooper was awarded the Flemingsburg Elementary bid at $211,300, and the fiscal court was asked for revenue bonds.

On November 9, 1957, the superintendent presented papers prepared to ask for official approval of the ten-room school building on the Rogers lot in the eastern part of the county. Emmons objected on the thought that both this building and the one at Tilton should be started at the same time and that $140,000 would not be enough for the building on Highway 32. Blair recommended seeking advice from the state office. Treasurer Scott was designated as the contact man between the architect and the county treasurer.

On December 14, 1957, the building status was discussed. No motion was made for approval. Chairman Blair suggested drilling for water first.

On January 11, 1958, the superintendent reported on the progress of Flemingsburg Elementary and asked if anything should be done on building near Rogers Park.

On May 12, 1958, the new building near Rogers Park was discussed. Another bond issue for $140,000 would be approved by the state.

On July 12, 1958, the superintendent was seeking topo maps for the school site near Rogers Park. The board paid Chesney H. Evans $190 for the maps. James Rogers and superintendent Frank Scott assisted Chesney Evans in the survey for Fox Valley School. James cut the weeds and watched for the snakes.

On August 9, 1958, the superintendent reported a general requirement of the state health department whereby they require a test well to produce the given amount of water submitted to the health department. Members of the board felt they would drill the well on the Rogers lot where it would be needed. In the event suitable water is not found, they would provide a cistern.

On September 13, 1958, kitchen plans for the building on 32 were discussed. The board voted to use two pot sinks and three openings in the serving table area.

On October 11, 1958, the board said there was no money for Tilton School at this time. The board paid one-half of the cost to rent an acre at the back of Tilton School to enlarge the playground.

On January 10, 1959, the board requested the fiscal court to advertise for construction bids.

On February 7, 1959, the bids for bulldozing were received, and the Alderman Company got the bid for $180.00. The building received the name Fox Valley School by a motion of Johnny Vise and seconded by Julian Atkinson.

On February 9, 1959, Flemingsburg Lumber Company had the lowest construction bid to the fiscal court.

On January 8, 1960, a second water sample from the Fox Valley well had been delivered to the health department in Louisville. The report said the water was usable but should have a softener to reduce soap usage. The board said no softener would be installed. Fox Valley School would be constructed.

The Last Students to Attend Goddard School in the Year 1959 to 1960

Students who attended Goddard School in the last year of operation are listed below.

Helen Barnett, Teacher of Grades One and Two:

Grade 1

Larry Lee Adkins
Evelyn Conley
Randall Curtis
Martha Emmons
Joyce Ann Fannin
Sterling Dean Hall
Nancy Mattox
Peter Acres McKee
Margaret Plummer
Larry Reeves
Brenda Roberts
Cathy Sloas
Justine Sloas
Jesse Leon Taylor
Peggy Taylor

Grade 2

Ruth Ann Adkins
Johnny B. Bowles
Jackie Wayne Conley
George Ray Cooper
Ruby Farrow
Sandra Greer
Jesse Price Gulley
Marcella Sue Gulley
Joyce Ann McKee

Sudie Ellen McKee
Marietta Parker
Julie Plummer
Jeri Lynn Sloas
James Ray Williams

Mrs. Lois Moore, Teacher, Grades 3, 4, 5

Grade 3

Kenny Adkins
Wesley Adkins
Shirley Butcher
Clarence Conley, Jr.
Lawrence W. Cooper
Charles Fannin
Melvin Lee Farrow
Linda Greer
Diana Gulley
Jimmy Gulley
John Robert Jones
Marious Mathison
Stanley Paul Mattox
J. Stewart McKee
Elaine Plummer
Tommy Reeves
Larry Roberts
Danny Williams
Shirley Williams

4th Grade

Judy Ann Bowles
Donna Butcher
Brenda Sue Conley
Denzil Conley

Kathy Sue Conley
Garnett Mae Gilliam
Larry Lee Mattox
Donna Jean McKee
Pauletta McKee
Roy Plummer
Ernie Reeves
Wilma Roberts

Grade 5

Kathy Adkins
Harold Ray Bays
Thomas Gorman
Billy Jett
Johnny Jett
Mabel Jeannie Jones
Larry Littleton
Shirley Ann Taylor Moore
Timothy Parker
Samuel Reeves
Kenneth Roberts
Elizabeth Sloas
Louella Sloas

Rev. Myron Barnett, Teacher, Grades 6, 7, 8

Grade 6

Wilburn Adkins
Sammy Braybant
Linda Butcher
Velma Cushard
Donna Farrow
Janice Gilliam
Ida Green

Eugene Hall
Billy Hamm
Mary Mathison
Sylvia Elaine Mattox
Sandra Parker
Larry Porter

Grade 7

Donald Bays
Joyce Conley
Edna Carolyn Mattox
Emerson Plummer
Patsy Roberts
Larry Swim

Grade 8

Margie Conley
Maxine Gorman
James Hall
John Acie Mattox
Ruth Ann Porter
Woodie Reeves
Joe Roberts

To prepare for the consolidation of schools, several activities were held on the last year at Goddard School. On September 4 and 5, 1959, an in-service was conducted for teachers. On October 2, school was dismissed for a school fair. Helen Barnett, former teacher, described it as more like a field day. Goddard students competed with students from other schools in sack races, hot jumping rope activities, and other events. It was a good way for students to be introduced to other students affected by the consolidation.

Mr. Barnett organized an inspiring eighth grade graduation for 1959 to 1960 at the Goddard Methodist Church.

Mr. Barnett gave the invocation, and student Bobby Mattox welcomed family and friends. A trio of Patsy Roberts, Mary Mathison, and Shirley Moore sang "Now Is the Hour." The flutophone band, with members Pauletta McKee, Shirley Moore, Elizabeth Sloas, Judy Bowles, Kathy Adkins, and Donna McKee, played some selections. Students sang "Oh, How Lovely is the Evening" and "Every Time I Feel the Spirit." Woodie Reeves gave the history of the class. Maxine Gorman, Joe Roberts, and John Acie Mattox offered a prophecy. James Lowell Hall presented the will. Ruth Porter gave the valedictory address, and Margie Conley the salutatory address. The class song was "May the Good Lord Bless and Keep You."

The Goddard School was closed after the school year ended in 1960, and the current students were transferred to the consolidated school at Fox Valley School. Ms. Nancy Staggs became the head cook at Fox Valley, and all three teachers, Mr. Myron Barnett, Mrs. Helen Barnett, and Lois Moore, were hired for teachers at Fox Valley.

Drew and Mary Lucy Emmons with Sherley Taylor
On the front porch of their new home,
built from wood of the Goddard School
1963

Chapter 18

Sale of Goddard School

At the June 14, 1960, school board meeting, it was announced that Goddard School, along with Muses Mill, Plummers Mill, Locust, McGregor's, Colfax, Johnson, Wallingford, and Flemingsburg Colored Schools, were all for sale.

The Goddard Cemetery Association added the Goddard School land after an auction on February 14, 1962, and made it part of the cemetery, where many local residents are now buried. The school building was purchased by Drewey G. and Mary Lucy Emmons of Goddard, Kentucky. Mr. Emmons sold the ball and Mitchell bell, Maysville, Kentucky, to Stewart McKee, also of Goddard. The bell had been located over the upper grades room, and a rope hung from the ceiling.

The bell remained in the McKee family until the bell was sold at Kevin Boling auctions. When Mr. McKee died, his wife, Frances, kept the bell. At her death, the bell was passed to the daughter, Lena McKee Reed. She sold the bell at Kevin Boling auctions on April 7, 2012, and it was purchased by Craig Stanfield, Tollesboro, Kentucky, for his museum.

After Drewey Emmons bought the school, he disassembled it and used the same 24 x 48-foot floor plan from the new section of the school building. The new part was built in 1935. He designed and built the four-bedroom Emmons family home, where they raised their seven children. A few changes were made, such as a basement under the home as well as porches, but the main part of the home came from the school. The weather boarding was poplar and would not hold paint, so Mary Lucy and Drew put aluminum siding on their home. They lived about one-half mile from the school and in sight of where the original Goddard School was. What a fitting location!

The remaining part, or the original section of the building, was sold to John and Tootsie (Mattox) Lowe who lived on Pea Ridge. They used that portion as the basic part of the home, where they raised their three daughters. That house was sold in recent years and is now home to Rickey and Tammi Riley and their three children. (1)

1. Mary Lucy Conn Emmons and Martha Emmons, "Whatever Happened to the Goddard School Building?" *Times Democrat,* September 18, 1991.

Chapter 19

Students Who Attended Goddard School by Decade

Goddard School Census Report 1911

Father's Name	Child's Name
William Bailey	Ella M. Bailey
	Frank E. Bailey
	Amy E. Bailey
	Jessie P. Bailey
Lizzie Binnon	Nellie M. Binnon
M.H. Campbell	Wells Campbell
	William Campbell
M. Carpenter	Morgan Carpenter
Reck Carpenter	Mabel Carpenter
	Paul Hifler Carpenter
	Pauline Carpenter
Dan Clark	Frank E. Clark
	William Clark

M. N. Davis	James Davis
	Adam S. Davis
Frank Dillion	Couttren Dillion
	C—R Dillion
	Viola Dillion
Sarah Evans	Guardian, Elmer O. Sanders
John W. Faris	Basil Faris
	Charles Faris
	Hettie Faris
	Guardian: Ruby Yazell
P. Freeman	Opal May Freeman
Harry Gaines	Nellie Gaines
	Estill Gaines
	Alma Gaines
Jas. Gooding	Stella B. Gooding
	Ethel Gooding
Thomas Hammond	Melvin Hammond
V. G. Hedges	Ollie Hedges
	Stanley Hedges
Peter Hitch	Clyde Hitch
J.W. Hunter	Hinton Hunter
	Ralph Hunter
	Elmae Hill Hunter
James Hurst	Lydie Hurst
	Bessie Hurst
	Nellie T. Hurst
T. T. Hurst	Verna Hurst
	Arthur Hurst
	Clarence Hurst
Thomas Ingram	Guardian: Maude Ingram

William Ingram

Vina I. Ingram
Kinsay Ingram
Sidney Ingram
Charles E. Ingram

O. James

Pearl James
Boswell James
Gituda James
Lehai James
Lucy James

W. E. James

Oscil James

W. J. James

Clarence James
Laman James
Agatha James

Ira Jones

Vera Jones
Oscil Jones

Frank T. Littleton, with children, Chester Littleton, Harley
Littleton, Lula Littleton, and Emma Maude Littleton

Students at Goddard School, 1911

J.H. Kufe

Luna A. Kufe
Matilda S. Kufe
Nora H. Kufe
Arthur R. Kufe

Mrs. L.P. Kuhus

Lena P. Kuhus
Ray Lee Kuhus

William Lawrence

May Lawrence

Frank T. Littleton

Harley Littleton
Chester Littleton
Lula Littleton
Emma M. Littleton

Chris Mattox

Ella Mattox
Lee Mattox

S. M. McClure

David McClure

E. S. Morrison

Nellie Morrison
Martha Morrison
Hyter Morrison

William H. Muse

Anna M. Muse
Alma Muse

Ben Plummer

Carl Plummer
Lester Plummer

Jno. Plummer

Jewell Plummer

E. Pugh

Guardian, Lena Gulley

John W. Pugh

Susan J. Pugh
Elihn J. Pugh
William Pugh

Leslie Reed

Mary Reed

T. J. Reed

Mame Reed

Claude M. Reeves	Clifford Reeves
	Nellie Reeves
	Kelly B. Reeves
G. W. Royse	Suddith Royse
V. C. Royse	Lena Royse
Ed Sorrell	Matilda Sorrell
C. W. Staggs	Mertie Staggs
James T. Staggs	Walter A. Staggs
	Axch Staggs
Louis Staggs	Joseph Staggs
	Irene Staggs
	Mayme Staggs
	Alma Staggs
Raleigh Staggs	Claude Staggs
	Harvey Staggs
	Darcos Staggs
	Howard Staggs
	Everett Staggs
William Stanter	Bruce P. Stanter
	Claude M. Stanter
John Thompson	Luther Thompson
William Welch	Lewis P. Morton
John H. Yazell	Luther Yazell
	Leshe Yazell
Nelson Yazell	Lina Yazell
	Clarence Yazell
	Earnest Yazell
	Veva Yazell
	Harold Yazell
	Roy Yazell

Census Report of School Children
Goddard School 1916

Page 226 of Record Book

Parent's Name	Child's Name	Birth Date
Celia Bailey	Ella Bailey	August 17, 1899
	Frank Bailey	April 18, 1920
	Amy Bailey	September 26, 1903
	Jessie Bailey	October 30, 1904
	Robert Bailey	
	Cecil Bailey	March 22, 1908
Lizzie Byron	Nellie Byron	August 25, 1900
R. M. Carpenter	Margie Carpenter	December 29, 1900
Reck Carpenter	Mabel Carpenter	June 5, 1895
	Paul Hifler Carpenter	October 12, 1900
	Pauline Carpenter	October 12, 1900
W. M. Claypool	Roy Claypool	December 14, 1900
Anderson Deatley	Anderson Deatley	February 1898
	Mary Deatley	January 1881
	Charles Deatley	February 1892
	Mandy Deatley	June 1893
	Emmitt Deatley	February 1894
John William Faris	Frank Faris	August 22, 1899
	Blanche Faris	December 15, 1901
	Mary Faris	September 4, 1906
	Vadie Faris	1909
Edward Fenton	Johnny Fenton	
James R. Gooding	Stella Gooding	April 29, 1899
	Ethel Gooding	December 22, 1900
	Pearl Gooding	October 8, 1906
	Golda Gooding	

William F. Gooding	Lillie Gooding	
	Austin Gooding	
	Ada Garr Gooding	February 6, 1909
Walter L. Hamm	Eckles Hamm	
	Helen Hamm	September 30, 1906
Alvin W. Hamilton	Everett Hamilton	January 24, 1897
	Maude Hamilton	January 15, 1899
	Flora Hamilton	October 9, 1905
	Bert Hamilton	March 3, 1908
George Hedges	Stella Hedges	July 5, 1909
Letha Huff	John Huff	April 11, 1908
D. F. Hurst	Clarence Hurst	June 10, 1897
James Hurst	Nellie Hurst	August 28, 1897
Oscar S. James	Lela James	October 24, 1896
W. S. James	Agatha James	August 15, 1899
Ira O. Jones	Lucy Jones	
	Verma Jones	January 4, 1902
	Theatrice Jones	March 30, 1905
	Emma Jones	January 28, 1905
Matilda Jordan	Willie D. Jordan	
Jessie W. Kirk	Arthur Kirk	July 20, 1897
	Sudie Kirk	June 19, 1899
	Harlan Kirk	February 3, 1901
	Jennie Kirk	
	Irene Kirk	July 7, 1906
Frank T. Littleton	Emma Littleton	October 16, 1900
M.F. Marshall	John Marshall	
	Dell Marshall	

Jennie M. Maddox (Mrs. Chris)	Ella Maddox	May 3, 1902
	Johnnie Maddox	July 27, 1904
	Alma Maddox	September 23, 1906
	Violet Maddox	August 1, 1908
Sam McClure	David McClure	February 6, 1896
	Carl McClure	
J. W. McIntire	Nellie McIntire	August 1, 1899
Mary S. McKee	Lola McKee	September 17, 1900
	Lester McKee	May 7, 1905
	Lucille McKee	May 7, 1908
Roscoe McKee	May McKee	
William B. McRoberts	James McRoberts	October 14, 1905
	Russell McRoberts	August 4, 1907
	Ethel McRoberts	March 18, 1908
E. S. Morrison	Frankie Morrison	June 7, 1889
Charles Newdigate	Jessie Newdigate	July 7, 1897
	Chester Newdigate	April 29, 1900
	Stella Newdigate	October 31, 1903
	Cecil Newdigate	May 2, 1906
	Josephine Newdigate	October 11, 1908
Benjamin Plummer	Carl Plummer	January 15, 1901
	Lester Plummer	November 3, 1903
	Hobert Plummer	April 2, 1907
	Ransom Plummer	
George Plummer	Jewell Plummer	June 17, 1902
	Russell Garr Plummer	March 26, 1907
	Lula Plummer	May 10, 1908
John F. Plummer	Ernest Plummer	September 16, 1904
J. M Plummer	Roy Plummer	

Claude M. Reeves	Clifford Reeves	May 25, 1897
	Nella Reeves	September 29, 1901
	Kelly Reeves	January 5, 1903
	Verna Reeves	March 14, 1906
	Glenn D. Reeves	May 3, 1908
Ulysses C. Royse	Lena Royse	November 13, 1896
	Russell Royse	September 9, 1898
	Lula Royse	May 3, 1902
	Frances Royse	September 16, 1906
Elizabeth (Lizzie) Staggs	Mamie Staggs	June 16, 1898
	Alma Staggs	December 20, 1901
Russell L. Staggs	Marie Staggs	
	Thomas Wood Staggs	December 1, 1907
Rawleigh Staggs	Harry Staggs	August 15, 1895
	Dorcas Staggs	October 21, 1899
	Howard Staggs	August 29, 1901
	Everett Staggs	June 27, 1905
Everett Thompson	Minnie Thompson	
Nelson Yazell	Clarence Yazell	March 6, 1897
	Ernest Yazell	November 13, 1898
	Vera Yazell	May 24, 1900
	Harold Yazell	June 28, 1902
	Roy Yazell	March 1, 1904
	Myrtle Yazell	October 8, 1905
	Mabel Yazell	June 21, 1907
	Melvin Yazell	December 19, 1908
	Dudley Yazell	

Goddard School Census Report 1918

Parent's Name	Child's Name	Birth Date
Conway Applegate	Will Nelson Applegate	January 20, 1905
	Mabel Applegate	November 19, 1908
Celia Bailey	Ella Bailey	August 17, 1899
	Frank Bailey	April 18, 1920
	Amy Bailey	September 26, 1903
	Jessie Bailey	October 30, 1904
	Herbert Bailey	March 27, 1906
	Cecil Bailey	March 22, 1908
	Nannie Bailey	October 15, 1910
Mrs. Virginia Boyse	Edna Boyse	August 2, 1905
Lizzie Bryson	Nellie Bryson	August 25, 1900
Reck Carpenter	Paul Hifler Carpenter	October 12, 1900
	Pauline Carpenter	October 12, 1900
Robert M. Carpenter	Margie F. Carpenter	December 29, 1902
William M. Claypool	Roy Claypool	March 15, 1902
John William Faris	Blanche Faris	December 15, 1901
	Mary Faris	September 4, 1906
	Ruth Faris	October 22, 1908
	Basil Faris	December 15, 1894
	Frank Faris	August 22, 1899
	Garr Faris	December 8, 1901
Elmer Gaines	Lorena Gaines	March 15, 1906
Robert H. Gaines	Estill Gaines	October 16, 1898
	Alma Gaines	August 16, 1900
	Irvin Gaines	January 29, 1907

James R. Gooding	Stella Gooding	April 29, 1899
	Ethel Gooding	December 22, 1900
	Pearl Gooding	October 8, 1906
	Golda Gooding	April 21, 1910
Sally Gooding	Foster Lee Gooding	August 20, 1911
	Melvin Hammonds	October 4, 1902
	Marie Hammonds	November 27, 1908
William F. Gooding	Zenith Gooding	November 27, 1905
	Minish Gooding	October 8, 1907
	Ada Garr Gooding	February 6, 1909
Alvin W. Hamilton	Flora Hamilton	October 9, 1905
	Myrtle Hamilton	September 14, 1895
	Everett Hamilton	January 24, 1897
	Maude Hamilton	January 15, 1899
	Bert Hamilton	March 3, 1908
Clyde Hamm	Mildred Hamm	September 17, 1908
	Alvin Hamm	December 28, 1910
Walter Hamm	Mary B. Hamm	July 7, 1900
	Helen Hamm	September 30, 1906
Nellie Hammond	Melvin Hammond	October 4, 1902
	Marie Hammond	November 23, 1907
Floyd Hedges	Stella Hedges	July 5, 1909
Hettie Hedges	Luther Hedges	September 2, 1911
Ed Hinton	John F. Hinton	March 9, 1909
	Lola M. Hinton	September 3, 1898
	Nellie B. Hinton	September 7, 1902
	Owen L. Hinton	June 11, 1906
John Howard	Lucy Howard	November 20, 1904
Letha Huff	John Huff	April 11, 1908
	Hershell Huff	July 5, 1911

James H. Humphries	Zetta Humphries	May 10, 1907
James Hurst	Nellie Hurst	August 28, 1897
	Bessie Hurst	June 11, 1895
Thomas F. Hurst	Clarence Hurst	June 10, 1897
William Ingram	Verna Ingram	August 15, 1900
	Pearl Ingram	November 6, 1901
	Sydney Ingram	June 4, 1903
	Charles Ellis Ingram	October 16, 1904
Jarred James	Agatha James	August 15, 1899
Oscar S. James	Lela James	October 24, 1896
	Gertha James	December 27, 1894
	Lucy James	March 29, 1899
Osel James	Rosa James	September 28, 1900
Roscoe James	Mabel James	June 15, 1895
Ira O. Jones	Verna Jones	January 4, 1902
	Theatrice Jones	March 30, 1905
	Helen Jones	September 30, 1907
	Emma Jones	January 28, 1905
Dodson Jordan	George W. Jordan	August 8, 1905
Jessie W. Kirk	Arthur Kirk	July 20, 1897
	Sudie Kirk	June 19, 1899
	Harlan Kirk	February 3, 1901
	Leona Kirk	March 30, 1895
	James F. Kirk	June 6, 1903
	Irene Kirk	July 7, 1906
	Noah Kirk	February 3, 1901
Mrs. L. F. Kirk	Lena Kirk	February 6, 1902
	Roy Lee Kirk	February 4, 1904
	Nellie M. Kirk	October 4, 1905

Frank T. Littleton	Emma Littleton	October 16, 1900
	Harley Littleton	September 28, 1896
Jennie M. Maddox	Ella Maddox	May 3, 1902
(Mrs. Chris)	Johnnie Maddox	July 27, 1904
	Alma Maddox	September 23, 1906
	Violet Maddox	August 1, 1908
Guardians	Alma Muse	November 22, 1903
	Owen Muse	December 1, 1905
Sam McClure	David McClure	February 6, 1896
J. W. McIntire	Nellie McIntire	August 1, 1899
Mary S. McKee	Lola McKee	September 17, 1900
	Lester McKee	May 7, 1905
	Lucille McKee	May 7, 1908
	Verna McKee	April 8, 1905
Sam McKee	Earl McKee	September 2, 1902
	Stewart McKee	June 17, 1907
William B. McRoberts	James McRoberts	October 14, 1905
	Russell McRoberts	August 4, 1907
	Ethel Humphries	March 18, 1908
	Melvin Humphries	November 23, 1914
E. S. Morrison	Mabel Nell Morrison	July 20, 1911
Elisha Morrison	Hyter Morrison	February 23, 1900
Charles Newdigate	Jessie Newdigate	July 7, 1897
	Chester Newdigate	April 29, 1900
	Stella Newdigate	October 31, 1903
	Cecil Newdigate	May 2, 1906
	Josephine Newdigate	October 11, 1908
Benjamin Plummer	Carl Plummer	January 15, 1901
	Lester Plummer	November 3, 1903
	Hobert Plummer	April 2, 1907
	Joseph Plummer	January 30, 1908

George Plummer	Jewell Plummer	June 17, 1902
	Russell Garr Plummer	March 26, 1907
	Lula Mabel Plummer	May 10, 1908
John F. and Carrie Plummer	Ernest Plummer	September 16, 1904
	William Plummer	June 14, 1895
J. M. Plummer	Helen Plummer	October 12, 1911
Claude M. Reeves	Clifford Reeves	May 25, 1897
	Nella Reeves	September 29, 1901
	Kelly Reeves	January 5, 1903
	Verna Reeves	March 14, 1906
	Glenn D. Reeves	May 3, 1908
	Clyde Reeves	February 5, 1911
C. C. Rigdon	Charles E. Rigdon	September 18, 1896
	Oliver Rigdon	July 10, 1898
	Archie D. Rigdon	January 11, 1901
	Nora B. Rigdon	September 13, 1904
	Frank Rigdon	March 13, 1908
Ulysses C. Royse	Lena Royse	November 13, 1896
	Russell Royse	September 9, 1898
	Ethel Frances Royse	September 16, 1906
	Lula B. Royse	May 3, 1902
Virginia Royse	Edna Royse	August 2, 1904
Mack Sparks	Estell Sparks	January 19, 1898
	George Sparks	February 9, 1900
Elizabeth (Lizzie) Staggs	Mamie Staggs	June 16, 1898
	Alma Staggs	December 20, 1901
	Irene Staggs	May 33, 1895
Hattie Staggs	Frances Staggs	April 12, 1910
James T. Staggs	Archie B. Staggs	July 26, 1895

Students at Goddard School

Nell Hammonds Plummer with children:
Melvin, Marie, Bernice, and Julia

Nell Hammond Plummer, dated November 30, 1918
Marie. Melvin, Bernice, Julia, and Nell Hammonds, 1915

Ollie Staggs	Ruby Staggs	November 15, 1909
	Hiriam Staggs	April 6, 1911
Rawleigh Staggs	Harry Staggs	August 15, 1895
	Dorcas Staggs	October 21, 1899
	Howard Staggs	August 29, 1901
	Everett Staggs	June 27, 1905
Russell Staggs	Thomas Wood Staggs	December 1, 1907
John Thompson	Osborne Thompson	March 9, 1907
Omer Vice	Nellie Vice	January 19, 1896
J. H. Yazell	Leslie Yazell	February 4, 1895
Nelson Yazell	Clarence Yazell	March 6, 1897
	Ernest Yazell	November 13, 1898
	Vera Yazell	May 24, 1900
	Harold Yazell	June 28, 1902
	Roy Yazell	March 1, 1904
	Myrtle Yazell	October 8, 1905
	Mabel Yazell	June 21, 1907
	Lena Yazell	September 24, 1894
	Melvin Yazell	December 19, 1908

Census Report of School Children Goddard School, Subdistrict Number 35 1920s

Parent	Child	Birth Date
Mont Arnold	Roy Arnold	1917
Jesse Bell	Geneva Bell	April 20, 1917
Walter Bramel	Pauline Bramel	November 26, 1919
	Bruce Bramel	January 3, 1922

Charles Campbell	Alice Garr Campbell	September 20 1922
	Clifton Campbell	April 7, 1912
	Clyde Campbell	April 17, 1914
Reck Carpenter	Gale Carpenter	February 4, 1920
Mrs. Ola Carpenter	Early Samuel Carpenter	March 8, 1915
(Markwell)	Eula B. Carpenter	June 28
Nelle Claypool	Oral G. Vise	August 17, 1913
Charles Claypoole	Charles Claypoole	July 4, 1915
	Claude Claypoole	1910
	Wilson Claypoole	1913
	Lois Vise	June 29, 1916
	Oral G. Vise	August 17, 1913
Preston Claypoole	Helen Claypoole	Feb. 9, 1917
	Marvin Claypoole	Feb. 2, 1919
T. C. Claypool	Stanley Claypool	
	Edna Claypool	
	Horace Claypool	
	Gladys Claypool	
	Florence Claypool	
	Arthur Crump	1913
Steve W. Dickens	John Dickens	September 7, 1911
	Eugene Dickens	December 2, 1913
	Mary Opal Dickens	October 6, 1922
Mrs. Rose	Ducie Downey	December 28, 1923
Downey (Baird)	Eula Downey	August 15, 1918
	Geneva Downey	1921
	Ollie Downey	May 6, 1922
W. Purn Doyle	Hazel Doyle	July 19, 1918
	Ruby Doyle	May 19, 1922

Thomas Emmons	Chester Emmons	March 23, 1921
	Edna Emmons	November 16, 1923
	Esther Ruth Emmons	August 4, 1927
	Estill Emmons	October 20, 1918
	Ola Mae Emmons	March 18, 1920
	Dorothy Fannin	December 14, 1914
Charles E. Faris	Lloyd Faris	February 17, 1917
	Wilson Faris	February 12, 1913
John W. Faris	Mary Faris	September 4, 1906
	Ruth Faris	October 22, 1908
	Johnnie Garr Faris	December 8, 1911
	Lutie Faris	June 4, 1914
Charles Flannery, guardian	Pauline Phillips	May 6, 1921
Dave Flora	Ruby Smitson	February 18, 1920
James Gardner	Arthur Gardner	March 12, 1922
	George Gardner	
Melvin Gardner	Hazel Gardner	September 26, 1919
	Helen Gardner	October 5, 1921
	Mary Gardner	December 1, 1917
Mrs. John Glenn	John Logan	October 10, 1916
Mrs. Della Gooding	Evalina Gooding	Feb. 21, 1922
	Ollie Gooding	March 31, 1919
	Jesse Gooding	April 12, 1921
	Victor Gooding	January 16, 1917
Mrs. Martha (Lazarus) Gooding	Brice Gooding	Dec. 21,
	Eugene Gooding	October 8, 1916
	Pearl Gooding	October 8, 1906
	Ola Gooding	April 21, 1910
William H. Gooding	Zenith Gooding	
	Minish Gooding	October 8, 1907
	Ada Garr Gooding	Feb. 6, 1909
	Nellie Gooding	June 15, 1914

Omar Gulley	Ernest Gulley	July 6, 1921
James Hamm	Helen Jones	
Alvin Hamilton	Bert Hamilton	March 3, 1908
	Flora Hamilton	October 9, 1905
	Beulah Hamilton	
	Earl Hamilton	
David Hamilton	Ellis Hamilton	March 25, 1916
	Fred Hamilton	October 22, 1912
Clyde Hamm	Mildred Hamm	13
	Alvin Hamm	11
	Josephine Hamm	9
	Eelria Hamm	6
James Hedger	Beulah Hedger	April 9, 1915
Hettie Hedges	Owen Muse	
	Thomas Hedges	Nov. 19, 1914
Howard Helphenstine	Virgil Helphenstine	Dec. 4, 1918
Oscar Helphinstine	Robert Lee Helphinstine	January 16, 1918
Ed F. Hinton	John Hinton	
	Thelma Hinton	November 13, 1913
Frank L. Hinton	Ruby Hinton	
	Frank Owen Hinton	
Mrs. D. Humphries	Maude B. Humphries	1913
James H. Humphries	Zetta Humphries	15
	Anna Humphries	13
	Luther Humphries	10
	Alsa Humphries	8
John R. Hurst	Herbert Garr Hurst	Jan. 17, 1914
	Wilbur Hurst	June 23, 1910

Mrs. Callie Hunter	Anna Ruby Hunter	January 31, 1915
	Esther Jesse	May 22, 1923
Osel James	Anna Bell James	July 30, 1921
	Raymond James	Dec. 3, 1916
W. R James	Larry James	
	Hildreth Johnson	
Samuel Jesse	Esther Jesse	May 22, 1923
J. Harvey Johnson	Laura B. Johnson	Sept. 12, 1909
Ben Jones	Curtis Jones	April 1913
	Henry Jones	April 26, 1914
	Hazel Ruth Jones	November 4, 1922
Calvert Jones	Edward Jones	March 20, 1924
	Hazel Jones	November 4, 1928
	James Jones	November 5, 1919
	Raymond Jones	March 20, 1924
	Ruth Jones	December 6, 1921
Ira L. Jones	Theatrice Jones	March 30, 1905
	Emma Jones	January 28, 1904
Dodson Jordan	Woodrow Jordan	
Jessie Kirk	Irene Kirk	July 7, 1906
Roy Landreth	Ruth Landreth	July 1, 1921
Ida Littleton	John Huff	April 11, 1908
Thomas Littleton	Emory Littleton	January 1, 1919
Alfred Manning	Darwin Sexton	1916
	Jewell Sexton	March 12, 1913
	Woodrow Manning	November 14, 1913
Elza Manning	Berry Manning	
	Plummer Manning	
	Randall Manning	

Robert Manning	Robert Manning	
	Woodrow Manning	Nov. 12, 1913
	Pearl Manning	July 19, 1919
J. W. McIntyre	Marie Hammond	
	Julia J. McIntyre	May 5
	Ransom Mattox	1910
Chris L. Maddox	John Maddox	July 27, 1904
	Alma Maddox	September 23, 1906
	Calvin Maddox	September 28, 1918
	Violet Maddox	August 1, 1908
	George Maddox	July 26, 1914
	Julia Maddox	June 27, 1916
Elijah Mattox	Glen Mattox	
	Mitchell Mattox	
Lee W. Mattox	Robert Price Mattox	April 23, 1916
	Lawrence McFadden	
Sam E. McKee	Stewart McKee	June 17, 1907
	Chastine McKee	Feb. 15, 1917
Robert McLain	Ruby McLain	1918
Mrs. Seth Mitchell	Seth Junior Mitchell	January 3, 1922
E. S. Morrison	Mabel Morrison	July 20, 1911
Nellie Muse	Robert Muse	March 5, 1919
	Ruth Muse	Nov. 2, 1915
Charles Newdigate	Cecil Newdigate	May 2, 1906
	Charles H. Newdigate	June 12, 1915
	Estill Newdigate	March 6, 1919
	Josephine Newdigate	October 11, 1908
	Sudie Newdigate	1912
	Hemler Neudigate	1915
Isom Wagoner	Phillip Oney	September 29, 1919
Adrien Owens	David Owens	November 12, 1922

221

Acie Perkins	Clarence Perkins	
	Edna Perkins	
	Stella Perkins	
Harrison Planck	Bessie Planck	1912
George Plummer	Russell Plummer	March 26, 1907
	Lulie Plummer	May 10, 1908
Ben Plummer	Delbert Plummer	July 15, 1916
	Robert Plummer	
	Joseph Plummer	January 30, 1908
	Helen Plummer	Oct 12, 1911
	Forest (Harlan) Plummer	Sept. 19, 1915
Ed Porter	Jesse Porter	1920
	Nellie P. Porter	1918
William Prince	Hazel Prince	April 15, 1921
	Mildred Prince	January 10, 1916
	Nevada Prince	May 2, 1923
	Wanda Prince	
	William Prince	September 5, 1915
C. M. and	Verna Reeves	March 14, 1906
Nettie Reeves	Glenn Darnald Reeves	May 3, 1908
	Clyde Reeves	
	Leona Blanche Reeves	August 23, 1913
	Woodrow Reeves	July 28, 1916
Richard Reeves	Roy Reeves	October 21, 1921
	William Reeves	August 17, 1920
William T. Riickert	Ernest Riickert	Sept. 29, 1911
	Roy Riicket	February 25, 1915
	Taft Riickert	1909
	LeRoy Riickert	

Amereicus Roberts	Addie Roberts	May 25, 1920
	Anne Mae Roberts	August 1923
	Austin Roberts	February 9, 1916
	James Roberts	April 13, 1926
	Leo Roberts	June 3, 1918
	Russell Roberts	June 1, 1923
	Kenneth Rourk	August 9, 1920
Aaron Royse	Stanley Royse	January 27, 1923
Arnold Royse	Arnold Royse, Jr.	1922
Morrison Saunders	Mary Frances Saunders	January 6, 1920
James Sexton	Darwin Sexton	
	James W. Sexton	1918
	Jewell Sexton	1913
	Willard Sexton	May 18, 1921
Bert L. Sparks	Harold P. Sparks	Nov. 29, 1915
J. Thomas Stacy	Flora Stacy	May 11, 1914
Thomas Stacy	Dorothy Stacy	March 13, 1919
	Leona Stacy	May 18, 1921
	Opal Stacy	March 12, 1916
	Raymond Stacy	February 25, 1921
	William Stacy	September 12, 1918
Mrs. Elizabeth Staggs	Ruth Plummer	May 16, 1917
Walter Staggs	Delbert Staggs	May 28, 1914
Hord Staggs	Frances Staggs	April 12, 1910
	John Lewis Staggs	Aug. 21, 1913
Russell N. Staggs	Thomas Wood Staggs	December 1, 1907
Shelman Swim	Emerson Swim	August 6, 1913
Elmer Thacker	Elsie Thacker	

Isa Thacker	Ottie Thacker	
	Lara Thacker	
Garey Todd	Maurice Todd	
	Steele Todd	November 5, 1922
	Wilma Todd	
	(moved to IL)	
Foster Vise	Elizabeth Vise	March 12, 1915
	Eula Vise	July 10, 1910
Rolla Vise	Charles Vise	August 5, 1917
	Opal Ruth Vise	April 26, 1919
	Wendel Vise	September 14, 1920
Isom Wagoner	Dan Wagoner	June 15, 1907
	Sam Wagoner	1909
	Dixie Wagoner	August 8, 1913
	Morrison Wagoner	
	Mona Wagoner	June 22, 1917
Robert Watson	Freda Watson	
	Willard Watson	January 4, 1919
Richard Whisman	Alvin Whisman	October 16, 1914
	Brooks Whisman	May 1, 1916
	Lettie Whisman	
	Roy Whisman	April 1, 1920
	Roya Whisman	April 28, 1919
Ephraim Wilson	Helen Wilson	Nov. 11, 1920
	Luellen Wilson	October 20, 1922
	Mildred Wilson	Jan. 12, 1912
	Robert Wilson	May 7, 1915
	Roy Wilson	January 16, 1918
Curtis Yazell	Hilda Yazell	September 29, 1921
Luther Yazell	Ruth Garr Yazell	November 26, 1921
Nell Vise Yazell	Oral Glenn Vise	August 12, 1913
	Lois Vise	June 29, 1917

Sarah Zornes	Nannie Zornes	
	Noah Zornes	
	Ethel Zornes	June 20, 1915
	Ithel Zornes	
	Muriel Zornes	February 1, 1917
	Willard Zornes	

*Please note, all dates are not given.

Students in the 1930's

Father	Student	Birth Date
Charles Armstrong	Douglas Armstrong	November 11, 1921
	Geneva Armstrong	July 30, 1928
William Arrasmith	Beulah Arrasmith	September 7, 1921
	Noble Arrasmith	June 27, 1919
Henry Back	Edward Back	June 8, 1926
	Gatewood Back	June 8, 1925
	Harold Back	January 30, 1929
	Johnnie Back	August 1, 1923
Edward Beard	Pauline Downey	May 6, 1921
Rose Baird (Beard?)	Eulah Downey	August 15, 1918
Mamie Boone	Marion Boone	July 1, 1929
Charles Bramel	Georgia Bramel	September 7, 1932
Walter Brammel	Stella Johnson	March 17, 1918
	Pauline Brammel	November 26, 1919
William Branham	Mary Alice Branham	March 1, 1920
Charlie Campbell	Alice Garr Campbell	September 20, 1922
Gilbert Caudill	Charles Caudill	August 13, 1931
	Edward Caudill	February 13, 1929
	Lovell Caudill	

C.P. Caywood	Virgin Herbert	June 15, 1924
Preston Claypoole	Charles Claypoole	July 10, 1931
	Mabel Garr Claypoole	January 19, 1928
	Maxine Claypoole	September 20, 1924
Mrs. (Thomas) Ruby Claypoole	Mary Jo Claypoole	January 29, 1929
Luther Conn	Mary Lucy Conn	October 23, 1928
William Cosbery	George Cosbery	March 14, 1921
Thomas Cunliff	Audra Cunliff	November 9, 1918
	Charles Cunliff	November 9, 1927
	Elsie Cunliff	June 21, 1922
John Curtis	Gilbert Curtis	September 21, 1929
Howard Daulton	Woodrow Smith	May 26, 1922
Emmit Deatley	Anderson Deatley	March 6, 1924
	Edna Deatley	
	Leonia Deatley	September 19, 1931
Faris Doolin	Deloris Doolin	
	Elizabeth Doolin	
	Golda Doolin	March 28, 1928
Frank Doulan	Elizabeth Doulan	July 17, 1920
William McRoberts	Gene Eden	
	Justin Eden	January 5, 1921
	Richard Eden	
Arthur Ellington	Anna Lewis Ellington	July 21, 1923
	Anna Louise Ellington	November 28, 1924
	Arthur Ellington	June 11, 1921
Edward Ellington	Eugene Ellington	August 31, 1928

Tom Emmons	Drew Emmons	July 26, 1927
	Gertrude Emmons	September 1, 1925
	Leonard Emmons	March 10, 1924
	Lloyd Emmons	August 7, 1930
	Thelma Emmons	September 1, 1925
Autie Fannin	Randolph Fannin	July 15, 1919
	Vernell Fannin	December 8, 1921
Robert Fizer	William Fizer	February 19, 1922
Dave Flora	Ruby Lee Smitson	February 18, 1920
James Flora	Dorothy Flora	August 28, 1929
	Georgia Flora	June 9, 1931
Sam Foudrey	John Glenn	June 17, 1920
Will Gallagher	Cecil Gallagher	January 13, 1926
Mrs. Mary Gallihier	Ceciel Wells	January 5, 1925
Chester Gardner	Archie Gardner	March 22, 1930
	Bruce Gardner	September 13, 1925
	Hazel J. Gardner	November 29, 1927
James Gardner	Estill Gardner	March 12, 1922
	Jessie Gardner	April 6, 1920
	Mabel Gardner	April 17, 1929
	Omar Gardner	March 18, 1918
	Ova Thomas Gardner	April 1, 1924
	Stella Mae Gardner	February 26, 1926
Melvin Gardner	Hazel Gardner	September 26, 1919
	Nellie Gardner	March 20, 1926
	Ruth Gardner	March 20, 1926
	Sadie Gardner	March 18, 1928
Lanch Gaskins	Mary Gaskins	May 1922
	Skinner Gaskins	May 1922
Edward Gillum	Edith Gillum	September 25, 1932
	Waneda Gillum	April 21, 1930

Mrs. Della Gooding (Gray)	Evalina Gooding Oral Gooding	February 21, 1923 August 18, 1925
Jesse Gray	Dorothy Gray John Glenn	November 11, 1925 June 17, 1920
Clem Gulley	Lillian Wilson	January 20, 1923
George Gulley	Kenneth Cooper	
Omer Gulley	Beulah Gulley Henry Thomas Gulley Omer Gulley, Jr. Ruby Gulley Tommy Gulley Wilbur Garr Gulley	August 16, 1925 January 7, 1930 December 25, 1927 May 28, 1924 January 7, 1930 January 27, 1933
Guardian	Junior Whaley	July 6, 1924
Butler Hall	Chancie Hall J. E. Hall Kenneth Hall Rubye Bell Hall Wendell Hall	November 30, 1929 1933 September 28, 1927 May 20, 1925 March 9, 1931
Mrs. Dillie Hall	Arnold Harris Donald Harris	July 10, 1918
Melvin (M.K.) Hall	Edgar Hall Marnie Hall Marvin Hall Marcus Hall William (Billie) Hall	March 27, 1918 August 24, 1920 May 18, 1923 December 6, 1925 May 18, 1923
Woodson Hall	Allie Florence Hall	September 28, 1929
Mrs. Ben C. Hamilton	Beulah Saunders Willard Saunders	July 20, 1927 February 3, 1924
Guy Hamilton	Christine Hamilton Volene Hamilton	May 27, 1931 April 5, 1933
Isaac Hamilton	Charles Hamilton Wilbur Hamilton	July 31, 1919 September 27, 1916

Lander Hamilton	Clarence Hamilton	August 21, 1928
	Ina Pearl Hamilton	January 3, 1925
	Lillian Hamilton	March 5, 1930
Mrs. C.P. Harmon	C.P. Harmon, Jr.	February 18, 1921
	George Robert Harmon	September 20, 1923
Nelle Harmon	Winona Harmon	June 12, 1929
Ruth Harmon	Charles F. Harmon	July 21, 1930
Bannie Helphenstine	Cressa Helphenstine	August 22, 1927
	Everett Helphenstine	March 27, 1923
	Geneva Helphenstine	January 17, 1925
Howard Helphenstine	Edward Helphenstine	August 21, 1933
Nunley Helphenstine	Archie Helphenstine	June 6, 1933
	Georgia Helphenstine	May 9, 1927
	Emma Louise Helphenstine	May 14, 1929
	Freddie Henderson	
William Hickerson	Archie Clyde Hickerson	April 5, 1919
Day Howell	Irene Howell	January 29, 1931
	Samuel Howell	January 17, 1928
Lee Huff	Mary Ann Smith	April 23, 1927
Orville B. Hughes	Buford Hughes	December 23, 1918
	Clayton Hughes	October 18, 1924
	Hazel Hughes	February 4, 1922
	Hubert Hughes	
Rubye Hunter, guardian	Jessie Gooding	April 12, 1921
Chester Garr Hurst	Anna Barbara Hurst	September 6, 1931
Elmo Hyatt	Robert McCane	July 26, 1932

Henry Ingram	Flora Sue Ingram	July 4, 1933
	James Ingram	
	Ruth Ann Ingram	July 8, 1930
	Tom Ingram	February 3, 1932
	William Ingram	
Osel James	Anna Bell James	July 30, 1921
	Jesse James	March 1, 1925
	Pauline James	February 26, 192
	Thelma James	July 19, 1928
W. Roscoe James	Morris Lee James	January 12, 1919
Iva Jesse	Floyd Jesse	February 22, 1927
	Howard Jesse	
	Raymond Jesse	January 24, 1926
Sidney Johnson	Preston Johnson	August 10, 1924
	Garnett Landreth	March 17, 1925
Calvert Jones	Dorothy Jones	July 19, 1928
	Edward Jones	March 20, 1924
	James Owen Jones	December 28, 1919
	Raymond Jones	July 10, 1925
Henry Jones	Anna Jones	August 26, 1920
	George Jones	August 23, 1924
James Kirk	James Kirk, Jr.	April 9, 1927
	Norma Jean Kirk	August 9, 1933
	Ramona Kirk	May 16, 1931
Mrs. Roy Landreth	Wayne Landreth	
(Emerritia)	Duane Landreth	June 11, 1925
William Little	Hershell Little	February 29, 1927
	Lester Little	January 23, 1925
	William Little	August 4, 1931
Emmit Littleton	Bernice Littleton	October 16, 1926
	Josephine Littleton	September 13, 1932

Sanford Long	Aldon Long	May 26, 1919
	Douglas Long	January 3, 1922
William Luman	Mary Elizabeth Luman	December 23, 1929
Elza Manning	Frazee Manning	January 14, 1923
	Kathleen Manning	April 27, 1925
	Raymond Manning	May 19, 1932
Robert Manning	Andrew Manning	November 25, 1924
	Blandenia Manning	November 28, 1927
	Deloris Manning	February 7, 1923
	Joe Manning	November 18, 1921
Dewey Marshall	Chester Marshall	March 19, 1928
	Dewey Marshall, Jr.	April, 26, 1930
	Estill Marshall	September 25, 1921
	Hazel Marshall	November 5, 1923
	Robert Marshall	December 22, 1931
	Thelma Marshall	July 30, 1925
John Mattox	Geniere Mattox	September 17, 1926
	Hilda Mattox	November 22, 1924
	Lily Mattox	August 15, 1928
Marvin McCall	Kenneth McCall	April 1, 1922
Mrs. Lovell McCane	Robert McCane	July 26, 1932
Charles McCormick	John McCormick	March 3, 192
	Samuel McCormick	July 15, 1921
Henry McKee	Anna Mary McKee	April 28, 1918
	Theodosia McKee	September 18, 1919
John McKee	Dorothy McKee	February 28, 1922
	Edgar McKee	
	Elwood McKee	July 3, 1925
	Harold McKee	November 15, 1928
	Orville McKee	March 24, 1927
	Roy McKee	February 7, 1931

Joseph McKee	Ernestine McKee	September 1, 1932
	Iolene McKee	January 18, 1921
	Joseph McKee, Jr.	January 7, 1923
	Mary Jeanette McKee	October 6, 1926
William McRoberts	Flora McRoberts	November 11, 1918
	Murdock McRoberts	April 23, 1917
	Sam McRoberts	April 23, 1917
	Willie McRoberts	December 16, 1920
	Willis McRoberts	December 16, 1920
Norman Meyers	Gertrude Meyers	July 17, 1923
	James Meyers	October 14, 1925
Henry Miller	Cecil Miller	September 6, 1922
	Delmar Miller	October 15, 1925
	Roger Miller	May 26, 1917
Ethel Moore Story	Fay Moore	January 1, 1925
	Eugene Moore	June 20, 1923
Willie Moore	Goldia Moore	November 12, 1922
	Lucy Lucille Moore	June 22, 1933
	Marnie Moore	August 31, 1930
	McKinley Moore	December 31, 1928
	Sterling Moore	September 22, 1924
	William, Jr.	July 7, 1926
Peter Morkiewiay	Mittie Price	October 3, 1925
Clyde Muse	Archie Muse	
	Artincie Muse	
	Edward Muse	June 2, 1925
	Orville Muse	September 1, 1929
	Sudie Mae Muse	December 25, 1922
	Thomas Lee Muse	July 20, 1927
Owen Muse	Kenneth Muse	October 29, 1928
Frank Oney	Frank Oney, Jr.	February 2, 1927

Adrian Owens	Anna Laura Owens	May 18, 1921
	Davis Owens	November 12, 1922
	Howard Owens	March 24, 1925
	Jack Owens	September 20, 1926
	Lula Margaret Owens	December 25, 1924
Carl Plummer	Crystal Plummer	January 2, 1932
Archie Potter	Dorothy Potter	May 14, 1929
	Genevive Potter	March 2, 1930
	Geraldine Potter	March 18, 1933
Lem Preston	Arthur Preston	July 2, 1933
	Dorothy Preston	August 9, 1930
	Jesse Preston	August 20, 1931
Eddie Frank Purcell	Rosa Purcell	June 18, 1928
Josh Purcell	Clyde Purcell	June 16, 1929
Clifford Reeves	Earl Reeves	September 9, 1930
	Helen Reeves	April 9, 1927
	Wilson Reeves	September 6, 1926
Kelley Reeves	Charles Reeves	1933
Robert Reeves	Emerson Reeves	November 23, 1927
	Evan Reeves	January 23, 1930
	Marvin Reeves	January 1927
William Reeves	Roy Reeves	October 21, 1921
	Thomas Reeves	January 13, 1924
	William Reeves, Jr.	August 17, 1920
Lee Rigdon	Edith Rigdon	
	Imogene Rigdon	May 13, 1921
	Walker Rigdon	October 22, 1924
	Nettie Thacker	January 8, 1929
William Riickert	Ruby Riickert	December 18, 1922
Americus Roberts	Addie M. Roberts	May 25, 1920
	James Roberts	April 13, 1926
	Rhoda Roberts	April 3, 1928

Lonnie Roberts	Elnora Roberts	April 10, 1928
	Eugene Roberts	January 6, 1933
	Robert M. Roberts	
Marcus Roberts	James Roberts	April 13, 1926
	Russell Roberts	June 2, 1923
Aaron Royse	Jackueline (Jackie) Royse	December 26, 1925
Arnold Royse	William Estill Royse	March 25, 1926
	Mildred Royse	February 5, 1918
Jesse Saunders	Alvin Parker	January 5, 1922
James Sexton	Clara Frances Sexton	May 20, 1927
	Holly Sexton	March 29, 1929
Bruce Snapp	Agnes Snapp	June 17, 1919
	Emma Snapp	September 11, 1923
	Reynolds Snapp	October 8, 1921
W.T. Sparks	Bernice Sparks	April 26, 1926
	Christine Sparks	September 10, 1929
	Clyde Sparks	April 14, 1924
Saint Staggs	Elizabeth Staggs	
	Nannie Staggs	April 5, 1928
	Wilson Staggs	August 30, 1923
Thomas Stanfield	Amos Stanfield	
	Daniel Stanfield	October 20, 1925
	Melvin Stanfield	August 26, 1929
	Lois Stephens	September 24, 1925
Ollie Stanfield	Frances Stanfield	September 8, 1930
Thomas Stanfield	Melvin Stanfield	August 26, 1929
Obeda Strode	Dorothy Strode	September 29, 1926
Raymond Strode	Catherine Turner	July 31, 1933
Donald Taylor	Herbert Virgin	

Horace Taylor	Edward Taylor	April 21, 1925
	Faustain Taylor	April 3, 1927
	Lawrence Taylor	September 29, 1932
	Luella Taylor	February 28, 1931
	Mildred Taylor	March 15, 1929
Jesse Thacker	Kenneth Thacker	November 15, 1921
	Thomas Thacker	May 12, 1925
	Raymond Thacker	
J.C. Tolliver, Sr.	J.C. Tolliver, Jr.	October 21, 1925
Rudolph Underwood	Paul Underwood	January 12, 1932
	Velma Underwood	May 15, 1928
Faris Vise	Margetta Vise	September 29, 1927
Dan Wagoner	Charles Wagoner	November 10, 1929
Isom Wagoner	Frank Oney	February 1, 1928
	Geneva Oney	December 28, 1922
Mart Wagoner	Bernice Wagoner	April 16, 1926
	Beulah Wagoner	April 19, 1926
	Will Isom Wagoner	September 18, 1924
Samuel Wagoner	Betty Jo Wagoner	February 9, 1932
	Nina Lewis Wagoner	August 24, 1930
Torn Whisman	Tom Whisman	1930
	Faye White	February 21, 1923
Emery Whitton	Bruce Whitton	October 10, 1927
	Charles T. Whitton	August 21, 1923
	Earnest C. Whitton	February 23, 1921
	Irvin Lee Whitton	August 6, 1930
	Mary Whitton	April 2, 1922
Mrs. Nell Williams	Gale Williams	April 10, 1926
	James Williams	April 29, 1924
Earl Wilson	Austin Earl Wilson	October 1, 1932

Earlalie G. Woosley	E.G. Woosley, Jr.	March 2, 1930
	Helen Louise Woosley	October 1, 1931
	Thelma Woosley	
	Woodford Woosley	April 12, 1922
	Charles York	
	Norma York	

Goddard School
Grades 1 to 8
1945

Mary Catherine Jones, Betty Claypoole, Terry Hurst, Jimmy Jones, Libby Wagoner, Gail Claypoole, George Littleton, Josephine Littleton, Anna Lee Preston, Donna Kay Duncan, Lewis Yazell, Faye Taylor, Charles Emmons, Eleanor Hall.

Patsy Gooding, Mildred Taylor, Dora B. Curtis, Lee Taylor, Marie Taylor, Ronnie Gooding, Beulah McKee, Evelyn Reeves, Ray Moore, Eddie Guy, Doris Thomas, Donna Ingram, Nancy Farrow, Lena Doyle, Anna Lewis, Orville Reed, Tommy Hall.

Geraldine Staggs, Beatrice Doyle, Jackie Back, Raymond Tally, Jimmy Conley, Betty Moore, Jewell Moore, Beulah Insko, James Conn, Ellis Plummer, Ronald Ingram, Norman Lewis, Archie Helphenstine, Louise Helphenstine.

Jack Williams, Tootsie Thomas, Doris Back, Georgia Bramel, Theodore Doyle, Wayne Reeves, Tommy Bowman, Jim Lewis, and Sadie Lewis. Teachers were Mrs. Jesse Hall, Mrs. Brooks Duncan, and Mrs. Maude Caywood.

Photo courtesy of Patsy Roberts Stacy and Gail Hinton.

1940s Students Some names smeared from flood damage. The 1947 books are missing.

Parent	Student	Birth Date
Ora Anderson	Edward Anderson	June 23, 1939
	Inaree Anderson	January 31, 1932
	Kenneth Anderson	July 15, 1934
	Samuel Anderson	January 15, 1937
	Thomas Anderson	November 12, 1941
Mrs. Charles Arnold	Clifton Walker	June 23, 1940
Henry Back	Doris Back	December 12, 1936
	Frank Owen Back	August 16, 1941
	James Isaac back	September 6, 1931
James H. Barker	Gary Gene Barker	November 26, 1943
	Phyllis C. Barker	December 24, 1939
	Roger (James) Barker	December 6, 1941
Johnnie Bays	Carl Dean Bays	February 28, 1941
D. Beyerleine	James Beyerleine	March 19, 1936
	Mary Lou Beyerlein	
	Susanne Beyerlein	
Elmer Botkin	Everette Douglas Botkin	March 1, 1935
Almyrtie Bowman	Thomas Bowman	October 6, 1938
Joseph Brabant	Joseph Isaac Brabant	
	Patricia Brabant	July 3, 1941
Logan Brown	Billy Ray Brown	March 29, 1935
Earle Burke	Charlotte Ann Burke	November 23, 1940
Claude Oral Carter	Evangeline Carter	June 22, 1938
	Treda Carter	April 14, 1940
Gilbert C. Caudill, Sr.	Gilbert Caudill, Jr.	June 5, 1934

238

Sam Caudill	Kenneth Caudill	
Thomas M. Charles	Clyde Charles	June 17, 1935
	Leslie William Charles	
Preston Claypoole	Betty Claypoole	May 26, 1939
	Gail Claypoole	October 28, 1936
	Wilson Claypoole	August 12, 1935
W. L. Conley	James Edward Conley	August 18, 1933
Luther Conn	James Conn	March 9, 1932
	Ruby Lee Conn	May 25, 1934
Odella Cooper	Yancey Cooper	June 7, 1936
John Curtis	Dora B. Curtis	April 18, 1934
	Gilbert Curtis	September 21, 1929
Tony (Floyd) Curtis	Avery Houston Curtis	July 26, 1938
	Ray D. Curtis	January 8, 1942
Hershel Daniel	Evelyn Daniel	January 8, 1935
	Marvin Daniel	May 22, 1933
John Day	Betty Day	October 11, 1936
	Gladys Day	
Faris Doolin	John Doolin	May 28, 1932
Jess Doyle	Billie Woosley Doyle	August 6, 1936
Luther Doyle	Beatrice Doyle	August 28, 1937
	Lena Doyle	
	Theodore Doyle	July 28, 1935
Conrad Duncan	Donna Kay Duncan	December 15, 1936
Andrew Jackson Dyer	Bonnie Jean Dyer	December 23, 1932
	Donald Dyer	January 1, 1935
Addison Emmons	Bellomany C.	October 18, 1934
	Emmons (B.C.)	

Thomas Emmons	Charles Emmons	March 30, 1934
Boyd Fannin	Boyd Fannin, Jr.	February 17, 1933
	Letha Fannin	July 17, 1938
	Wilma Fannin	January 26, 1934
Nancy Farrow	Nancy Farrow	February 20, 1939
Marvin Farrow	James T. Farrow	January 27, 1942
Thomas Farrow	James Farrow	March 4, 1934
	Robert Farrow	March 4, 1936
	Rubye Farrow	
	William Farrow	February 7, 1940
Louie Flannery	Retta Flannery	January 4, 1937
Mollie Flora	Dorothy Flora	August 28, 1929
	Albert Gallagher	
	Ruby May Flora	
Earl Thomas Flora	Bobby (Robert Allen) Flora	February 12, 1942
	Calvin Flora	November 1, 1943
Guardian	Charles Willis Harmon	December 15, 1938
William Galliher	Jackie Galliher	January 28, 1938
James Gardner	Beulah Gardner	December 22, 1937
	Ervin Eugene Gardner	February 10, 1935
	Mabel Gardner	February 23, 1930
Henry Gillum	Billie Gillum	January 18, 1935
(Mrs. Stella)	Glenna Gillum	October 3, 1932
	Madeline Gillum	December 20, 1933
Melvin Gooding	Paul Gooding	December 14, 1943
Minish Gooding	Patsy Gooding	April 6, 1936
	Ronnie Wayne Gooding	November 28, 1939
Willie Grayson	Arlene Grayson	November 2, 1931
	Florida Grayson	July 2, 1934
Florence Greene	Christine Greene	June 11, 1929

Omar Gulley, Sr.	Henry Thomas Gulley	August 18, 1926
	Wilbur Gulley	January 27, 1933
Boone Guy	Edward Guy	December 16, 1937
Creed Hall	Ralph Hall	July 27, 1934
Milford L. Hall	Elinor Hall	September 10, 1933
Robert Ham	James W. Ham	February 25, 1934
	Tommy (Milford) Hall	March 4, 1935
Oakley Hamilton, guardian	Preston Hamilton	
	Avery Hamilton	July 14, 1942
	Bonnie Keeton	December 26, 1937
	Johnny Keaton	October 13, 1942
	Cora E. Hamilton	June 26, 1938
Edmond Hamm	Florence Gleason	January 20, 1935
Oscar Hamm	Eugene Hamm	June 9, 1933
Thomas Hedges	Anna Opal Hedges	September 9, 1936
	Tom Hedges	August 21, 1940
Johnnie Helphenstine	Charlotte Fay Helphenstine	October 1, 1940
	Donald Helphenstine	August 23, 1935
Nunley Helphenstine	Shirley Helphenstine	November 11, 1937
Robert Helphinstine	Frances Louise Helphinstine	October 19, 1941
Lyde Holbrook	Gerald Holbrook	July 23, 1938
	Ramona Holbrook	May 1, 1937
Day Howell	Irene Howell	
	Samuel Howell	January 17, 1927
Curtis Hunt	Billie Joe Hunt	May 9, 1936
	John C. Hunt	August 21, 1940
	Samuel Thomas Hunt	June 19, 1938
	Wanda Marie Hunt	June 21, 1943

Garr Hurst	Terry Hurst	November 13, 1938
Howard Ingram	Donna Ingram	August 11, 1938
	Patty Ingram	October 30, 1940
	Ronald Ingram	December 29, 1936
William M. Insko	Beulah Insko	April 22, 1933
	Ida Mae Insko	January 29, 1931
	Olive Ann Insko	June 1, 1934
Edward Jesse	Betty Jesse	March 21, 1933
	Peggy Joy Jesse	September 30, 1937
	JoAnn Jennings (9 days)	
Rosie C. Johnson, guardian	Dorotha Carrozza	July 24, 1937
	Raymond Carrozza	October 1, 1939
Sidney Johnson	Charles Edward Johnson	December 23, 1934
James Jones	Clarence Jones	August 26, 1935
	James Jones	October 22, 1938
Melvin Jones	Donald Jones	May 5, 1930
	Eugene Jones	May 5, 1930
	Irvin Samuel Jones	February 26, 1935
William Clyde Jones	Anna Florence Jones	June 2, 1942
	Billy Jones	October 4, 1940
	Clarence Jones	August 26, 1935
	James P. Jones	October 22, 1938
	Mary Catherine Jones	October 11, 1937
	William Hixson Jones	October 4, 1940
Goldie Jordan	Nona Mae Johnson	
Woodrow Jordan	Omar Jordan	May 14, 1943
Alvin Keaton	Roger Keaton	November 17, 1942
Earl Keaton	Bonnie Keaton	December 26, 1936
	Johnnie Keaton	October 13, 1940
	Mary Jane Keaton	June 24, 1939

James Kirk	Edna Olive Kirk	December 14, 1941
	James Kirk	April 9, 1927
	Nellie Kirk	January 23, 1936
	Norma Jean Kirk	August 28, 1933
	William Wayne Kirk	October 26, 1939
Frank Lewis	Jimmy Lewis	May 1, 1936
	Norman Lewis	July 12, 1937
	Sadie Lewis	June 26, 1939
Glen Lewis	Anna M. Lewis	January 20, 1934
	Clell Lewis	December 22, 1937
	Marie Lewis	February 2, 1932
	Mary Magdeline Lewis	May 5, 1941
	Anna Myrl Lewis	January 20, 1933
John Lewis	Callie Lewis	February 9, 1932
	Charles Allen Lewis	April 5, 1934
	Dewey Lewis	August 11, 1928
	Fidella Lewis	February 9, 1930
	Herman Lewis	December 10, 1936
Troy Lewis	Frances Lewis	January 16, 1935
	John Lewis	April 6, 1931
	Dottie Lewis	March 7, 1933
Walter Little	Louise Little	April 14, 1937
Elwood Littleton	Clifford Eugene Littleton	November 12, 1943
	James Thomas Littleton	April 8, 1942
	Thelma Faye Littleton	July 25, 1950
Emmit Littleton	George Littleton	May 18, 1937
	Josephine Littleton	September 13, 1931
	Ronald Littleton	October 7, 1943
	Wanda Littleton	October 14, 1940
Harley Littleton	Alberta Littleton	August 26, 1937
	Frank Owen Littleton	October 19, 1940
Millard Luman	Cecil Edford Luman	July 30, 1931
	Clifton Lee Luman	August 29, 1933

243

Dewey Marshall	Robert Marshall	December 22, 1931
George Mattox	George Mattox	July 8, 1940
	Lillian Mattox	April 9, 1938
	Violet (Tootsie) Mattox	December 29, 1935
	Wanda Mattox	1943
Claude McCormick	Raymond W. McCormick	January 18, 1934
	Roberta McCormick	July 26, 1936
Clyde McCormick	Mary McCormick	December 23, 1938
Charles McKee	Johnny Charles (J.C.) McKee	December 29, 1940
Mrs. Herbert McKee	Mildred McKee	January 12, 1942
Russell McKee	Beulah McKee	January 22, 1934
William McKee	Carol Jean McKee	December 20, 1935
James Meade	James Lacey Meade	July 1, 1942
	Lillian Meade	March 17, 1935
Garvie Million	Josephine Million	October 26, 1937
	Ruth Million	April 27, 1936
James H. Mineer	Emma Finley	May 29, 1933
	Mary Finley	October 24, 1935
William Moore	Betty Jean Moore	June 20, 1934
	(Anna) Jewell Moore	March 21, 1939
	Lucy Moore	June 22, 1933
	Martha Carolyn Moore	November 12, 1940
	Ray Moore	October 13, 1938
	Wesley Moore	November 7, 1936
Archie Muse	Jennie Porter	May 3, 1935
Clyde Muse	Allie Frances Muse	July 17, 1933
	Harold Muse	October 7, 1931
	Orville Muse	September 1, 1929
	Thomas Muse	July 20, 1927

Owen Muse	Joyce Dean Muse	September 29, 1934
Carl Plummer	Dorothy Plummer	February 20, 1937
	Freda Plummer	October 12, 1934
Delbert Plummer	Clyde R. Plummer	October 23, 1942
	Robert Plummer	February 13, 1940
	Virginia Plummer	February 17, 1938
Forest Plummer	Edna Plummer	February 19, 1938
	Edward Plummer	January 14, 1940
	Ellis Plummer	October 7, 1934
	Elsie Plummer	July 17, 1936
	Erlene Plummer	September 30, 1942
Hobert Plummer	Helen Plummer	February 21, 1939
	Ida Plummer	April 9, 1938
	Maude Plummer	March 15, 1937
Jesse Porter	Donnie Glenn Porter	February 11, 1942
	Jerry Lee Porter	August 7, 1943
W.E. Presley	James Presley	February 11, 1940
	Jeanetta Presley	August 12, 1943
	Woodrow Presley	
Craig Preston	Billy Gene Preston	April 9, 1942
	Ruby Anita Preston	April 9, 1933
L. N. Preston	Arthur Preston	July 2, 1933
	Donald Preston	June 6, 1935
	Dorothy Preston	August 9, 1930
	Jesse Thomas Preston	August 20, 1931
Thomas Reed and	Bessie Reed	January 30, 1943
Mrs. Thomas	Kenneth Reed	September 25, 1938
	Orville Reed	May 23, 1937
	Walter Reed	May 9, 1941
Clifford Reeves	Dorothy Reeves	November 20, 1943
	Evelyn Reeves	April 15, 1935
Clyde Estil Reeves	Mary Estil Reeves	July 29, 1935

Eck Reeves	Wayne Reeves	August 1937
Kelly Reeves	Kelly Bruce Reeves	July 17, 1942
Ruby Reeves	Charles Reeves	May 6, 1933
	Gobel Reeves	August 22, 1936
Hesikah Richmond	Bennie Richmond	March 14, 1935
	Bobby Richmond	May 5, 1942
	Charles Richmond	June 6, 1933
	Donald Richmond	July 19, 1941
	Mabel Richmond	June 23, 1937
Charles Rigdon	Omar Rigdon	December 25, 1927
Frank Rigdon	Billie Rigdon	May 12, 1933
Ollie Rigdon	Earl Rigdon	January 25, 1933
	Leonard Rigdon	April 11, 1930
Lonnie Roberts	Eugene Roberts	January 6, 1933
	Robert Roberts	August 30, 1930
Ernest Rogers	James Lloyd Rogers	March 21, 1941
Claude Roseberry	Christine Roseberry	April 12, 1927
Richard Ross	Betty Jewell Ross	February 8, 1934
	Frances Ross	July 19, 1930
Isaac Routt	Emma Keaton	November 2, 1939
	Joy Ann Keaton	December 24, 1941
James Sexton	Arthur Sexton	October 4, 1933
Erma Sloss	Bobby Sloas	November 18, 1942
	Donnie Sloas	February 19, 1938
	Glennis Sloas	February 25, 1936
Winfred Sluss	Beatrice Sluss	September 11, 1939

Henry Smedley	Christine Smedley	October 8, 1942
	Leslie Smedley	January 16, 1939
	Virginia Faye Smedley	October 4, 1937
	Wendell Smedley	January 13, 1941
Ovie Smith	Carolyn Sue Smith	May 7, 1943
	Nancy JoAnn Smith	July 5, 1941
Delbert Staggs	Geraldine Staggs	July 3, 1939
	Norman Staggs	April 5, 1937
	Wendell Staggs	March 1, 1934
Hattie Staggs	Elizabeth Wagoner	December 22, 1938
Samuel Stephens	Lonnie Ronald Stephens	November 13, 1938
George Swim	Diane Sue Swim	August 26, 1943
James Tackett	Eula Tackett	October 25, 1935
	Lowell Tackett	
Lucien Talley	Raymond Talley	May 23, 1937
Donald Taylor	Clarence Lee Taylor	March 8, 1935
	Ethel Marie Taylor	June 5, 1933
Horace Taylor	Bobby Taylor	October 24, 1939
	Charlene Faye Taylor	February 5, 1937
	Horace Franklin Taylor	October 24, 1939
	Sherley Taylor	December 19, 1942
Allen Thacker	Adrian Thacker	May 27, 1934
	Helen Thacker	February 13, 1932
	Ida Thacker	August 13, 1930
	Iva Thacker	August 13, 1930
Grant Thomas	Leanna Thomas	September 19, 1932
	William Thomas	March 2, 1930
Roy Thomas	Doris Jean Thomas	December 25, 1938
	Louranie Thomas	July 27, 1934

Rudolph Underwood	Mary Jewell Underwood	September 8, 1935
	Paul Underwood	January 12, 1932
George Viars	Faris Viars	January 11, 1937
	George Viars, Jr.	October 11, 1939
	Raymond Viars	January 30, 1942
Robert C. Vice	Ida E. Vice	October 21, 1943
	Robert C. Vice, Jr.	October 21, 1943

**Joyce Meade, Kathy Meade, and Betty Claypool
in front of Goddard School around 1952.
Photo courtesy of Joyce Snider.**

Grades 7 to 8
1950 to 1951

Row 1:
1. Teacher, Nora Meade
2. Donnie Sloas
3. Polly Gilliam

Row 2:
1. George Littleton
2. Faye Taylor
3. Norman Staggs
4. Betty Claypoole
5. Benny Richmond

Row 3:
1. Anna Lee Preston
2. Marilyn James
3. Alberta Littleton
4. Patsy Gooding
5. Ruby Lee Conn

Photo courtesy of Patsy Roberts and Taylor Stacy.

John Henry Wallace	Cecil Ray Wallace	October 24, 1938
	Clayton Wallace	March 9, 1940
	Frances Wallace	November 17, 1941
	Johnny Wallace	March 22, 1943
Mrs. Williams-Tony Curtis	Hale Williams	February 6, 1930
	Jackie Williams	February 11, 1935
	Ronald Wayne Williams	April 14, 1932
	Wilder Williams	
Earl Wilson	Bonnie Wilson	March 6, 1934
	Charles Thomas Wilson	September 17, 1935
	Donnie Wilson	March 6, 1934
	Earl Wilson, Jr.	October 5, 1932
	Julia Pearl Wilson	August 11, 1937
Ray Wright	Chelsa Wright	January 3, 1941
	Donnie Wright	July 1, 1934
	Jeanette Wright	September 11, 1938
Curtis Yazell	Lewis Yazell	June 5, 1934
	Louise Yazell	January 21, 1939
Clarence Zornes	Angillee Zornes	October 6, 1940

Please note: If students attended in two decades, they may be only listed in one.

Since birth certificates were not required for enrollment, the birth date may be different.

1950s Students

Lester Adkins	Kathy Adkins	May 28, 1949
	Kenny Adkins	July 9, 1950
	Larry Lee Adkins	
	Ruth Ann Adkins	October 1, 1952
Richard Adkins	Elta Adkins	November 2, 1941
	Wilburn Adkins	January 28, 1947

Wesley Adkins	Larry Lee Adkins	April 21, 1953
	Wesley Adkins, Jr.	March 17, 1951
Clarence Alexander	Bennie Alexander	
	Clarine Alexander	April 30, 1940
	Gayle Alexander	April 7, 1943
	Wayne Alexander	November 27, 1941
Henry Back	Allen Back	June 11, 1945
	Bobby Back	August 8, 1949
James Barker	Garry Barker	November 26, 1943
Richard Basford	Dale Basford	December 4, 1950
	Sue Basford	February 19, 1948
Johnnie Bays	Donald Bays	June 15, 1946
	Garnett Faye Bays	February 4, 1944
	Harold Ray Bays	September 20, 1948
Jack Bivens, guardian	Kenneth Richmond	May 3, 1947
	Shirley Richmond	October 14, 1944
Elmer Botkins	Donald Botkin	September 24, 1941
	Ruth Anne Botkins	May 17, 1945
Harley Edward Bowles	Johnny Burlin Bowles	September 5, 1951
	Judy Ann Bowles	February 2, 1949
Joe Braybant	Sammy Braybant	June 18, 1945
Willie Burton	Barbara Jo Burton	June 29, 1951
	Dixie Burton	August 30, 1949
	Joyce Burton	October 14, 1946
	Steven Burton	November 20, 1947
	Willie Ray Burton	December 28, 1944
Claude Bussel	Brenda Bussel	November 16, 1949
	Donna Marie Bussel	October 22, 1950
Gano Bussel	Gary Mackel Vance	December 7, 1950

Alvin Forest Butcher	Donna Butcher	January 7, 1950
	Linda Butcher	October 29, 1948
	Shirley Butcher	July 11, 1951
John H. Carpenter	Wayne Carpenter	August 22, 1945
Oral Carter	Austin Carter	February 5, 1944
Pershing and June Caudill	William Caudill	January 7, 1947
Clarence Conley	Brenda Sue Conley	February 1950
	Clarence Conley, Jr.	July 21, 1951
	Denzil Conley	February 13, 1948
	Evelyn Conley	May 13, 1953
	Margie Conley	December 31, 1945
Johnnie Conley	Billy Gene Conley	January 3, 1944
	Jackie Wayne Conley	December 18, 1952
	Joyce Conley	March 27, 1947
	Kathy Sue Conley	October 23, 1950
Luther Conn	Charles Elmer Conn	April 5, 1944
Douglas J. Cooper	George Ray Cooper	July 18, 1952
	Lawrence Wayne Cooper	December 29, 1950
Floyd Curtis, Jr.	Randall Curtis	November 21, 1951
Isabel Curtis	Herbert Reed	March 16, 1945
Tony Curtis	Densil Ray Curtis	January 8, 1942
Vada Dyer	Opal Dyer	September 1, 1944
	Shirley Dyer	November 4, 1940
George Elam	Freda Elam	December 7, 1941
	Roy Elam	July 4, 1945
Clarence Eldridge	Donald Eldridge	December 16, 1941
Drewey Emmons	Martha Beulah Emmons	August 27, 1953

Boyd Fannin	Charles E. Fannin	May 19, 1949
	Joyce Ann Fannin	March 18, 1953
Roy Fannin	Eugene Fannin	April 11, 1938
	Everett Fannin	March 4, 1941
	Lavonna Fannin	May 22, 1943
	Roy Fannin, Jr.	
	Wilbur Fannin	May 4, 1939
Roy Faris	Charles Faris	July 26, 1944
	Eldred Faris	June 17, 1937
	Mildred Faris	October 3, 1942
	Shirley Faris	November 20, 1952
Harley Farrow	Donna Farrow	October 28, 1948
	Melvin Lee Farrow	March 17, 1951
	Ruby Farrow	September 29, 1952
Garrett Feltner	Molly Ann Feltner	September 16, 1947
Thomas Flora	Calvin Flora	November 1, 1943
	Ruby Mae Flora	January 12, 1940
Dewey Garris	Carolyn Sue Garris	December 16, 1944
	Charles Garris, Jr.	September 7, 1948
	Donna Garris	August 25, 1947
Ernie Gilliam	Garnett Mae Gilliam	September 18, 1950
	Janice Lee Gilliam	February 22, 1948
Stanley Gilliam	Darrel Gilliam	March 19, 1951
	Joe Gilliam	August 10, 1948
	Lovene Gilliam	April 6, 1950
	Pat Gilliam	June 21, 1946
	Paul Gilliam	December 31, 1945
	Rudolph Gilliam	April 29, 1952
Lon Gorman	Maxine Gorman	December 28, 1946
	Thomas Allen Gorman	February 17, 1949
Christine Green	Ida Lee Green	March 4, 1946

M.C. Greer	Linda Ann Greer	November 7, 1949
	Sandra Greer	July 3, 1952
Alvin Gulley	Diana Gulley	November 23, 1950
	James Alvin Gulley	May 13, 1949
	Jesse Price Gulley	November 28, 1952
Charles Gulley	Marcella Sue Gulley	August 29, 1952
Myrtle Gulley	Paul Richmond	May 3, 1947
Orville Gulley	Shirley Gulley	July 2, 1944
Boone Guy	Patricia Guy	January 29, 1944
	Russell Guy	November 2, 1943
Milford Hall	Carl Eugene Hall	November 3, 1948
	James Lowell Hall	February 6, 1946
Thomas Hall	Sterling Dean Hall	March 18, 1953
Hazel/Virgil Hamm	Beryl Hamm	February 4, 1940
	Billie Hamm	October 25, 1941
	Douglas Hamm	June 8, 1945
	Gail Hamm	July 25, 1943
	Joe Hamm	December 31, 1946
William Hamm	Billy Wayne Hamm	January 19, 1948
William Hardin	Bertie Lee Hardin	August 30, 1948
Ad Hardy/ Della Hardy	Beatrice Hardy	March 4, 1946
	Elsie Hardy	June 19, 1941
	William Hardy	March 5, 1943
Donald Harris	Phillip Harris	August 26, 1949
	Richard Harris	November 27, 1939
Robert Helphinstine	Frances Louise Helphinstine	October 19, 1941
	Virginia Lee Helphinstine	October 6, 1945
Lloyd Henson	James Franklin Henson	February 11, 1947

Willie Howard	Johnny Howard	January 11, 1945
	Tommy Howard	May 9, 1941
Charlie Hunt	Ronnie Hunt	October 23, 1948
Curtis Hunt	Billy Jo Hunt	May 9, 1936
	Jackie Hunt	June 5, 1944
	John C. Hunt	August 21, 1940
	Wanda Marie Hunt	June 21, 1943
Winfred Isom	Elza Isom	December 1, 1945
	Irene Isom	February 15, 1942
	Wanda Lou Isom	July 3, 1943
Clara James	Linda Hamm	May 26, 1944
Loright James	Gerald James	October 24, 1943
	Judith James	February 11, 1945
	Marilyn Deloris James	February 8, 1937
Gene Jett	Billy Jett	June 18, 1948
	Johnny Jett	April 28, 1949
Benjamin Johnson	Clarence Ernie Johnson	November 5, 1950
	Donovan Johnson	May 25, 1947
	Yvonne Johnson	May 19, 1949
Elmer/Rosie Johnson	Dorotha Carrozza	July 24, 1937
	Raymond Carrozza	October 1, 1937
(William) Clyde Jones	Elizabeth Carolyn Jones	October 4, 1944
	John Robert Jones	November 4, 1951
	Mabel Jean Jones	April 22, 1946
	William H. Jones	October 4, 1940
Woodrow Jordan	Omar Jordan	
	Lillie Jordan	January 13, 1946
James Kirk	Ronald Kirk	May 23, 1945
Lorene Kirk	Edna Kirk	December 14, 1941
	William Wayne Kirk	October 26, 1939

Robert Sam Lee	David Lee	May 4, 1942
	Thelma Jean Lee	August 1, 1938
Glen Lewis	Madeline Lewis	May 5, 1942
Cluster Little	Delma Little	October 5, 1946
	Mary Rachel Little	November 1, 1948
James Little	Alma Little	February 5, 1942
	Dallas Green	May 17, 1937
	Delma Green	February 8, 1939
Clifford Elwood Littleton	Larry Littleton	February 3, 1949
Emmit Littleton	Ronnie Littleton	October 7, 1943
Harley Littleton	Imogene Littleton	July 27, 1944
	Willie Gene Littleton	July 27, 1944
Olaf Mathison	Marius E. Mathison	September 5, 1950
	Mary Ellen Mathison	July 31, 1947
	Oscar Mathison	June 30, 1944
George Mattox	John Acie Mattox	June 5, 1945
	Stanley Paul Mattox'	October 23, 1951
	Sylvia Elaine Mattox	September 1, 1948
	Wanda Sue Mattox	June 23, 1943
John Mattox	Danny Mattox	December 4, 1944
Price Mattox	Edna Carolyn Mattox	October 10, 1947
	Larry Lee Mattox	December 18, 1949
	Nancy Mattox	December 26, 1953
	Robert Mattox	April 21, 1946
John McClurg	Charles McClurg	October 19, 1936
	Hilda McClurg	July 27, 1941
	Lloyd McClurg	June 23, 1937
	Rilda McClurg	July 27, 1940
	Roy Earl McClurg	March 23, 1944
Charles McKee	Pauletta McKee	April 24, 1950

Elwood McKee	Donna Jean McKee	July 5, 1950
Henry McKee	William Harold McKee	June 9, 1938
J. Stewart McKee	Velma Cushard	
	J. Stewart McKee	September 30, 1950
	Peter Acres McKee	July 4, 1953
	Sudie Ellen McKee	December 22, 1951
Roy McKee	Joyce Ann McKee	October 21, 1952
Paul McKenzie	Elva Dotson	
Eugene McRoberts	Raymond Lee McRoberts	March 10, 1944
James L. Meade	Joyce Ann Meade	January 27, 1946
	Leonard Meade	March 11, 1944
Garvey Million	Josephine Million	October 26, 1937
	Ruth Million	April 27, 1936
Mrs. Kermit Moore	Shirley Ann Taylor Moore	November 29, 1949
Ed Muse	Jennie Mae Muse	January 23, 1949
	Thomas Muse	September 3, 1946
	Vernice Muse	October 15, 1943
Espie Muse	Archie Muse	July 19, 1945
	Henry Dallas Muse	November 1, 1947
	Hobert Muse	September 13, 1939
	Jeanette Muse	March 6, 1942
	John Robert Muse	June 22, 1950
Charles Owens	Howard Owens	March 12, 1938
	James Owens	October 12, 1943
	Myrtle Owens	December 2, 1941
Edgar Owens	Thomas J. Kiser	January 19, 1940
Grant Owens	Buford Owens	June 7, 1943
	Floyd Owens	February 19, 1940
	Roger Owens	September 14, 1944

Wayman Parker	Marietta Parker	August 31, 1952
	Sandra Parker	May 16, 1947
	Timothy Parker	October 9, 1948
Taylor Pence, Jr.	Janie Pence	September 27, 1951
Joe Perkins	Myrtle Perkins	February 4, 1946
	Phyllis Mae Perkins	October 5, 1948
Leota Perkins	Eddie Perkins	January 22, 1940
James Peyton	Faye Peyton	September 15, 1939
	Nathan Peyton	
Delbert Plummer	Clyde Plummer	October 23, 1943
	Kathleen Plummer	January 11, 1945
	Patsy Ann Plummer	March 2, 1947
	Robert Plummer	February 13, 1940
Forest Plummer	Edith Plummer	June 26, 1947
	Elloise Elaine Plummer	June 27, 1951
	Emerson Plummer	October 20, 1945
	Erleen Plummer	September 30, 1941
Hobert Plummer	Julie Plummer	July 1951
	Margaret Plummer	July 11, 1952
	Ralph Plummer	June 5, 1944
	Roy Plummer	January 10, 1948
	Thomas Plummer	December 6, 1946
Jesse Porter	Jerry Lee Porter	August 7, 1943
	Larry Porter	December 29, 1946
	Ruth Ann Porter	April 24, 1945
Elza Presley	James Presley	February 11, 1940
	Janetta Presley	August 12, 1943
	Woodrow Presley	October 25, 1938
Thomas Reed	Bessie Reed	
Isabel Reed	Martha Ann Reed	November 21, 1948
Clifford Reeves	Dorothy Reeves	November 20, 1943

Earl Reeves	Jackie Ray Reeves	November 1, 1951
Kelly Reeves	Jimmy Reeves	March 14, 1947
Woodrow Reeves	Ernie Reeves	June 12, 1948
	Larry Reeves	July 14, 1952
	Samuel Reeves	December 8, 1946
	Tommy Reeves	June 25, 1950
	Woodie Reeves	June 11, 1945
Eugene Richmond	Ronald Richmond	June 5, 1943
	Shirley Richmond	October 14, 1944
	William Richmond	September 28, 1939
Hessie Richmond	Bobby Richmond	April 5, 1943
	Donald Richmond	July 19, 1941
	Jimmy Richmond	September 9, 1945
Ollie Riddle	Lloyd Riddle	September 27, 1940
Elmo Lee Roberts	Brenda Roberts	February 10, 1953
	Jimmy Roberts	October 5, 1943
	Joseph Leroy Roberts	September5, 1945
	Kenneth Roberts	January 8, 1949
	Larry Roberts	July 2, 1951
	Patricia Carolyn Roberts	February 12, 1947
	Wilma Roberts	March 12, 1950
Mrs. Gladys Robinson	Gloria Robinson	July 8, 1943
Isaac N. Routt	Sammy Braybant	June 18, 1944
	Anita Keeton	August 9, 1944
	Clifford Keeton	April 30, 1946
	Danny Keeton	March 14, 1948
	Roger Keeton	November 7, 1942
	Charles Routt	December 16, 1946
	George Routt	October 7, 1945
James Routt	Ballard Mulwee, Jr.	October 31, 1942
Berlin Sloas	Justine Sloas	September 4, 1953
	Louella Sloas	November 21, 1947

Erma Sloas	Elizabeth Frances Sloas	September 15, 1949
	Jeri Lynn Sloas	October 30, 1952
Wendell "Elmo" Sloas	Cathy Sloas	February 23, 1953
Winfred W. Sluss	Beatrice Sluss	October 11, 1941
	Ronald Sluss	March 17, 1943
	Wilford Sluss	October 17, 1940
Ovie Smith	Carolyn Sue Smith	May 7, 1943
	Nancy Jo Ann Smith	July 5, 1941
William Smith	Bonnie Sue Smith	November 25, 1947
	Earl Dean Smith	July 1, 1949
Noah Spencer	Donald Spencer	April 24, 1939
	Noah Spencer, Jr.	July 14, 1942
	Roger Spencer	
Luther Stamper	Alice Stamper	July 13, 1941
Ballard Stephens	Marie Stephens	June 22, 1947
	Ruth Stephens	
Eldon Stevens	Jeraldine Stevens	March 25, 1943
	John Stevens	July 19, 1945
	Lurina Stevens	February 12, 1940
	Ruth Stevens	June 22, 1947
Ossie Stiltner	Clarence Davis	November 27, 1948
	Roy Davis	February 12, 1946
Ruby Stine	James Reeves	February 14, 1941
George Swim	Larry Swim	October 19, 1947
Mrs. Elish (Pete) Taylor	Jesse Leon Taylor	November 16, 1952
	Peggy Taylor	December 15, 1953
	Linda Hamm	May 30, 1944
Stella Taylor	Myrtle Ed Gillum	June 25, 1941
	Pauline Gillum	August 6, 1937

Walter Thacker	Beverly Thacker	May 26, 1939
	Monte Thacker	July 25, 1947
	Patsy Thacker	May 16, 1943
	Pauline Thacker	April 26, 1941
	Wilma Thacker	April 26, 1941
Paul Tranbarger	Richard Tranbarger	March 25, 1948
	Vickie Tranbarger	February 7, 1952
George Viars	Raymond Viars	January 30, 1941
Luther Wagoner	Addie Wagoner	November 10, 1943
	Billie Scott Wagoner	August 20, 1937
	Ivis Wagner	February 2, 1939
	Mary Ethel Wagoner	August 26, 1941
	Pauline Wagoner	February 2, 1939
Marshall Walker	Kenneth Ray Walker	March 28, 1941
John Henry Wallace	Cecil Wallace	October 24, 1938
	Clayton Wallace	March 9, 1940
	Frances Wallace	November 17, 1941
	Johnny Wallace	March 23, 1944
	Olive Wallace	March 25, 1937
Frank Watson	Anna Watson	June 5, 1945
Humphrey Watson	Wayne Watson	April 19, 1947
Alta Wentz	Daniel Wentz	February 4, 1942
William Wilburn	Tracy Wilburn	August 1, 1944
John Williams	Eleanor Williams	February 5, 1943
	James Oscar Williams	September 25, 1948
	Loretta J. Williams	September 26, 1946
Leslie Williams	Nancy Carol Williams	May 4, 1949
	Phyllis Williams	March 6, 1952
	Terry Lee Williams	February 16, 1947
Wilder Williams	Danny Williams	September 13, 1949
	James Ray Williams	May 24, 1952
	Shirley Williams	February 26, 1951

Chapter 20

Marriages of Goddard School Students

(This does not include all marriages.)

Romance was in the air at Goddard School. When Kathy Adkins enrolled in Goddard School in the fifth grade in the 1950s, she saw Larry Swim sitting on the cistern top. She thought he was so cute and remarked to a friend, "I will marry him someday." Larry loved her Ohio accent and teased her about it. Their friendship developed, and a few years after graduation, they were married. At the Goddard School reunion in October 2019, Kathy reported that after fifty-three years of marriage, they are still in love.

Another couple that married young were Patsy Roberts and Sherley Taylor. Sherley spotted Patsy when she walked across the porch at Goddard School. She also had transferred from another school. Sherley was working on a motor and stuck the wire out and shocked Patsy as she passed. She thought he was mean at first, but she soon learned he had a loving heart. They were married when she was fourteen and lived together until his sudden death on July 31, 2005. Other couples that were students at Goddard School and married are the following:

Pauletta McKee and Denzil Conley
Nancy Mattox and Charles Elmer Conn
Beulah Insko and Leonard Emmons
Bernice Littleton and Virgil Helphenstine

Maxine Morrison and Frank Owen Hinton
Gail Hinton and Frank Owen Hinton (second marriage)
Elaine Plummer and Willie Gene Littleton
Helen Reeves and Ed McKee
Ruth Ann Porter and Johnny Charles McKee
Evelyn Reeves and Roy McKee
Artinsie Muse and Delbert Plummer
Bernice Muse and Edward Plummer
Joyce Conley and Donnie Porter
Shirley Williams and Larry Porter
Mae Lawrence and Clifford Reeves
Ginny Helphinstine and Woodie Reeves
Dorothy McKee and Woodrow Reeves
Maxine Gorman and Ronnie Richmond
Sadie Gardner and Willard Saunders
Kathy Adkins and Larry Swim
Patsy Roberts and Sherley Taylor
Polly Thacker and Hale Williams
Jean Kirk and Wilder Williams
Bessie Hurst and Curtis Yazell

The Goddard School children had a common rural background. They played together, and they had a sense of identity. Teachers were loving and supportive, and students were appreciative of teachers' efforts. Their dedication and enthusiasm was something to be admired. Older children helped younger students with their lessons, or bright children could look ahead at the next classes' lessons. Students had time and opportunities to explore their passions and to use their imaginations. Students were taught to work hard and had similar jobs and chores on the farm—taking care of cattle, working in tobacco and hay, gathering eggs, cooking, helping with laundry, carrying in wood, and others. An atmosphere was created where children wanted to learn. Students had something to look forward to each day. For some, it was Mrs. Moore's flannel board stories; for others, a hot lunch and the story after lunch or playing ante-over with Mr. Barnett and friends. School was fun. Faye Taylor expressed it well. "I always admired and looked up to my teachers. Teaching was important to them, and learning was important to me. I cried on my first day of school and cried when school was over.[1'] Teachers continued to carry out the common school motto: "Train up a child the way he should go, and when he is old, he will not depart from it" (Proverbs 22:6). Students got a good basic education and had productive lives. Many went on to advanced degrees and became college professors, dentists, teachers, nurses, and television actors. Parents had community pride. The building was primitive, but relationships were built and friendships made that will last a lifetime.

Index of Students
Who Attended Goddard School

Please note that a few record books were missing or water-stained. The 1947 book is missing. Teachers may list a student by their nickname while others by their given name. Birth dates may vary.

Elta Adkins, 1950s

Kathy Adkins, 1950s

Kenny Adkins, 1950s

Larry Lee Adkins, 1950s

Ruth Ann Adkins, 1950s

Wesley Adkins, Jr., 1950s

Wilbur Adkins, 1950s

Bennie Alexander, 1950s

Clarine Alexander, 1950s

Gayle Alexander, 1950s

Wayne Alexander, 1950s

Edward Anderson, 1940s

Inaree Anderson, 1940s

Kenneth Anderson, 1940s

Samuel Anderson, 1940s

Thomas Anderson, 1940s

Douglas Armstrong, 1930s

Geneva Armstrong, 1930s

Eddie Arnold, 1898

Frank Arnold, 1898

Lula M. Arnold, 1898

Ottie Arnold, 1898

Roy Arnold, 1920s

Beulah Arrasmith, 1930s

Noble Arrasmith, 1930s

Allan Back, 1950s

Bobby Back, 1950s

Doris Back, 1940s

Edward Back, 1930s

Frank Back, 1957

Gatewood Back, 1930s

Harold Back, 1930s

Jackie Back, 1940s

James Isaac Back, 1940s

Johnnie Back, 1930s

Amy Bailey, 1911, 1916

Cecie Bailey 1916

Ella Bailey, 1911, 1916

Frank Bailey, 1911, 1916

James Bailey, 1907

Jessie Bailey, 1911, 1916

Robert Bailey, 1916

Ben Baird, 1903

Charles Baird, 1898

Grover Cleveland Baird, 1898
James Edward Baird, 1898
Stella Baird, 1903
Gary Gene Barker, 1940s, 1950s
Phyllis C. Barker, 1940s
Roger James Barker, 1940s
Dale Basford, 1950s
Sue Basford, 1950s
Theodore Bass, 1898
Carl Bays, 1940s, 1956
Donald Bays, 1950s
Garnet Faye Bays, 1958
Harold Ray Bays, 1950s
Charlotte Beckett, 1898
Iva B. Beckett, 1898
John S. Beckett, 1898
Laura Beckett, 1898
Geneva Bell, 1920s
James Beyerlein, 1940s
Mary Lou Beyerlein, 1940s
Susanne Beyerlein, 1940s
Nellie M. Binnon, 1911
Lillie B. Bolin, 1903
Marion Boone, 1930s
Donald Botkin, 1950s
Everette Douglas Botkin, 1940s
Ruth Ann Botkin, 1950s
Johnny Burlin Bowles, 1950s
Judy Ann Bowles, 1950s
Thomas Bowman, 1940s
Ida Bramble, 1898
Mary Bramble, 1903, 1907
Ora Bramble, 1903
Anna Bramel, 1898
Betty Bramel, 1898
Bruce Bramel, 1920s

Calla Bramel, 1898
Dora Bramel, 1898
Emma Bramel, 1898
Georgia Bramel, 1930s
Ira Bramel, 1907
Kirby Bramel, 1898
Lester Bramel, 1907
Marie Bramel, 1898
May D. Bramel, 1903
Milford Bramel, 1903
Minnie Bramel, 1907
Pauline Bramel, 1920s, 1930s
Mary Alice Branham, 1930s
Arthur Bratton, 1898
Clarie Bratton, 1899
Joe Braybant, 1956
Patricia Braybant, 1955
Sammy Braybant, 1950s
Ida Bristow, 1898
Billy Ray Brown, 1940s
Charlotte Ann Burke, 1940s
Barbara Jo Burton, 1950s
Dixie Burton, 1950s
Joyce Burton, 1950s
Steven Burton, 1950s
Willie Ray Burton, 1950s
Brenda Bussel, 1950s
Donna Marie Bussel, 1950s
Donna Butcher, 1950s
Linda Butcher, 1950s
Shirley Butcher, 1950s
Nellie Byron, 1907, 1916
Anna G. Calvert, 1907
Dean Calvert, 1907
Letcher Calvert, 1907
Lullie Calvert, 1907

Maude M. Calvert, 1907
Alice Garr Campbell, 1920s, 1930s
Clifton Campbell, 1920s
Clyde Campbell, 1920s
Gale Campbell, 1920s
Wells Campbell, 1911
William Campbell, 1911
Alice Carpenter, 1898
Belt Carpenter, 1898
Clarence Carpenter, 1898
Early Samuel Carpenter 1898, 1920s
Emma Carpenter, 1898
Eula B. Carpenter, 1920s
Eva Carpenter, 1898
Fay Carpenter, 1898
Goldie Carpenter, 1898
Mabel Carpenter, 1911, 1916
Mirtle Carpenter, 1898
Morgan Carpenter, 1911
Orval Carpenter, 1898
Oscar Carpenter, 1898
Paul Hifler Carpenter, 1911, 1916
Pauline Carpenter, 1911, 1916
Virga Carpenter, 1916
Wayne Carpenter, 1950s
Dorotha Carrozza, 1940s, 1950s
Raymond Carrozza, 1940s, 1950s
Austin Carter, 1950s
Evangeline Carter, 1940s
Treda Carter, 1940s
Charles Caudill, 1930s
Edward Caudill, 1930s
Gilbert Caudill, Jr., 1940s
Kenneth Caudill, 1940s
Lovell Caudill, 1930s
William Caudill, 1950s

Clyde Charles, 1940s
Leslie William Charles, 1940s
Frank E. Clark, 1911
William Clark, 1911
Betty Claypoole, 1952
Charles Claypool, 1920s, 1930s
Claude Claypool, 1920s
Edna Claypool, 1922
Florence Claypool, 1920s
Gladys Claypool, 1922
Helen Claypool, 1920s
Horace Claypool, 1922
Mabel Garr Claypool, 1930s
Marvin Claypool, 1920s
Mary Jo Claypool, 1930s
Maxine Claypool, 1930s
Millard Claypool, 1907
Roy Claypool, 1916
Stanley Claypool, 1922
Velda Gail Claypool, 1940s
Wilson Claypool, 1920s
Wilson Claypool, 1940s
Maty B. Cline, 1898
Sida W. Cline, 1898
Billy Gene Conley, 1950s
Brenda Sue Conley, 1950s
Clarence Conley, Jr., 1950s
Denzil Conley, 1950s
Evelyn Conley, 1950s
Jackie Wayne Conley, 1950s
James Edward Conley, 1940s
Jimmy Conley, 1940s
Joyce Conley, 1950s
Kathy Sue Conley, 1950s
Conley, Marjorie, 1950s
Charles Elmer Conn, 1950s

Mary Lucy Conn, 1930s
James Conn, 1940s
Ruby Lee Conn, 1940s
George Ray Cooper, 1950s
Lawrence Wayne Cooper, 1950s
Kenneth Cooper, 1930s
Yancey Cooper, 1940s
George Cosbery, 1930s
Calvin Craig, 1909
Charles Craig, 1909
Mary Craig, 1909
Mattie Craig, 1909
Arthur Crump, 1920s
Audra Cunliff, 1930s
Charles Cunliff, 1930s
Elsie Cunliff, 1930s
Avery Houston Curtis, 1940s, 1950s
Denzil Ray Curtis, 1958
Dora B. Curtis, 1940s
Gilbert Curtis, 1930s, 1940s
Randall Curtis, 1950s
Ray D. Curtis, 1958
Velma Cushard, 1950s
Evelyn Daniel, 1940s
Marvin Daniel, 1940s
Adam S. Davis, 1911
James Davis, 1911
Betty Day, 1940s
Gladys Day, 1940s
Eddie Dearing, 1898
Levada Dearing, 1898
Maiy Dearing, 1907
Una Mae Dearing, 1898
Yantis Dearing, 1907
Anderson Deatley, 1916, 1930s
Charles Deatley, 1916

Edna Deatley, 1930s
Emmitt Deatley, 1916
Leonia Deatley, 1930s
Maudy Deatley, 1916
Maurice Deatley, 1916
Eddie DeBusch, 1898
Frank DeBusch, 1898
Omar DeBusch, 1898
Rillie DeBusch, 1898
Eugene Dickens, 1922
John Dickens, 1922
Mary Opal Dickens, 1920s
Couttren Dillion, 1911
C—R Dillion, 1911
Viola Dillion, 1911
Deloris Doolin, 1930s
Elizabeth Doolin, 1930s
Golda Doolin, 1930s
John Doolin, 1940s
Elva Dotson, 1950s
Elizabeth Doulin, 1930s
Ducie Downey, 1920s
Eulah Downey, 1930s
Geneva Downey, 1920s
Ollie Downey, 1920s
Pauline Downey, 1930s
Alice Doyle, 1898
Beatrice Doyle, 1940s
Billie Woosley Doyle, 1940s
Elias Doyle, 1898
Elmer Doyle, 1898
Frank Doyle, 1898
Hazel Doyle, 1920s
Irvin Doyle, 1898
John Doyle, 1907
Lena Doyle, 1940s

Lula Doyle, 1898
Mary Doyle, 1898
Rolla Doyle, 1898
Ruby Doyle, 1920s
Theodore Doyle, 1940s
Donna Kaye Duncan, 1940s
Bonnie Jean Dyer, 1940s
Donald Dyer, 1940s
Opal Dyer, 1950s
Shirley Dyer, 1950s
Gene Eden, 1930s
Justin Eden, 1930s
Richard Eden, 1930s
Freda Elam, 1950s
Roy Elam, 1950s
Donald Eldridge, 1950s
Anna Lewis Ellington, 1930s
Anna Louise Ellington, 1930s
Arthur Ellington, 1930s
Eugene Ellington, 1930s
Bellomany (B.C.) Emmons, 1940s
Charles Emmons, 1940s
Chester Emmons, 1920s
Drew Emmons, 1930s
Edna Emmons, 1920s
Esther Ruth Emmons, 1920s
Estill Emmons, 1920s
Gertrude Emmons, 1930s
Leonard Emmons, 1930s
Lloyd Emmons, 1930s
Martha Beulah Emmons, 1950s
Ola Mae Emmons, 1920s
Thelma Emmons, 1930s
Chester Evans, 1898
William Evans, 1898
Boyd Fannin, Jr., 1940s

Charles E. Fannin, 1950s
Dorothy Fannin, 1920s
Eugene Fannin, 1950s
Everett Fannin, 1950s
Joyce Ann Fannin, 1950s
Lavonna Fannin, 1950s
Letha Fannin, 1940s
Randolph Fannin, 1930s
Roy Fannin, 1950s
Vemell Fannin, 1930s
Wilbur Fannin, 1950s
Wilma Fannin, 1940s
Anabell Faris, 1903
Basil Faris, 1911
Blanche Faris, 1916
Carl Faris, 1903
Charles Faris, 1911
Charles Faris, 1950s
Eldred Faris, 1950s
Estella Faris, 1907
Eunice Faris, 1907
Frances Faris, 1916
Garr Faris, 1922
Gertrude Faris, 1898
Hettie Faris, 1911
Janies Gordan Faris, 1898
John B.Faris, 1903
John Ransome Faris, 1898
Johnnie Garr Faris, 1920s
Lloyd Faris, 1920s
Lutie Faris, 1922
Mabel Faris, 1907
Mary Faris, 1916, 1922
Maude Faris, 1907
Mildred Faris, 1950s
Myrtle Faris, 1907

Ransom Faris, 1898
Ruth Faris, 1922
Shirley Faris, 1950s
Stella Faris, 1898
Unis Faris, 1903
Vadie Faris, 1916
William B. Faris, 1899
Wilson Faris, 1920s
Donna Farrow, 1950s
James Farrow, 1940s
James T. Farrow, 1940s
Melvin Lee Farrow, 1950s
Nancy Farrow, 1940s
Robert Farrow, 1940s
Ruby Farrow, 1950s
Rubye Farrow, 1940s
William Farrow, 1940s
Molly Ann Feltner, 1950s
Johnny Fenton, 1916
M. W. fieman, 1909
Emma Finley, 1940s
Mary Finley, 1940s
Alice Fischer, 1903
William Fizer, 1930s
Retta Flannery, 1940s
Bobby (Robert Allen) Flora, 1940s
Calvin Flora, 1940s, 1950s
Dorothy Flora, 1930s, 1940s
Georgia Flora, 1930s
Ruby Mae Flora, 1940s
Opal May Freeman, 1911
Alma Gaines, 1911
Elbridge Gaines, 1898
Elmer Gaines, 1898
Estill Gaines, 1911
Mary Gaines, 1898

Muriel Gaines, 1898
Nellie Gaines, 1911
Albert Gallagher, 1940s
Cecil Gallagher, 1930s
Jackie Galliher, 1940s
Archie Gardner, 1930s
Arthur Gardner, 1920s
Beulah Gardner, 1940s
Bruce Gardner, 1930s
Ervin Eugene Gardner, 1940s
Estill Gardner, 1930s
George Gardner, 1920s
Hazel Gardner, 1920s
Helen Gardner, 1920s
Jessie Gardner, 1930s
Mabel Gardner, 1930s
Mary Gardner, 1920s
Nellie Ruth Gardner, 1930s
Omar Gardner, 1930s
Ova Thomas Gardner, 1930s
Sadie Gardner, 1930s
Stella Mae Gardner, 1930s
Carolyn Sue Garris, 1950s
Charles Garris, Jr., 1950s
Donna Garris, 1950s
Mary Gaskins, 1930s
Skinner Gaskins, 1930s
Darrel Gilliam, 1950s
Edith Gilliam, 1930s
Garnett Mae Gilliam, 1950s
Janice Gilliam, 1950s
Joe Gilliam, 1950s
Lovene Gilliam, 1950s
Pat Gilliam, 1950s
Paul Gilliam, 1950s
Rudolph Gilliam, 1950s

Waneda Gilliam, 1930s
Billie Gillum, 1940s
Glenna Gillum, 1940s
Madeline Gillum, 1940s
Myrtle Ed Gillum, 1950s
Pauline Gillum, 1950s
Florence Gleason, 1940s
John Glen, 1930s
Ada Gar Gooding, 1916, 1922
Austin Gooding, 1916
Brice Gooding, 1920s
Emma Gooding, 1898
Estella Gooding, 1907
Ethel Gooding, 1911, 1916
Eugene Gooding, 1932
Evalina Gooding, 1920s
Frances Gooding, 1920s
Golda Gooding, 1916
Hattie Gooding, 1898
Jesse Gooding, 1920s, 1930s
Lillie Gooding, 1916
Minish Gooding, 1922
Minnie Gooding, 1898
Nellie Gooding, 1922
Ola Gooding, 1922
Ollie Gooding, 1922
Oral Gooding, 1930s
Patsy Gooding, 1940s, 1951
Paul Gooding, 1940s, 1957
Pearl Gooding, 1916, 1922
Retha Gooding, 1898
Ronnie Wayne Gooding, 1940s, 1955
Solomon Gooding, 1898
Stella B. Gooding, 1911, 1916
Susan Gooding, 1898
Thomas Gooding, 1898

Victor Gooding, 1920s
Zenith Gooding, 1922
Elder Gorman, 1898
Maxine Gorman, 1960
Roberta Gorman, 1950s
Thomas Allen Gorman, 1950s
William Gorman, 1898
Dorothy Gray, 1930s
Arlene Grayson, 1940s
Amet Grayson, 1898
Doss Grayson, 1898
Florida Grayson, 1940s
Joseph Grayson, 1898
Omar Grayson, 1898
Ora Grayson, 1903
Dallas Green, 1950s
Delma Green, 1950s
Christine Greene, 1940s
Ida Lee Green, 1950s
Linda Ann Greer, 1950s
Sandra Greer, 1950s
Beulah Gulley, 1930s
Diana Gulley, 1950s
Ernest Gulley, 1920s
Henry Thomas Gulley, 1940s
James Alvin Gulley, 1950s
Jesse Price Gulley, 1950s
Lena Gulley, 1911
Marcella Sue Gulley, 1950s
Matilda Gulley, 1898
Omar Gulley, Jr., 1930s
Rachel Gulley, 1898
Ray Gulley, 1960s
Ruby Gulley, 1930s
Shirley Gulley, 1950s
Tommy Gulley, 1930s

Wilbur Garr Gulley, 1930s, 1940s
Edward Guy, 1940s
Patti Guy, 1950s
Russell Guy, 1950s
Allie Florence Hall, 1930s
Carl Eugene Hall, 1950s
Chancie Hall, 1930s
Edgar Hall, 1930s
Elinor Hall, 1940s
J.E. Hall, 1930s
James Lowell Hall, 1950s
Kenneth Hall, 1930s
Mamie Hall, 1930s
Marcus Hall, 1930s
Marvin Hall, 1930s
Ralph Hall, 1940s
Rubye Bell Hall, 1930s
Sterling Dean Hall, 1950s
Tommy Milford Hall, 1947
Wendell Hall, 1930s
William (Billie) Hall, 1930s
Allen Ham, 1898
Amy Ham, 1903
Carie Ham, 1898
Clyde Ham, 1898
Essey Ham, 1898
Ethel Ham, 1903
Ewin Ham, 1907
Gilbert Ham, 1903
Hattie Ham, 1898
Jack Ham, 1898
Minnie Ham, 1898
Thomas Ham, 1898
Avery Hamilton, 1940s
Bert Hamilton, 1922
Best Hamilton, 1916

Beulah Hamilton, 1922
Charles Hamilton, 1930s
Christine Hamilton, 1930s
Clarence Hamilton, 1930s
Cora E. Hamilton, 1940s
Earl Hamilton, 1922
Ellis Hamilton, 1920s
Esseto Hamilton, 1916
Flora Hamilton, 1916, 1922
Fred Hamilton, 1920s
Ina Pearl Hamilton, 1930s
Lillian Hamilton, 1930s
Maude Hamilton, 1916
Volene Hamilton, 1930s
Wilbur Hamilton, 1930s
Alsin Hamm, 1922
Beryl Hamm, 1956
Billie Hamm, 1957
Billie Wayne Hamm, 1950s
Douglas Hamm, 1950s
Eckles Hamm, 1916
Eelria Hamm, 1922
Eugene Hamm, 1940s
Gail Hamm, 1957
Helen Hamm, 1916
James W. Hamm, 1940s
Joe Hamm. 1950s
Josephine Hamm, 1922
Linda Hamm, 1950s
Mildred Hamm, 1922
Brice Hammonds, 1907
Early Hammond, 1899
Emma Hammond, 1899
Harry Hammond, 1907
Harvey Hammond, 1899
Marie Hammond, 1922

Julia Hammond, 1922

Melvin Hammond, 1911

Nellie Hammond, 1903

Bertie Lee Hardin, 1950s

Beatrice Hardy, 1950s

Bill Hardy, 1958

Elsie Hardy, 1950s

C. P. Harmon, Jr., 1930s

Charles F. Harmon, 1930s

Charles Willis Harmon, 1940s

George Robert Harmon, 1930s

Winona Harmon, 1930s

Arnold Harris, 1930s

Donald Harris, 1930s

Phillip Harris, 1950s

Richard Harris, 1950s

U. G. Hawkins, 1907

Beulah Hedger, 1920s

Anna Opal Hedges, 1940s

Arthur Hedges, 1898

Edgar Hedges, 1903

Floyd Hedges, 1898

Lloyd Hedges, 1898

Mary Hedges, 1898

Ollie Hedges, 1911

Stanley Hedges, 1911

Stella Hedges, 1916

Tom Hedges, 1940s

Thomas Hedges, 1922

Archie Helphenstine, 1930s

Charlotte Fay Helphenstine, 1940s

Cressa Helphenstine, 1930s

Donald Helphenstine, 1940s

Edward Helphenstine, 1930s

Everett Helphenstine, 1930s

Geneva Helphenstine, 1930s

Georgia Helphenstine, 1930s

Louise Helphenstine, 1930s

Sherley Helphenstine, 1940s, 1953

Virgil Helphenstine, 1920s

Frances Helphinstine, 1940s, 1955

Ginny Helphinstine, 1950s

Robert Lee Helphinstine, 1920s, 1930s

Freddie Henderson, 1930s

James Franklin Henson, 1950s

Virgin Herbert, 1930s

Archie Clyde Hickerson, 1930s

Charles Hickerson, 1899

Clarence Hickerson, 1898

Paul Hifler, 1911, 1916

Elmond Hill, 1898

Orville Hill, 1898

Ida Hines, 1898

John Hines, 1898

Ollie Hines, 1898

Robert P. Hines, 1898

Bruce Hinton, 1898

Callie Hinton, 1898

Frank Owen Hinton, 1922

Ina E. Hinton, 1898

John Hinton, 1922

Lonnie Hinton, 1898

Mary Hinton, 1898

Nellie Hinton, 1898

Ollie Hinton, 1898

Robert Hinton, 1898

Rosa Hinton, 1898

Ruby Hinton, 1922

Thelma Hinton, 1920s

Clyde Hitch, 1911

Gerald Holbrook, 1940s

Ramona Holbrook, 1940s

Johnny Howard, 1950s
Tommy Howard, 1950s
Irene Howell, 1930s, 1940s
Samuel Howell, 1930s, 1940s
Blanche A. Huff, 1903
John Huff, 1916, 1922
Lettie Huff, 1907
Buford Hughes, 1930s
Clayton Hughes, 1930s
Eunice Hughes, 1898
Hazel Hughes, 1930s
Hubert Hughes, 1930s
Minnie Hughes, 1903
Alsa Humphries, 1922
Anna Humphries, 1922
Luther Humphries, 1922
Maude B. Humphries, 1920s
Zetta Humphries, 1922
Billie Joe Hunt, 1940s
Jackie Hunt, 1950s
John C. Hunt, 1940s
Samuel Thomas Hunt, 1940s
Wanda Marie Hunt, 1940s
Anna Ruby Hunter, 1920s
Elmae Hill Hunter, 1911
Hinton Hunter, 1911
Lulie Hunter, 1898
Morgan Hunter, 1898
Nellie Hunter, 1898
Ralph Hunter, 1911
Alice Hurst, 1899
Anna Barbara Hurst, 1930s
Arthur Hurst, 1911
Bessie Hurst, 1911
Clarence Hurst, 1911, 1916
Dudley Hurst, 1899

Herbert Garr Hurst, 1920s
Howard Hurst, 1898
Lula W. Hurst, 1898
Lydie Hurst, 1911
Nellie Hurst, 1911, 1916
Nelson Hurst, 1899
Rhoda Hurst, 1898
Robert Hurst, 1898
Roy Hurst, 1898
Terry Hurst, 1940s
Verna Hurst, 1911
Wilbur Hurst, 1920s
Charles E. Ingram, 1911
Donna Ingram, 1940s
Flora Sue Ingram, 1930s
James Ingram, 1930s
Kinsay Ingram, 1911
Maude Ingram, 1911
Patty Ingram, 1940s
Ronald Ingram, 1940s
Ruth Ann Ingram, 1930s
Sidney Ingram, 1911
Tom Ingram, 1930s
Vina I. Ingram, 1911
William Ingram, 1930s
Beulah Insko, 1940s
Ida Mae Insko, 1940s
Olive Ann Insko, 1940s
Elza Isom, 1950s
Irene Isom, 1950s
Wanda Lou Isom, 1950s
Omer Jackson, 1898
Robert Jackson, 1898
Agatha James, 1911, 1916
Anna Bell James, 1920s
Annie James, 1903

Armor James, 1898
Arthur James, 1898
Bertha James, 1898
Bessie James, 1898
Boswell James, 1911
Clarence James, 1911
Ethel James, 1898
Fannie James, 1898
Gerald James, 1950s
Girtha James, 1898
Gituda James, 1911
Hittum James, 1898
Iva James, 1898
Jesse James, 1930s
Judy James, 1959
Lana C. James, 1907
Lanman James, 1911
Larry James, 1922
Laura James, 1903
Lela James, 1911, 1916
Lida B. James, 1907
Linda James, 1959
Lucy James, 1911
Marilyn Deloris James, 1950s
Millard James, 1898
Morris Lee James, 1930s
Omar James, 1898
Ora James, 1898
Osel James, 1911
Ottn James, 1898
Pauline James, 1930s
Pearl James, 1911
Raymond James, 1920s
Roscoe James, 1898
Thelma James, 1930s
Thomas James, 1903

William R. James, 1903
JoAnn Jennings, 1940s
Betty Jesse, 1940s
Esther Jesse, 1920s
Floyd Jesse, 1930s
Howard Jesse, 1930s
Peggy Joy Jesse, 1940s
Raymond Jesse, 1930s
Billy Jett, 1950s
Johnny Jett, 1950s
Charles Edward Johnson, 1947
Clarence Ernie Johnson, 1950s
Donovan Johnson, 1950s
Hildreth Johnson, 1920s
Laura B. Johnson, 1920s
Nona Mae Johnson, 1940s
Preston Johnson, 1930s
Stella Johnson, 1930s
Yvonne Johnson, 1950s
Anna Jones, 1930s
Anna Florence Jones, 1940s, 1957
Betty (Elizabeth Carolyn) Jones, 1950s
Billy Jones, 1940s, 1956
Beatrice Jones, 1916
Clarence Jones, 1940s
Curtis Jones, 1920s
Donald Jones, 1940s
Dorothy Jones, 1930s
Edmund Jones, 1930s
Edward Jones, 1920s
Emma Jones, 1916, 1922
Eugene Jones, 1940s
George Jones, 1930s
H. Walter Jones, 1899
Hazel Jones, 1920s
Hazel Ruth Jones, 1920s

Helen Jones, 1922
Henry Jones, 1920s
Irvin Samuel Jones, 1940s
James Jones, 1920s
James Owen Jones, 1930s
James P. Jones, 1940s, 1954
John Robert Jones, 1950s
Lucy Jones, 1916
Mabel Jean Jones, 1950s
Mary Katherine Jones, 1952
Oscil Jones, 1911
Raymond Jones, 1930s
Theatrice Jones, 1922
Verna Jones, 1911, 1916
William Hixson Jones, 1940s
Barton Jordan, 1909
Blanche Jordan, 1909
Dow Jordan, 1898
Gertrude Jordan, 1898
Lillie Jordan, 1909, 1950s
Louis Jordan, 1898
Lulin Jordan, 1898
Mage Jordan, 1898
Omar Jordan, 1898, 1950s
Otis Jordan, 1898
Willie D. Jordan, 1916
Woodrow Jordan, 1920s
Anita Keaton, 1960s
Bonnie Keaton, 1940s
Clifford Keaton, 1950s
Danny Keaton, 1950s
Emma Keaton, 1953
Johnny Keaton, 1940s
Joy Ann Keaton, 1955
Mary Jane Keaton, 1940s
Roger Keaton, 1958

Arthur Kirk, 1916
Charles Kirk, 1898
Edna Olive Kirk, 1940s, 1956
Harlan Kirk, 1916
Irene Kirk, 1916, 1922
James Kirk Jr., 1930s, 1940s
Jennie Kirk, 1916
Leona Kirk, 1903
Maiy Kirk, 1903
Matilda Kirk, 1907
Nellie Kirk, 1940s
Norma Jean Kirk, 1930s, 1940s
Ramona Kirk, 1930s
Sudie Kirk, 1916
William Wayne Kirk, 1940s, 1955
Emma H. Knapp, 1899
Estella Knapp, 1903
Eva L. Knapp, 1899
Irvin H. Knapp, 1899
Millie Knapp, 1899
Nellie Knapp, 1903
Rulla Knapp, 1899
Stella Knapp, 1899
Arthur R. Kufe, 1911
Luna A. Kufe, 1911
Matilda S. Kufe, 1911
Nora H. Kufe, 1911
Lena P. Kuhus, 1911
Ray Lee Kuhus, 1911
Duane Landreth, 1930s
Garnett Landreth, 1930s
Ruth Landreth, 1920s
Wayne Landreth, 1930s
May Lawrence, 1911
Alonzo Leaverball, 1898
David Lee, 1950s

Thelma Jean Lee, 1950s
Anna Myrl Lewis, 1940s
Callie Lewis, 1940s
Charles Allen Lewis, 1940s
Clell Lewis, 1940s
Dewey Lewis, 1940s
Dottie Lewis, 1940s
Fidelia Lewis, 1940s
Frances Lewis, 1940s
Herman Lewis, 1940s
Jimmy Lewis, 1940s
John Lewis, 1940s
Madeline Lewis, 1950s
Marie Lewis, 1947
Mao Magdeline Lewis, 1940s
Norman Lewis, 1940s
Sadie Lewis, 1940s
Alma Little, 1950s
Delma Little, 1950s
Hershell Little, 1930s
Lester Little, 1930s
Louise Little, 1940s
Mary Rachel Little, 1950s
William Little, 1930s
Bernice Littleton, 1930s
Birdie (Alberta) Littleton, 1951
Charles Littleton, 1899
Chester Littleton, 1911
Clifford Eugene Littleton, 1957
Emma Maude Littleton, 1911, 1916
Emory Littleton, 1932
Frank Owen Littleton, 1954
George Littleton, 1951
Harley Littleton, 1911
Imogene Littleton, 1959
James Thomas Littleton, 1940s

Josephine Littleton, 1930s
Larry Littleton, 1950s
Lula Littleton, 1911
Ronnie Littleton, 1950s
Thelma Faye Littleton, 1940s
Wanda Littleton, 1940s
Willie Gene Littleton, 1959
James Littleton, 1956
Josephine Littleton,
Thelma Littleton, 1955
Wanda Littleton, 1954
John Logan, 1920s
Aldon Long, 1930s
Douglas Long, 1930s
Cecil Edford Luman, 1940s
Clifton Lee Luman, 1940s
Mary Elizabeth Luman, 1930s
Andrew Manning, 1930s
Anna Manning, 1898
Berry Manning, 1920s
Blandena Manning, 1930s
Deloris Manning, 1930s
Emma Manning, 1898
Frazee Manning, 1930s
Gleanor Manning, 1898
Joe Manning, 1930s
Kathleen Manning, 1930s
Minnie Manning, 1898
Pearl Manning, 1920s
Plummer Manning, 1920s
Randall Manning, 1920s
Raymond Manning, 1930s
Robert Manning, 1920s
Rosa Manning, 1898
Woodrow Manning, 1920s
Chester Marshall, 1930s

Dell Marshall, 1916
Dewey Marshall Jr., 1930s
Estill Marshall, 1930s
Hazel Marshall, 1930s
John Marshall, 1916
Robert Marshall, 1930s, 1940s
Thelma Marshall, 1930s
Daugherty Mathews, 1898
Jennie Mathews, 1898
Mammie Mathews, 1898
Marius E. Mathison, 1950s
Mary Ellen Mathison, 1950s
Oscar Mathison, 1950s
Alma Mattox, 1916, 1922
Bobby Mattox, 1960s
Calvin Mattox, 1920s
Danny Mattox, 1950s
Edna Carolyn Mattox, 1950s
Ella Mattox, 1911, 1916
Geniere Mattox, 1930s
George Mattox, 1922
George Mattox, 1940s, 1955
Glen Mattox, 1920s
Hilda Mattox, 1930s
John Acie Mattox, 1960s
John Mattox, 1922
Johnnie Mattox, 1916
Julia Mattox, 1922
Larry Lee Mattox, 1950s
Lee Mattox, 1911
Lillian Mattox, 1954
Lily Mattox, 1930s
Mitchell Mattox, 1920s
Nancy Mattox, 1950s
Ransom Mattox, 1920s
Robert Mattox, 1950s

Robert Price Mattox, 1922
Stanley Paul Mattox, 1950s
Sylvia Elaine Mattox, 1950s
Tootsie (Violet) Mattox, 1940s
Violet Mattox, 1916, 1922
Wanda Mattox, 1940s, 1957
Clark Maxey, 1899
Kenneth McCall, 1930s
Robert McCane, 1930s
Carl McClure, 1916
David McClure, 1911, 1916
Charles McClurg, 1950s
Hilda McClurg, 1950s
Lloyd McClurg, 1950s
Rilda McClurg, 1950s
Roy Earl McClurg, 1950s
John McCormick, 1930s
Mary McCormick, 1940s
Raymond W. McCormick, 1940s
Roberta McCormick, 1940s
Samuel McCormick, 1930s
Lawrence McFadden, 1920s
Nellie McIntire, 1916
Julia J. McIntyre, 1920s
Anna Mary McKee, 1933
Beulah McKee, 1940s
Carol Jean McKee, 1940s
Chastine McKee, 1920s
Donna Jean McKee, 1950s
Dorothy McKee, 1930s
Edgar McKee, 1930s
Elwood McKee, 1930s
Ernestine McKee, 1930s
Harold McKee, 1930s
Iolene McKee, 1930s
J. Stewart McKee, 1950s

Johnny Charles (J.C.) McKee, 1940s, 1956
Joseph McKee, Jr., 1930s
Joyce Ann McKee, 1950s
Lester McKee, 1916
Lola McKee, 1916
Lucille McKee, 1916
Mary Jeanette McKee, 1930s
May McKee, 1916
Mildred McKee, 1940s
Orville McKee, 1930s
Pauletta McKee, 1950s
Peter Acres McKee, 1950s
Roy McKee, 1930s
Stewart McKee, 1922
Sudie Ellen McKee, 1950s
Theodosia McKee, 1930s
William Harold McKee, 1950s
Ruby McLain, 1920s
Ethel McRoberts, 1916
Flora McRoberts, 1933
James McRoberts, 1916
Mary McRoberts, 1898
Murdock McRoberts, 1930s
Raymond Lee McRoberts, 1950s
Russell McRoberts, 1916
Samuel McRoberts, 1933
Willie McRoberts, 1920s, 1930s
James Lacey Meade, 1940s, 1956
Joyce Meade, 1950s
Kathy Meade, 1950s
Leonard Meade, 1950s
Lillian Meade, 1940s
Gertrude Meyers, 1930s
James Meyers, 1930s
Cecil Miller, 1930s

Delmar Miller, 1930s
Roger Miller, 1930s
Josephine Million, 1940s
Ruth Million, 1940s
Seth Junior Mitchell, 1920s
(Anna) Jewell Moore, 1940s
Betty Jean Moore, 1940s
Eugene Moore, 1930s
Fay Moore, 1930s
Goldia Moore, 1930s
Lucy Lucille Moore, 1930s, 1940s
Mamie Moore, 1930s
Martha Carolyn Moore, 1940s
McKinley Moore, 1930s
Ray Moore, 1940s
Shirley Ann Taylor Moore, 1950s
Sterling Moore, 1930s
Wesley Moore, 1940s
William, Jr. Moore, 1930s
Eliza Maude Morrison, 1899
Fiom Morrison, 1916
Frankie Morrison, 1899
Hyter Morrison, 1911
Lida Morrison, 1899
Mabel Morrison, 1922
Martha Lyons Morrison, 1911
Mary L. Morrison, 1899
Nellie Steele Morrison, 1911
Charles Morton, 1903
Lewis P. Morton, 1911
Ballard Mulwee Jr., 1950s
Allie Frances Muse, 1940s
Alma Muse, 1911
Anna Muse, 1911
Archie Muse, 1950s
Artincie Muse, 1930s

Edward Muse, 1930s
Harold Muse, 1940s
Henry Dallas Muse, 1950s
Hobert Muse, 1950s
Jeanette Muse, 1950s
Jennie Mae Muse, 1950s
John Robert Muse, 1950s
Joyce Dean Muse, 1940s
Kenneth Muse, 1930s
Orville Muse, 1940s
Owen Muse, 1922
Robert Muse, 1920s
Ruth Muse, 1932
Sudie Mae Muse, 1930s
Thomas Muse, 1940s, 1950s
Vernice Muse, 1950s
Cecil Newdigate, 1916
Cecial Newdigate, 1922
Charles Newdigate, 1920s
Chester Newdigate, 1916
Estill Newdigate, 1920s
Hemlor Neudigate, 1922
Jessie Newdigate, 1916
Josephine Newdigate, 1916, 1922
Stella Newdigate, 1916
Sudie Neudigate, 1922
Frank Oney Jr., 1930s
Geneva Oney, 1930s
Phillip Oney, 1933
Anna Laura Owens, 1930s
Buford Owens, 1950s
David Owens, 1920s
Floyd Owens, 1950s
Howard Owens, 1950s
Jack Cooper Owens, 1930s
James Owens, 1950s

Lula Margaret Owens, 1930s
Myrtle Owens, 1950s
Roger Owens, 1950s
Alvin Parker, 1930s
Early A. Parker, 1898
Green Parker, 1898
Iva Parker, 1898
John S. Parker, 1898
Marietta Parker, 1950s
Sandra Parker, 1950s
Steley M. Parker, 1898
Timothy Parker, 1950s
Marshall Parks, 1898
Janie Pence, 1950s
Clarence Perkins, 1920s
Eddie Perkins, 1950s
Edna Perkins, 1920s
Myrtle Perkins, 1950s
Phyllis Perkins, 1950s
Stella Perkins, 1920s
Faye Peyton, 1950s
Nathan Peyton, 1950s
Bessie Planck, 1920s
Ann Plummer, 1899
Aussiee Plummer, 1916
Carl Plummer, 1911, 1916
Clyde R. Plummer, 1940s, 1957
Crystal Plummer, 1930s
Delbert Plummer, 1920s
Donnie Plummer, 1907
Dorothy Plummer, 1940s
Edith Plummer, 1950s
Edna Plummer, 1940s
Edward Plummer, 1940s, 1954
Elbert Plummer, 1899
Elloise Elaine Plummer, 1950s

Ellis Plummer, 1940s

Elsie Plummer, 1940s

Emerson Plummer, 1950s

Erlene Plummer, 1940s, 1957

Ernest Plummer, 1916

Forest Plummer, 1922

Freda Plummer, 1940s

Helen Plummer, 1922

Helen Plummer, 1940s, 1957

Hiriam Plummer, 1899

Hobert Plummer, 1916

Ida Plummer, 1940s

Jewell Plummer, 1911, 1916

Joseph Plummer, 1922

Julie Plummer, 1898, 1950s

Kathleen Plummer, 1959

Lester Plummer, 1911, 1916

Lula Plummer, 1916

Lucie Plummer, 1898

Lutie Plummer, 1922

Margaret Plummer, 1950s

Marshall Plummer, 1899

Maude Plummer, 1940s

Minnie Plummer, 1898

Omer S. Plummer, 1899

Patsy Plummer, 1950s

Ralph Plummer, 1950s

Ransom Plummer, 1916

Robert Plummer, 1899, 1922

Robert Plummer, 1940s, 1957

Roy Plummer, 1916

Roy Plummer, 1950s

Russell Plummer, 1922

Ruth Plummer, 1920s

Thomas Plummer, 1950s

Virginia Plummer, 1940s

William Plummer, 1907

Donnie Glenn Porter, 1940s, 1956

Jerry Lee Porter, 1950s

Jesse Porter, 1920s

Larry Porter, 1960s

Nellie P. Porter, 1920s

Ruth Ann Porter, 1960s

Dorothy Potter, 1930s

Genevive Potter, 1930s

Geraldine Potter, 1930s

James Presley, 1940s

Jeanetta Presley, 1940s

Woodrow Presley, 1940s

Anna Lee Preston, 1947

Arthur Preston, 1930s

Billy Gene Preston, 1940s

Donald Preston, 1940s

Dorothy Preston, 1930s

Jesse Thomas Preston, 1930s, 1940s

Ruby Anita Preston, 1940s

Mittie Price, 1930s

Hazel Prince, 1920s

Mildred Prince, 1920s

Wana Prince, 1920s

William Prince, 1920s

Elihn J. Pugh, 1911

Jane Pugh, 1907

Luther Pugh, 1898

Pearl Pugh, 1907

Susan Pugh, 1911

William Pugh, 1911

Clyde Purcell, 1930s

Rosa Purcell, 1930s

Bessie Reed, 1958

Herbert Reed, 1950s

Kenneth Reed, 1940s, 1954

Marne Reed, 1911
Martha Ann Reed, 1950s
Mary Reed, 1911
Orville Reed, 1940s
Walter Reed, 1956
Charles Reeves, 1930s, 1940s
Clifford Reeves, 1911, 1916
Clyde Reeves, 1922
Darnald Reeves, 1922
Dorothy Reeves, 1950s
Earl Reeves, 1930s
Emerson Reeves, 1930s
Ernie Reeves, 1950s
Evan Reeves, 1930s
Evelyn Reeves, 1940s
Glenn D. Reeves, 1916
Gobel Reeves, 1940s
Helen Reeves, 1930s
Jackie Ray Reeves, 1950s
James Reeves, 1950s
Jimmy Reeves, 1950s
Kelly Reeves, 1911, 1916
Kelly Bruce Reeves, 1957
Larry Reeves, 1950s
Leona Reeves, 1922
Marvin Reeves, 1930s
Mary Estil Reeves, 1940s
Nella Reeves, 1911, 1916
Roy Reeves, 1930s
Sammy Reeves, 1950s
Thomas Reeves, 1930s
Tommy Reeves, 1950s
Verna Reeves, 1916, 1922
Wayne Reeves, 1940s
William Reeves Jr., 1930s
Wilson Reeves, 1930s

Woodrow Reeves, 1920s
Woodie Reeves, 1950s
Bennie Richmond, 1940s
Bill Richmond, 1958
Bobby Richmond, 1958
Charles Richmond, 1940s
Donald Richmond, 1957
Jimmy Richmond, 1950s
Kenneth Richmond, 1950s
Mabel Richmond, 1955
Paul Richmond, 1950s
Ronald Wayne Richmond, 1959
Shirley Richmond, 1959
William Richmond, 1950s
Donna Rickert, 1899
George Rickert, 1907
Hattie Rickert, 1907
Lela Rickert, 1899
Mattie Rickert, 1899
Ona Rickert, 1899
Stella Lee Rickert, 1899
William Rickert, 1899
Lloyd Riddle, 1950s
Billie Rigdon, 1940s
Earl Rigdon, 1940s
Edith Rigdon, 1930s
Imogene Rigdon, 1930s
Leonard Rigdon, 1940s
Omar Rigdon, 1940s
Walker Rigdon, 1930s
Ernest Riickert, 1920s
LeRoy Riickert, 1920s
Roy Riickert, 1920s
Ruby Riickert, 1930s
Taft Riickert, 1920s
Addie M. Roberts, 1930s

Anne Mae Roberts, 1920s
Brenda Roberts, 1950s
Elnora Roberts, 1930s
Eugene Roberts, 1930s, 1940s
James Roberts, 1930s
Jimmy Roberts, 1950s
Joe Roberts, 1950s
Kenneth Roberts, 1950s
Larry Roberts, 1950s
Leo Roberts, 1920s
Patsy Carolyn Roberts, 1950s
Rhoda Roberts, 1930s
Robert M. Roberts, 1930s, 1940s
Russell Roberts, 1920s
Wilma Roberts, 1950s
Gloria Robinson, 1950s
James Lloyd Rogers, 1940s, 1956
Christine Roseberry, 1940s
Betty Jewell Ross, 1940s
Frances Ross, 1940s
Kenneth Rourk, 1920s
Charles Routt, 1950s
George Routt, 1950s
Arnold Royse Jr., 1920s
Erma L. Royse, 1903
Estella Royse, 1899
Estill Royse, 1930s
Frances Royse, 1916
George Royse, 1899
Jacqueline Royse, 1930s
Lena Royse, 1911, 1916
Lula Royse, 1916
Mildred Royse, 1933
Omer F. Royse, 1903
Ray S. Royse, 1909
Russell Royse, 1916

Ruth M. Royse, 1903
Stanley Royse, 1920s
Suddith Royse, 1911
Willie Samuels, 1898
Elmer O. Sanders, 1911
Beulah Saunders, 1930s
Mary Frances Saunders, 1933
Willard Saunders, 1930s
Arthur Sexton, 1940s
Clara Frances Sexton, 1930s
Darwin Sexton, 1920s
Holly Sexton, 1930s
James W. Sexton, 1920s
Jewell Sexton, 1920s
Alice Shepherd, 1899
Ames Shepherd, 1899
Bess Shepherd, 1899
Ethel Shepherd, 1899
Hittum Shepherd, 1899
A. L. Shoemaker, 1909
John Skeen, 1898
Bobby Sloas, 1940s, 1956
Cathy Sloas, 1950s
Donnie Sloas, 1940s
Elizabeth Frances Sloas, 1950s
Glennis Sloas, 1940s
Jeri Lynn Sloas, 1950s
Justine Sloas, 1950s
Louella Sloas, 1950s
Beatrice Sluss, 1955
Ronald Sluss, 1958
Wilford Sluss, 1956
Christine Smedley, 1940s
Leslie Smedley, 1940s
Virginia Faye Smedley, 1940s
Wendell Smedley, 1940s

Bonnie Sue Smith, 1950s
Carolyn Sue Smith, 1940s, 1950s
Earl Dean Smith, 1950s
Mary Ann Smith, 1930s
Nancy Jo Ann Smith, 1940s, 1950s
Woodrow Smith, 1930s
Ruby Lee Smitson, 1930s
Agnes Snapp, 1930s
Emma Snapp, 1930s
Reynolds Snapp, 1930s
Matilda Sorrell, 1911
Bernice Sparks, 1930s
Christine Sparks, 1930s
Clyde Sparks, 1930s
Harold P. Sparks, 1920s
Donald Spencer, 1950s
Noah Spencer Jr., 1950s
Roger Spencer, 1950s
Dorothy Stacy, 1920s
Flora Stacy, 1920s
Leona Stacy, 1920s
Opal Stacy, 1920s
Raymond Stacy, 1920s
William Stacy, 1920s
Alma Staggs, 1911, 1916
Archie Staggs, 1898
Axch Staggs, 1911
Bussel Staggs, 1898
Claude Staggs, 1911
Cora Staggs, 1898
Darcos Staggs, 1911
David Staggs, 1898
Delbert Staggs, 1920s
Dorean Staggs, 1916
Elizabeth Staggs, 1930s
Everett Staggs, 1911, 1916

Frances Staggs, 1916, 1922
Frank Staggs, 1898
Geraldine Staggs, 1940s
Harvey Staggs, 1911
Harry Staggs, 1916
Harvey Staggs, 1911
Hattie Staggs, 1898
Hord Staggs, 1898
Howard Staggs, 1911
Irene Staggs, 1898, 1911
Jessie Staggs, 1898
John Lewis Staggs, 1922
Joseph Staggs, 1911
Koware Staggs, 1916
Laura Staggs, 1898
Lutie Staggs, 1907
Mamie Staggs, 1911, 1916
Marie Staggs, 1916
Marvin Staggs, 1898
Mertie Staggs, 1911
Nannie Staggs, 1930s
Norman Staggs, 1940s
Ollie Staggs, 1898
Pearl Staggs, 1898
Russell Staggs, 1903
Stewart Staggs, 1898
Tulley Staggs, 1898
Walter Staggs, 1898, 1911
Ward Staggs, 1898
Wendell Staggs, 1940s (left in third grade, returned in fifth)
William Staggs, 1898
Wilson Staggs, 1930s
Wood Staggs, 1916, 1922
Alice Stamper, 1950s
Amos Stanfield, 1930s

Daniel Stanfield, 1930s
Frances Stanfield, 1930s
Melvin Stanfield, 1930s
Bruce P. Stanter, 1911
Claude M. Stanter, 1911
Lois Stephens, 1930s
Lonnie Ronald Stephens, 1940s
Marie Stephens, 1950s
Ruth Stephens, 1950s
Jeraldine Stevens, 1950s
John Stevens, 1950s
Lurina Stevens, 1950s
Pearl Story, 1899
Dorothy Strode, 1930s
Diane Sue Swim, 1957
Emerson Swim, 1920s
Larry Swim, 1950s
Eula Tackett, 1940s
Lowell Tackett, 1940s
Raymond Talley, 1940s
Bobby Taylor, 1954
Clarence Lee Taylor, 1940s
Edward Taylor, 1930s
Ethel Marie Taylor, 1940s
Faustain Taylor, 1930s
(Charlene) Faye Taylor, 1940s
Horace Franklin Taylor, 1940s
Jesse Leon Taylor, 1950s
Lawrence Taylor, 1930s
Luella Taylor, 1930s
Mildred Taylor, 1930s
Peggy Taylor, 1950s
Sherley Taylor, 1940s, 1957
Adrian Thacker, 1940s
Annie Thacker, 1898
Beverly Thacker, 1950s

Denzil Thacker, 1898
Elsie Thacker, 1922
Frank Thacker, 1898
Helen Thacker, 1940s
Ida Thacker, 1940s
Iva Thacker, 1940s
Jeanette Thacker, 1898
Kenneth Thacker, 1930s
Lara Thacker, 1922
Monte Thacker, 1950s
Ottie Thacker, 1922
Patsy Thacker, 1950s
Pauline Thacker, 1950s
Thomas Thacker, 1930s
Wilma Thacker, 1950s
Doris Jean Thomas, 1940s
Leanna Thomas, 1940s
Louranie Thomas, 1940s
William Thomas, 1940s
Evert Thompson, 1898
Jessie Thompson, 1898
Luther Thompson, 1911
Minnie Thompson, 1916
Lizzie Tincher, 1898
Mahala Tincher, 1898
Maurice Todd, 1920s
Wilma Todd, 1920s
J.C. Tolliver Jr., 1930s
Richard Tranbarger, 1950s
Vickie Tranbarger, 1950s
Catherine Turner, 1930s
Mary Jewell Underwood, 1940s
Paul Underwood, 1930s
Velma Underwood, 1930s
Gary Mackel Vance, 1950s
Faris Viars, 1940s, 1956

George Jr. Viars, 1940s, 1956

Raymond Viars, 1940s, 1958

Ida E. Vice, 1940s

Robert C. Vice Jr., 1940s

Herbert Virgin, 1930s

Ann Vise, 1899

Charles Vise, 1920s

Elizabeth Vise, 1920s

Eula Vise, 1920s

Glenn Vise, 1922

Lois Vise, 1922

Margetta Vise, 1930s

Ola Vise, 1899

Omer Vise, 1899

Opal Ruth Vise, 1920s

Oral G. Vise, 1920s

Rola Vise, 1899

Tullie Vise, 1899

Wendel Vise, 1920s

Alice Waddle, 1899

Clifford Waddle, 1899

LaVada Waddle, 1899

Major R. Waddle, 1899

Addie Wagoner, 1950s

Bernice Wagoner, 1930s

Betty Jo Wagoner, 1930s

Beulah Wagoner, 1930s

Billie Scott Wagoner, 1950s

Charles Wagoner, 1930s

Dan Wagoner, 1922

Dixie Wagoner, 1922

Ivis Wagoner, 1950s

Libby (Elizabeth) Wagoner, 1940s, 1953

Mary Ethel Wagoner, 1950s

Mona Wagoner, 1920s

Morrison Wagoner, 1922

Nina Lewis Wagoner, 1930s

Pauline Wagoner, 1950s

Sam Wagoner, 1922

Will Isom Wagoner, 1930s

Kenneth Ray Walker, 1950s

Cecil Ray Wallace, 1940s, 1950s

Clayton Wallace, 1940s, 1950s

Frances Wallace, 1940s, 1950s

Johnny Wallace, 1940s, 1950s

Olive Wallace, 1950s

Charles Waltz, 1898

Robert Waltz, 1898

Anna Watson, 1950s

Freda Watson, 1920s

Wayne Watson, 1950s

Willard Watson, 1920s

Ben Welch, 1898

Burt (Albert) Welch, 1898

John Welch, 1898

Matilda Welch, 1898

Mary Welch, 1903

Morton Welch, 1898

Rachel Welch, 1898

Sarah Welch, 1898

William Welch, 1898

Ceciel Wells, 1930s

Daniel Wentz, 1950s

Junior Whaley, 1930s

Alvin Whisman, 1920s

Annie Bessie Whisman, 1903

Brooks Whisman, 1920s

Lettie Whisman, 1920s

Roy Whisman, 1920s

Tom Whisman, 1930s

Faye White, 1930s

Bruce Whitton, 1930s

Charles T. Whitton, 1930s
Earnest C. Whitton, 1930s
Irvin Lee Whitton, 1930s
Mary Whitton, 1930s
Tracy Wilburn, 1950s
Ben Williams, 1898
Danny Williams, 1950s
Dora Williams, 1899
Eleanor Williams, 1950s
Flora Williams, 1898
Gale Williams, 1930s
George Williams, 1899
Golda Williams, 1907
Hale Williams, 1940s
Ida Williams, 1898
Jack Williams, 1940s
James Oscar Williams, 1950s
James Ray Williams, 1950s
Loretta J. Williams, 1950s
Lula Williams, 1907
Millie Williams, 1898
Nancy Carol Williams, 1950s
Nora Williams, 1899
Phyllis Williams, 1950s
Roland Wayne Williams, 1940s
Shila Williams, 1898
Shirley Williams, 1950s
Stella Williams, 1898
Terry Lee Williams, 1950s
Thomas Williams, 1898
Wilder Williams, 1940s
Austin Earl Wilson, 1930s
Bonnie Wilson, 1940s
Charles Thomas Wilson, 1940s
Donnie Wilson, 1940s
Earl Jr. Wilson, 1940s

Helen Wilson, 1920s
Julia Pearl Wilson, 1940s
Lillian Wilson, 1930s
Luellen Wilson, 1920s
Mildred Wilson, 1920s
Robert Wilson, 1920s
Roy Wilson, 1920s
E. G. Woosley Jr., 1930s
Helen Louise Woosley, 1930s
Thelma Woosley, 1930s
Woodford Woosley, 1930s
Chelsa Wright, 1940s
Donnie Wright, 1940s
Jeanette Wright, 1940s
Thomas Yantis, 1898
Abby Yazell, 1903
Ally Jane Yazell, 1899
Charley Yazell, 1898
Clarence Yazell, 1911, 1916
Curtis Yazell, 1899
Dudley Yazell, 1916
Edna Yazell, 1909
Ernest Yazell, 1911, 1916
Harold Yazell, 1911, 1916
Hilda Yazell, 1920s
James T. Yazell, 1899
John Samuel Yazell, 1899
Joseph M. Yazell, 1899
Leonard Yazell, 1909
Leshe Yazell, 1911
Leslie Yazell, 1898
Lethia Yazell, 1898
Lewis Yazell, 1940s
Lina Yazell, 1911
Louise Yazell, 1940s, 1954
Luther Yazell, 1898, 1911

Lutie Yazell, 1898
Mabel Yazell, 1916
Melvin Yazell, 1916
Melvina Yazell, 1903
Minnie Yazell, 1899
Myrtle Yazell, 1916
Riley Yazell, 1907
Roy Yazell, 1911, 1916
Ruby Yazell, 1911
Ruth Garr Yazell, 1920s
Vera Yazell, 1911, 1916

William Yazell, 1899
Charles York, 1930s
Norma York, 1930s
Angillee Zornes, 1940s
Ethel Zornes, 1920s
Ithel Zornes, 1920s
Muriel Zornes, 1920s
Nannie Zornes, 1922
Noah Zornes, 1922
Willard Zornes, 1920s

Goddard School Bibliography

A letter to Mrs. Garr Hurst from the late Mrs. Maude M. Helphinstine.
Atlas of Bath and Fleming County. Kentucky. D. J. Lake and Company, 1884, p. 59.

Baldwin, Yuvonne Honeycutt. *Coral Wilson Stewart and Kentucky's Moonlight Schools: Fighting for Literacy in America.* Lexington, Kentucky: University Press of Kentucky, 2006, pp. 44, 51.

Barker, Garry. *Humor Is as Humor Does.* Ashland, Kentucky: Jesse Stuart Foundation, pp. 12, 126.

Columbia, James R. *Civil War Stories from the Buffalo Trace.* Northeastern Kentucky Genealogical Research Services, 2015, pp. 121, 195, 243, 268.

Cotterill, Robert. *History of Fleming County. Kentucky: The First One-Hundred Years. 1780 to 1880.* p. 192, 243 to 263, 335. (Fleming County Public Library)

Greenup, Christopher. *Executive Journal. 1804 to 1808.* MSS, in possession of Kentucky State Historical Society, Frankfort, Kentucky.

Gulliford, Andrew. *America's Country Schools.* National Trust for Historic Preservation, 1984, p. 88.

Helphinstine, Maude Morrison. "Along the Old Buffalo Trail." Goddard, Kentucky: c Frances Helphinstine and Virginia Helphinstine Reeves.

Jenchs. and Riesman. D. *The Academic Revolution.* Garden City, New York: Doubleday, 1968.

Journal of the Senate of the Commonwealth of Kentucky 1816. Frankfort: Gerard and Kendall, 1816, pp. 18 to 19.

Lathrop, J.M. and J.H. Summers. Actual Surveys. Published by D.J. Lake & Company. Assistants: H.C. Mead, E.W. Dison and W. R. Wands. General Office: 27 South Sixth Street, Philadelphia, PA, 1884.

Lewis, Alvin. *History of Higher Education in Kentucky.* Washington, 1899, p. 31.

Mann, Horace. *Twelfth Annual Report.* New York: Dutton and Wentworth, 1849, p. 107.

Rawlings, James. "History of Mason County, Kentucky Schools." Maysville, Kentucky, unpublished, p.2. (Available at Kentucky Gateway Museum Center, Maysville, Kentucky.)

Ray, M.D., Joseph. *Intellectual Arithmetic by Induction and Analysis.* Cincinnati: Sargent, Wilson, & Hinkle, 1860, pp. 7 to 8.

Report of the Superintendent of Public Instruction of the State of Kentucky for Two Scholastic Years ended June 30, 1897. Louisville: George F. Felter Printing Company, 1897, p. 351.

Web

"Country Life Commission." Standford.edu./group/rural/West

National Weather Service. "The Great Appalachian Storm of 1950," weather.gov/jkl/events

Northcott, Rev. H.C. *Early History of Hillsboro,* http://KyKinfolk. org.Fleming. pgs. 12, 15.

P.L. 690, 83rd Congress, August 28, 1954,68 Stat, 900.; www.fns. usda.gov/nslp/history 11

"Sacred Harp Movement," Wikipedia.org

www.huffpost.com/entry/1912-eighth-grade-exam

www.stanford.edu/group/rural west

Newspapers:

Dickey, J.J. "Fleming County History." *The Fleming Gazette,* February 24, 1931.

"Goddard School Principal Assaulted by Two Men in School Yard Wednesday." *Flemingsburg Times Democrat.* February 4, 1954.

"Project Receives Approval." *Fleming Gazette.* December 9, 1936, No. 6.

Spradling, Ruby Hinton. "Letter to the Editor." *Flemingsburg Times Democrat.*

Story, Ben H., Sr., "Story's Stories." *Flemingsburg Times Democrat.* September 18, 1969; March 12, 1970.

Leaflet:

4-H 1008 Booklet, Lexington, Kentucky: University of Kentucky, 1955.

Fleming County, Kentucky Court Records:

Deed Book U, p. 24.
Fleming County Court Order Book G, pp. 83 to 85.
Fleming County Settlement Book 4, p. 307.

Fleming County School Records:

School Board Minutes 1899 to 1960
School Board Financial Ledgers 1900 to 1960
Goddard School Teachers Record Books

Interviews with Robert and Dixie Helphinstine, Dr. Fran Helphinstine, Mrs. Garr Hurst, Mrs. Jim Meade, Mr. Luther Yazell, Miss Nancy Staggs, Mrs. Myrtle Hamm, Mrs. Leo Royse, Mrs. Frank L. Hinton, Mrs. Loright James, Mrs. Martin L. Kennedy, Wells Campbell, Edward and Bernice Muse Plummer, Elizabeth Sloss Wagner, Elaine Hinton Logan, Jane Hinton Lands, Imogene Littleton Wheeler, Jimmy Jones, Anna Florence Jones, Helen Barnett, Terry Hurst, Kelly Bruce Reeves, Dorothy Reeves, Louise Yazell, Kenny Roberts, Patsy Roberts Stacy, Larry Swim, Kathy Swim, Donald Bays, Margie Conley Bays, Edith Plummer, Garnet Bays Hall, James Lloyd Rogers, Wyndell Staggs, Crystal Plummer Sapp, Dorothy Plummer Briggs, Hilda Mattox Muse McKenzie,

Faye Taylor Hill, Joyce McKee Richmond, Tom Muse, Archie Muse, Greg Helphinstine, Woodie Reeves, Sammy Reeves, Ervin Gardner, Eugene Hall, George Littleton

Many are deceased at this time.

General Index

Academy at Flemingsburg 14

Adkins, Kathy 188, 197,262

Adkins, Wes 155

Alderman Company 192

Alexander, Theo. 21

Allen, Wm. 20

Allison, Mary 125, 128

American Legion 85

Andrews, Mae 84, 127

Arnold, Lee 73

Art 115

Atchison, Julia 26

Atkinson, Alberta 118

Atkinson, Julian 192

Autograph Books 170

Babbs, William 16

Back, Frank 178

Back, Gatewood 99

Back, Henry 72

Barker, Garry 112

Barnett, Charles 190

Barnett, David 153, 156

Barnett, Helen 72, 95, 109, 111, 118, 125, 131, 145, 152, 153, 178, 196, 197

Barnett, Myron 68, 70, 87, 92, 93, 94,95, 101, 109,111, 125, 131, 148, 149, 152, 153, 154, 155, 156, 163, 169, 170, 178, 180, 182, 196, 197,263

Bartley, James   17
Baseball   170
Bays, Carl   170, 178
Bays, Donald   98, 149, 169, 170
Bays, Garnett Faye   93, 183
Bays, Harold   148, 149, 169, 170
Bell, school   198
Bell, J.D.   15
Blair, C.D.   128, 132, 190, 191
Boling, Kevin Auction   198
Bon Ton Restaurant   94
Botkin, Flora   125, 126
Bowles, Judy   197
Braybant, Joe   100, 139
Braybant, Patricia   139, 177
Brown, Elkin   187
Browning, Charles   67
Bryant, Bailey   21
Bubble lights   164
Burke, Catherine   129
Bus Plan   187
Busy Day Cake   172
Campbell, G. M.   89
Campbell, Harley   121
Campbell, Maggie   26, 124
Campbell, Verna   24, 66, 117
Campbell, Wells   24, 71, 132, 184
Carpenter, Alma Muse   126
Carpenter, Brooks   127
Carpenter, J.J.   60
Carpenter, John R.   21
Carpenter, Marion   60, 85, 109
Carpenter, Reck   77
Carpenter, Wat   73

Cartmell, W. W.	20
Catrell, T. M.	20
Caven, John A.	14
Caywood, Clarence P.	99, 124,125, 127
Caywood, Maude	100, 125, 129, 134
Caywood, Miss Nellie	124
Chadwick, A. B.	20
Christmas	164
Circus	185
Cistern	70, 133
"Civil War School Days"	27
Clark, Sheriff	139
Clarke, Mrs.	21
Clary, Naomi	118, 132
Class rings	178
Claypool, Betty	117, 135
Claypool, Dora	160
Claypool, Gail	90, 135, 176
Claypool, Naomi	144
Colgan, D. C.	77
Common School Composition	114
Common School Graduation	84
Common School Graduation Certificates	64, 83
Common School Ordinances	1869 108
Common School Teacher Contract	32
Compton, Lloyd	139
Coney Island	154
Conley, Billy	170, 178
Conley, Denzil	148
Conley, Dorothy Reeves	71

Conley, Jimmy   176
Conley, Marjorie   68, 101, 181, 197
Conley, William   102
Conn, Mary Lucy   96, 188
Conrad, Mrs.   16
Conway, Wm. F.   19
Cooper and Company   69, 71, 87
Cooper, Carmie   131, 145
Cooper, Charley   97
Cooper, Cleo   66, 186, 187
Cooper, E. L.   191
Cooper, George   93
Cooper, Helen   186
Cooper, Nettie   156, 157
Cord, J. P.   20
Cord, L. J.   21
Cormack, Loma   15
Country Life Commission 59
Cowan, Charles   190
Cox, Andrew   15
Crain, Wm.   18
Crawford, William   189, 190
Creighton   14
Cropper, Mrs.   125
Cummins, James   68
Curtis, Avery   170
Curtis, Ray   178
Daniels, Herschel   186, 187
Daulton, Howard B.   68, 125, 127
Davis, Bell   21
Davis, Id   16
Davis, Nell   26, 124
Davis, Mabel   121
Davis, Morton   26, 124

Dawson, James	20
Dearing, Mrs.	17
Denton, Maxine	190
Dickey, M. Eva	21
Dickey, Mr.	67
Dillon, Isiah	20
Discipline	98, 99
Dixie's Peanut Butter Fudge	182
Donaldson, John	14
Dorsey, Mr.	89
Doyle, Billy	176
Doyle, Hazel	66
Doyle, John	16
Duncan, Brooks	99, 109, 124, 129, 134
Dye, Jack	190
Eckman, D. I.	19
Eighth Grade Examination	61
Electricity	71
Ellington, Eugene	96
Emmons, B.C.	99
Emmons, Charles	110
Emmons, Chester	98
Emmons, Drewey Garr	197, 198
Emmons, Lowell Lee	60, 190, 191
Emmons, Mary Lucy Conn	197, 198, 199
Emmons, St. Clair	16, 17
Emmons, William	16
Estill, O.	21
Evans, Allen	20
Evans, Amanda	75
Evans, Chesney H.	192
Evans, Miss Erie	26, 31
Evans, Frank	26
Evans, Griffin	17

Evans, Ida	121
Evans, Jack	26
Evans, Jesse	17
Evans, Lulu	79, 121
Evans, Marvin	58, 59, 67, 78, 97, 186
Evans, Mattie	76
Evans, Scioto	15
Evans, Uhlan	67, 71, 190
Eyler, Emery	190
F & N Railroad	71
4-H Club	171
Fant, Nelson	17
Faris, Basil	64
Faris, Caroline	118
Faris, Dunbar	118
Faris, Floyd	83
Faris, J. W.	75, 76, 77
Faris, James	16
Faris, Mary	70, 111, 125, 127,128, 129
Farrow, James	176
Feed Sacks	159
Ferguson, N. J.	60
Fem, Helen	118, 180
Fem, Kenneth	85, 190
Ferry, Maysville, Ky.	185
Field Schools	14
Fields, Freda	118
Fields, Hershel	118
Filson, S. F.	121
Flannery, Clyde	26, 124
Flannery, Louie	187
Fleming, Thomas	14
Fleming County Public School Corporation	84

298

Fleming-Mason RECC 71
Flora, Estill 191
Flutophone band 197
Foudraysburg 15
Fountain, Andrew 20
"Four Eyes" 112
Freeman, Gamaliel 16
Fried, Noah 89
Fried, Sam 68
Frost, Jack 183
Fryman, Woodie 170
Gaines, Nell 64
Gaines, Harold 190
Gardner, A. 16
Gardner, Archie 96
Gardner, Bruce 96
Gardner, Ervin 134
Gardner, Jim 70
Gardner, J. W. 25
Gardner, Sadie 96
George, Wm. H. 20
Gilliam, Ed 90
Gillmore, Charlie 121
Glascock, R. H 69
Glenn, Beryl 68, 127, 128
Goddard, J.W. 60
Goddard Covered Bridge 66
Goodan, Charles 76
Gooding, Elizabeth 128, 129
Gooding, Eugene 83
Gooding, Lovell 173
Gooding, Ronnie 177
Gooding, Wes 74, 75, 76, 108
Gooding, William A. 25

Gordon, J. W.	21
Gorman, Maxine	68, 181, 197
Gorman, Tommy	169
Graham, Tom	20
Graham, Wm. S.T.	17
Grannis, Jack	89
Gray, Lucille	125, 127
Gray, Maggie Hiner	116
Gray, Roy	71, 77, 87
Green, Mary Ellen	26
Greenup, Governor Christopher	13
Gross, A. D.	20
Gulley, Alvin	152, 188
Gulley, Diane	152
Gulley, Orville	67
Gulley, Shirley	112, 154, 170, 173, 178, 180
Gulley, S. K.	25
Guy, Eddie	139
Hall, Allen	85, 145
Hall, Eugene	71, 101, 155, 169
Hall, James Lowell	181, 197
Hall, Jesse	70, 96, 98, 99, 100, 110, 125, 129, 131, 144, 145, 162, 165
Hall, Tom T.	117, 118, 182
Halloween	162
Ham, Charles	75, 76
Ham, James	74, 75
Ham, W. K.	25, 32, 74, 77
Hamm, E. F.	20
Hammond, J. W.	25, 77
Hammonds, Thomas	65
Hampton, Beulah	160
Hams, Wilson	121

Hardy, Elsie — 92, 177

Harmon, Amos — 71, 177

Hart, Nancy B. — 157

Hart, Wm. — 20

Hartley, Ben — 16

Hawkins, Anna — 79

Hayes, Nelva — 129

Hedges, U. G. — 75, 76, 77

Hellard, Mabel — 125, 131

Helphenstine, Sherley — 176

Helphinstine, Dixie — 137, 176, 182, 183

Helphinstine, Ed — 116

Helphinstine, Fran — 92, 112, 117, 133,135, 136, 138, 140, 144, 158, 160, 165, 173, 175, 177, 181, 186

Helphinstine, Ginny — 70, 94, 109, 112, 135, 136, 137, 143,144, 146, 150, 154, 155, 156, 160, 172, 173, 178, 180, 186

Helphinstine, Marion — 116

Helphinstine, Mary Bell — 116

Helphinstine, Oscar — 25, 116, 117

Helphinstine, Robert Lee (Bob) — 66, 67, 83, 84, 89, 98, 99, 110, 124, 184, 185, 188

Henderson, Mollie — 101

Hickerson, Myrtle — 26, 124

Hillsboro High School — 64, 65, 158

Hiner, Harvey — 116

Hiner, Jesse — 116

Hiner, Maggie — 116

Hinsch, Charles A. Co.

Hinton, Elora — 60

Hinton, Enos — 185

Hinton, Frank L. — 66, 67, 107, 185

Hinton, Frank Owen — 189

Hinton, H. B. and Son — 72

Hinton, Maxine — 189, 190

Hinton, O. L.   60

Hinton, Mrs. Richard   190

Hinton, Ruby   66

Hinton, Russ   73, 75, 76

Home Visitations   98

Huff, R. B.   60

Hughes, Ella   160

Hull, L.N   73, 102

Hull, Sam   21

Hunt, Mr.   70

Hunt, Mrs. Emery   190

Hunt, Henry   186, 187

Hunter, J. W   60, 81, 102, 103

Hunter, Ruby   68, 127, 128

Hunter, Wallace   25, 124

Hurst, Alice   121, 122, 123, 124, 126

Hurst, Bazil   17

Hurst, Christine   171, 173

Hurst, Frankie Nell   67, 125, 126, 127

Hurst, H. P.   121

Hurst, J. R.   71

Hurst, Terry   164, 171

Hurst, Tom F.   24, 26, 31, 32, 74, 75, 76, 77, 121, 122, 124, 125

Hurst, Verna   122, 123, 125, 126

Hurst, William   16

Idyner, Mrs.   16

Ingram and Jones   69

Iound, John   16

Issac, Sutton   17

James, C. B.   122, 125

James, Elsie   125

James, George   75

James, Gerald   157

James, J. P. 74
James, Linda 154
James, Loright 69, 71, 89, 187, 188
James, O. S. 75
James, Roscoe 26, 124
James, Virginia 90, 91
James, W. R. 122
Jesse, Floyd 96
Jett, Billy 149, 169
Jett, Johnny 169
Johns, Hattie 121
Johnson, Ben 72
Johnson, Charles Edward 134
Johnson, Helen 131
Jones, Allie Lewis 26, 31
Jones, Anna Florence 165, 178, 188
Jones, Betty 154, 173, 180
Jones, Billy 100, 178
Jones, Mrs. Charles 26
Jones, E. 21
Jones, Jas. 21, 177
Jones, Jimmy 133, 134, 177, 188
Jones, Walter 116
Jones, Zeke 25, 27
Jordan, Mrs. 16
Jordan, C. A. 76
Jordan, Edgar 75
Joyland Park 154
Junior Conservation Club 171
Keaton, Emma 176
Keaton, Joy Ann 177
Kemper, Harry 15
Kentucky 10th Calvary 25
Kentucky 16th Infantry 25

Kentucky Travelers	117
Kirk, Mrs.	16
Kirk, J.	21
Kirk, Nellie	117
Kizer, Norman	131
Knapp, J. S.	74, 75,76, 77
"Lazy Bones"	163
Leahy, G.W.	22
Lee, Rena	125
LeForgee, Lewis	16
Lewis, Glen	71
Lewis, William	16
Lewman, Emma	75
Littleton, Bill	118, 147, 154, 180
Littleton, Birdie	99
Littleton, Bruce	25
Littleton, Charles	25
Littleton, Columbus	25
Littleton, Doshia	94
Littleton, Emory	83, 117, 124
Littleton, Eugene	178
Littleton, Eva	90
Littleton, Frank	177, 203
Littleton, Gene	165
Littleton, George Wayne	71,90, 91, 99, 176
Littleton, Imogene	70, 94, 101, 146, 149, 154, 162, 180
Littleton, J. F.	74
Littleton, James	178
Littleton, Jesse	25
Littleton, Mike	124
Littleton, Minnie	25
Littleton, Ronnie	90, 178
Littleton, Rose Ann	25
Littleton, Thelma Faye	173, 177

Littleton, Wanda	173, 177
Littleton, William	25, 66, 124
Lloyd, Mrs.	17
Lowe, John and Tootsie	199
Lunchroom	86
Madden, S. C.	20
Mann, Horace	14
Marshall, Miss	125
Mason, Gertrude	121
Mathews, J. H.	74, 76
Mathison, Mary	197
Mathison, Oscar	154, 170, 180
Mattox, Bobby	181,197
Mattox, C. L.	71
Mattox, Calvin	124
Mattox, Danny	69, 93,118, 154, 173, 180
Mattox, George	71, 89, 140, 177
Mattox, Hilda	86, 96
Mattox, John	89, 165, 187,188
Mattox, John Acie	70, 181, 197
Mattox, Lillian	177
Mattox, Price	150, 170
Mattox, Violet	176
Mattox, Wanda	178
Maxey, Wanda	157
May Day	134
McCall, M.O	68
McCall, Pearl	116
McDaniel, Margaret	25
McDonald, Lloyd	95
McDonald, Mrs. Marvin	190
McGregor, Himmer	26, 121, 124
McGuffey, William	14

McIntyre, Brooks Hammond   116, 117

McIntyre, J. W.   25

McKee,?   20

McKee, Anna Mary   83

McKee, Charlie   71

McKee, Donna Jean   149, 197

McKee, Dora   75

McKee, Elias   20

McKee, Frances   94, 198

McKee, George W.   75

McKee, J.C.   178

McKee, J. Stewart   198

McKee, Lena   198

McKee, Lucy   178, 180

McKee, Pauletta   197

McKee, Ruby   90

McNeil, Anna Lou   118

McNeil, Pete   171

McRoberts, Alexander   16

McRoberts, Flora   83

McRoberts, Gene Austin   188

McRoberts, Glenn   187

McRoberts, Samuel   83

McRoberts, Willie   98

Meade, Jim   170, 171, 187

Meade, Nora   89, 100, 109, 125, 129, 130, 131, 135, 136, 137, 146, 162, 164, 166, 173, 176, 182, 189

Middleton, Grace   129

Miller, Harvey   16

Miller, Jim Wayne   112

Money, R. D.   20

Moonshine Stills   99

Moore, Lois	71, 72, 109, 119, 125, 131, 146, 147, 148, 149, 150, 156, 162, 177, 178, 197, 263
Moore, Shirley Ann Taylor	197
Moreland, Samuel	17
Morly, Mrs.	20
Morrison, Anna	25
Morrison, Elisha S.	25, 73, 74, 77, 121, 123, 124, 125, 126, 127
Morrison, Emma	121, 123
Morrison, H. C.	73
Morrison, Heytor	25, 123
Morrison, Lulu	25, 26, 31
Morrison, Mamie	171
Morrison, Martha	64
Morrison, Mary	123
Morrison, Mathas	16
Morrison, Maude	25, 26, 27, 30, 31
Morrison, Milton	25
Morrison, W.A.	19
Mosely, Ann	156
Muse, Bell	31
Muse, George	116
Muse, H.B. and Company	60
Muse, James	16
Muse, Joyce	68
Muse, Kenneth	68
Muse, Mary	185
Muse, Owen	184, 185, 187
Muse, Ruth	83
Muse, Bernice	177, 178
National School Lunch Program	86
Nealis, Charles	17
Norriee, John	16

North Central Surplus Army Disposal Organization	89
Northcutt, Rev. H.C.	17
O'Bannon, Dr. J.B.	60
Oney, Phillip	83
Outhouses	67
Overley, Milford	20, 21
Owens, Kirk	190
Palmer, E.L. (Bud)	72, 186
Palmer's Guide to Business Writing	112
Panic of 1819	13
Patterson, Jesse	16
Pea Ridge Mountain	96
Pendland, Thurl	71
Perkins, Hazel	128
Phelps, Y.	20
Pleak, Miss Lucky	21
Planck, Lillian Carpenter	125
Planck, Mrs. S. F	68, 126
Plummer, Bernice Muse	92, 93, 145, 154
Plummer, Clyde	109
Plummer, Crystal	69, 86, 109
Plummer, Dorothy	160
Plummer, Edith	146
Plummer, Edward	177
Plummer, Emerson	156
Plummer, George	68
Plummer, J. F.	75
Plummer, Joseph Malin	16, 26, 56, 59, 74
Plummer, Lucy	26
Plummer, Minnie	26
Plummer, Ransom	71

Plummer, Roy	149
Plummer, Thomas	60
Porter, Andrew	125, 128
Porter, Donnie	178
Porter, Jean	24
Porter, Larry	24
Porter, Mollie	76
Porter, Ruth Ann	68, 94, 181, 197
Porter, Thomas	14
Potato Candy	90
Prater, Junior	93
Prather, M. E.	20
Preston, Anna Lee	134,186
Primer, Tor	20
P.T.A. (Parent Teachers Association)	28, 87,137, 181, 182
P.T.A. of the Olden Days	28
Reed, Kenneth	177
Reeves, Charles	137,164
Reeves, Claude	117
Reeves, Clifford	72
Reeves, Dorothy	94, 147, 173, 178, 180
Reeves, Dorothy McKee	160
Reeves, Eck	117
Reeves, Evelyn	69
Reeves, Goble	164
Reeves, James	20
Reeves, Kelly Bruce	156, 178
Reeves, Onie	117
Reeves, Sammy	162, 169
Reeves, Sudie	74, 75
Reeves, Woodie	98, 171, 181, 197
Reeves, Woodrow, Sr.	109, 117
Rice, G.T.	69, 71

Rice, Mary 97, 140, 157
Richeson, Thomas 19
Richmond, Bennie 188
Riickert, Ruby 160
Riley, Rickey and Tammi 199
Roberts, Rev. Earl 68, 92, 93, 94, 100, 109, 125, 131, 139, 140, 143, 169, 182
Roberts, Joe 163, 181, 197
Roberts, Kenny 148, 149, 150, 151, 165, 166, 169
Roberts, Patsy 68, 167, 168, 197, 262
Robinson, E. 20
Rogers, Ernest 190
Rogers, James Lloyd 93, 100, 133, 134, 139, 157, 166, 178, 192
Rogers, Virgie 90
Rogers, W. F. 19
Roosevelt, President Teddy 59
Ross, Bess 79
Ross, J.M. 60
Routt, Bryant 17
Routt, Isaac 139
Routt, O.N. 100
Routt, Sam 139
Royse, Aaron 184
Royse, Ben 77
Royse, Lena 64
Royse, Leo 185, 187, 190
Royse, Martha 100, 125, 131, 138
Royse, Mildred 83
Royse, H.C 60, 74
Runyon, W. J. 60
Russ, Johnson 20
Ryan, John K. 97
Sacred Harp Movement 116
Samuels, John 19

Sapp, Crystal   98

Saunders, Earlyne   125, 128

Saunders, Mary Frances   83

Saunders, Robert   139

Scarlett Fever   98

School Lunch Program   86, 87

Schools (Early):   15
Burn School

Columbia   15

Fant's Schoo   14, 15

Lewis Crain   15

Sylvan Shade School   15

Temperance School   15

Woodlawn   83

Scott, Frank, Supt.   92, 100, 158, 192

Seacrest, Joseph   16

Sebree, Kathryn   173

Selective Service   98

Shrout, Herd   85

Simdrian, J.   20

Singing Schools   116

Six, Anna   60

Slaughter, Gov. Gabriel   13

Sloas, Bobby   139, 178

Sloas, Cathy   188

Sloas, Elizabeth   148, 152, 153, 188, 197

Sloas, Erma   187, 188

Sloas, Glennis   176

Sloas, Jeri   94, 152

Snow   97

Sorrell, John   77

Sousley, Jas.   20

Sousley, R. J.   103

Spencerian Key to Practical Penmanship	112
Staggs, Alice	21, 76
Staggs, C. W.	32, 75, 77
Staggs, D. E.	25
Staggs, H.P.	74
Staggs, Hattie	66, 90, 183
Staggs, Hord	66, 68, 69
Staggs, Irene	64
Staggs, John Lewis	66, 71, 91, 147, 160, 173, 186, 188
Staggs, John	188
Staggs, Lewis	32,76, 77
Staggs, Lillian	66
Staggs, Nancy	91, 92, 93, 94, 153, 156, 178
Staggs, Nanny	121
Staggs, Noreen	118, 138, 157, 158, 182
Staggs, Thomas	16
Staggs, Wendell	99, 134, 176
Staggs, William	116
Stamper, J. W.	20
Stanfield, Craig	198
Stewart, Cora Wilson	79
Stewart, Robert	15
Stockton, D.K	14
Story, B.H.	121
Story, Elijah	17
Story, Ethel	97, 125, 127
Story, James	17
Story, Owen	25, 98, 111, 125, 127
Subscription schools	14, 26
Sugar rationing	78
Summitt, John	17
Summons, Jesse	16
Sutton, Amos	16

Swim, Diane   169,178

Swim, Larry   149, 165, 262

Swinging Bridge   65, 66

Tackett, Helen   125, 129, 131

Tackett, Lillian   129

Taylor, Bobby   177

Taylor, Faye   107, 117, 131, 135, 173, 263

Taylor, Horace   66, 70, 90, 162, 181

Taylor, Sherley   101, 168, 178, 197, 262

Teacher Contracts   32

Teacher Institutes   22

Teacher Retirement   158

Teegarden, Christine   125, 128

Ten Commandments   70, 109

Textbook Dealer   107

Textbook Lists   104

Thacker, G. T.   74, 75

Throop, James   20

Throop, Phares   20

Tom Thumb Wedding   133

Truman, President Harry S.   86

Tuberculosis Tests   78

Vansandt, William   16

Viars, Faris   100, 137, 138

Viars, George, Sr.   100

Viars, George, Jr.   100

Viars, Raymond   100

Vice, Johnny   191, 192

Vize, Foster   76

Wagner, Elizabeth Sloas   94, 145

Wagoner, Charles   186

Wagoner, Dan   184, 187

Wagoner, Dewey   90, 185, 186

Wagoner, Libby   176

Walton, Jonathan   17
Walton, Noel   190
Waltz, John   121
Waltz, Molly   25, 31, 73, 74, 75
Ward, Ersil   125, 128
Ward, Mary Faris   125, 134
Warren, Mabel   145, 152
Watson, D.A.   171
Watson, Harlan   190
Watson, Ruby   125, 132
Weather Service   97
Wentz, Alta   71, 125, 131, 146
Whaley, C.G.   21, 22
Wheat, George   75
Whitten, Irvin   96
Wild West Show   185
Williams, Hale (Bye)   183
Williams, Jack   99
Williams, Lutie Palmer   84
Williams, S. O.   20
Williams, William H.   25
Winn, Douglas J.   17
Wood, Wm. A.   20
Wright, Donnie   99, 176
Yates, Mrs.   20
Yazell, Bessie   86, 101, 147, 149, 164, 165
Yazell, Curt   86, 164, 186
Yazell, Lewis   176
Yazell, Louise   86, 92, 135, 139, 160, 165, 169, 177, 186
Young, Gordie   189
Zimmerman, May   26, 124
Zornes, John   74, 184

About the Author

Ginny Reeves, author of *Goddard School Memories*, is a former student of Goddard School and a native of Fleming County, Kentucky. Ginny experienced a rewarding rural education from caring teachers in the 1950s at Goddard School, a time when communities and families came together to celebrate the achievements of their students, a time to share what they had with their friends and neighbors. Ginny was influenced by her Goddard School teachers to read award-winning books as a child and became a school librarian for forty-four years.

Recognized as one of Indiana's foremost educators and researchers, Ginny received the American Legion Teacher of the Year award and the Indiana Library Media Specialist of the Year award and was recognized by the Indiana Historical Society with the Dorothy Riker Hoosier Historian award, She also received the Sagamore of the Wabash and Kentucky Colonel awards. She has B.S. and M.A. degrees from Morehead State University, Morehead, Kentucky, with additional work at Indiana University and Purdue University.

She has written articles for the Encyclopedia of Northern Kentucky and dozens of articles for historical newspapers and magazines. After retirement, Ginny has returned to her roots in Kentucky and continues to do historical research. She and her husband, Woodie, live on the family farm at Goddard, Kentucky, near the site of the Goddard School.

CPSIA information can be obtained
at www.ICGtesting.com
Printed in the USA
LVHW010815300321
682936LV00009B/85